Hardship and Happiness

THE COMPLETE WORKS OF LUCIUS ANNAEUS SENECA

Edited by Elizabeth Asmis, Shadi Bartsch, and Martha C. Nussbaum

Seneca
Hardship and Happiness

TRANSLATIONS BY
ELAINE FANTHAM,
HARRY M. HINE,
JAMES KER, AND
GARETH D. WILLIAMS

The University of Chicago Press CHICAGO AND LONDON

ELAINE FANTHAM was the Giger Professor of Latin at
Princeton University from 1986 to 1999. She has written
many books and commentaries on Latin literature, including
Seneca's *Troades*. HARRY M. HINE is honorary professor
in the School of Classics at the University of St Andrews in
Scotland and the translator of Seneca's *Natural Questions*, also
in the series. JAMES KER is associate professor of classical
studies at the University of Pennsylvania and the editor of *A
Seneca Reader: Selections from Prose and Tragedy*. GARETH D.
WILLIAMS is the Violin Family Professor of Classics
at Columbia University and the author of many books,
including *The Cosmic Viewpoint: A Study of Seneca's "Natural
Questions."*

The University of Chicago Press, Chicago 60637
The University of Chicago Press, Ltd., London
© 2014 by The University of Chicago
All rights reserved. Published 2014.
Printed in the United States of America

23 22 21 20 19 18 17 16 15 14   1 2 3 4 5

ISBN-13: 978-0-226-74832-0 (cloth)
ISBN-13: 978-0-226-10835-3 (e-book)
DOI: 10.7208/9780226108353.001.0001

Library of Congress Cataloging-in-Publication Data

Seneca, Lucius Annaeus, approximately 4 B.C.–65 A.D., author.
    [Works. Selections. English. 2014]
    Hardship and happiness / Seneca ; translations by
Elaine Fantham, Harry M. Hine, James Ker, and
Gareth D. Williams.
        pages   cm. — (Complete works of Lucius
        Annaeus Seneca)
    Includes bibliographical references and index.
    ISBN 978-0-226-74832-0 (hardcover : alkaline paper) —
ISBN 978-0-226-10835-3 (e-book)   1. Conduct of life—
Early works to 1800.   2. Happiness—Early works to 1800.
I. Title.   II. Series: Seneca, Lucius Annaeus, approximately
4 B.C.–65 A.D. Works. English. 2010.
B615.E5 2014
188—dc23

                                    2013020404

♾ This paper meets the requirements of ANSI/NISO Z39.48–
1992 (Permanence of Paper).

Contents

On Providence
TRANSLATED BY JAMES KER

Seneca and His World

ELIZABETH ASMIS, SHADI BARTSCH, AND MARTHA C. NUSSBAUM

Seneca once remarked of Socrates that it was his death by hemlock that made him great (*Letter* 13.14). With reason: Socrates' death demonstrated the steadfastness of his philosophical principles and his belief that death offered nothing to fear. When Seneca himself, then, was ordered to commit suicide by Nero in 65 CE, we might well believe Tacitus's account in his *Annals* (15.63) that the Roman Stoic modeled his death on that of Socrates, discoursing calmly about philosophy with his friends as the blood drained out of his veins. In Tacitus's depiction we see, for once, a much-criticized figure living up to the principles he preached.

Seneca's life was mired in political advancement and disappointment, shaped by the effects of exile and return, and compromised by his relationship with the emperor Nero—first his pupil, then his advisee, and finally his murderer. But his many writings say little about his political career and almost nothing about his relationship with Nero except for what can be gleaned from his essay *On Clemency*, leaving us to turn to later sources for information—Tacitus, Suetonius, and Dio Cassius in particular. We know that Seneca was born to a prominent equestrian family in Corduba, Spain, some time between 4 and 1 BCE. He was the second of three sons of Helvia and Lucius Annaeus Seneca (the youngest son, Annaeus Mela, was the father of the poet Lucan). The elder Seneca had spent much of his life in Rome, and Seneca himself was brought to Rome as a young boy. There he was educated in rhetoric and later became a student of the philosopher Sextius. But his entry into political life was delayed, and when he did enter upon the *cursus honorum* late in Tiberius's reign, his ill health (he had asthma and possibly tuberculosis) was a source of difficulty. In any case his career was cut short. He survived Caligula's hostility, which the sources tell us was thanks to his talents in oratory, but was sent into exile on Corsica by Claudius shortly after Caligula's death in 41 CE. The charge, almost certainly false, was adultery with Caligula's younger sister, Julia Livilla. Seneca spent his time in exile in philosophical and natural study and wrote the *Consolations* to Helvia (his mother) and to Polybius (Claudius's freedman secretary), revealing in the latter how desperately he hoped to be recalled to Rome.

When Seneca did return in 49 CE, it was under different auspices. Claudius had recently remarried, to Germanicus's daughter Agrippina, and she urged him to recall Seneca as tutor to her son, the twelve-year-old Nero. Claudius already had a younger son, Britannicus, but it was clear that the wily Agrippina wished to see her own flesh and blood on the throne. When Claudius died five years later, Agrippina was able to maneuver Nero into position as emperor—and Britannicus was dispatched by poison shortly after, in 55 CE.

From 54 until his influence waned at the end of the decade, Seneca acted as Nero's adviser, together with the praetorian prefect Sextus Afranius Burrus. We know he wrote a speech on clemency for Nero to deliver to the Roman senate soon after his accession, and Seneca's own essay *On Clemency* may contain some inkling of his strategy to keep the young emperor from running amok. Seneca's use of the term *rex*, or king, applied to Nero by analogy in this piece, is surprising from a Roman senator, but he seems to have hoped that flattering Nero by pointing to his limitless power and the value of clemency would be one way to keep him from abusing that power. Both Seneca and Burrus also helped with the civil and judicial administration of the empire.

Many historians, ancient and modern, feel that this early part of Nero's reign, moderated by Seneca and Burrus, represented a period of comparative good rule and harmony (the "*quinquennium Neronis*"). The decline started in 59 CE with Nero's murder of Agrippina, after which Seneca wrote the emperor's speech of self-exculpation—perhaps the most famous example of how the philosopher found himself increasingly compromised in his position as Nero's chief counsel. Certainly as a Stoic, Seneca cuts an ambiguous figure next to the others who made their opposition to Nero clear, such as Thrasea Paetus and Helvidius Priscus. His participation in court politics probably led him to believe that he could do more good from where he stood than by abandoning Nero to his own devices—if he even had this choice.

In any case, Seneca's influence over Nero seems to have been considerably etiolated after the death of Burrus in 62. According to Tacitus, Seneca tried to retire from his position twice, in 62 and 64. Although Nero refused him on both occasions, Seneca seems to have largely absented himself from the court after 64. In 65 CE came the Pisonian conspiracy, a plot to kill Nero and replace him with the ringleader, C. Calpurnius Piso. Although Seneca's nephew Lucan was implicated in this assassination attempt, Seneca himself was probably innocent. Nonetheless, Nero seized the opportunity to order his old adviser to kill himself. Seneca cut his own veins, but (so Tacitus tells us) his thinness and advanced age hindered the flow of blood. When a dose of poison also failed to kill him, he finally sat in a hot bath to make the blood flow faster. His wife, Pompeia Paulina, also tried to commit suicide but was saved on orders from Nero.

Because of his ethical writings, Seneca fared well with the early Christians—hence the later forging of a fake correspondence with St. Paul—but already in antiquity he had his fair share of critics, the main charge arising from the apparent contradiction between his Stoic teachings on the unimportance of "externals" and his own amassing of huge wealth. Perhaps for this reason he never gained the respect accorded the "Roman Socrates," the Stoic C. Musonius Rufus, banished by Nero in 65, even though Seneca's writings have had far more influence over the centuries. In Seneca's own lifetime one P. Suillius attacked him on the grounds that, since Nero's rise to power, he had piled up some 300 million sesterces by charging high interest on loans in Italy and the provinces—though Suillius himself was no angel and was banished to the Balearic Islands for being an embezzler and informant. In Seneca's defense, he seems to have engaged in ascetic habits throughout his life and despite his wealth. In fact, his essay *On the Happy Life* (*De vita beata*) takes the position that a philosopher may be rich as long as his wealth is properly gained and spent and his attitude to it is appropriately detached. Where Seneca finally ranks in our estimation may rest on our ability to tolerate the various contradictions posed by the life of this philosopher in politics.

A Short Introduction to Stoicism

Stoicism is one of the world's most influential philosophical movements. Starting from the works and teaching of the three original heads of the Greek Stoic school—Zeno of Citium (335–263 BCE),

Cleanthes (331–232 BCE), and Chrysippus (ca. 280–207 BCE)—it became the leading philosophical movement of the ancient Greco-Roman world, shaping the development of thought well into the Christian era. Later Greek Stoics Panaetius (ca. 185–109 BCE) and Posidonius (ca. 135–51 BCE) modified some features of Stoic doctrine. Roman thinkers then took up the cause, and Stoicism became the semiofficial creed of the Roman political and literary world. Cicero (106–43 BCE) does not agree with the Stoics on metaphysical and epistemological matters, but his ethical and political positions lie close to theirs, and even when he does not agree, he makes a concerted effort to report their positions sympathetically. Roman Stoics Seneca, Epictetus (mid-first to early second century CE), Musonius Rufus (ca. 30–ca. 102 BCE), and the emperor Marcus Aurelius (121–80 CE, emperor 161–80) produced Stoic works of their own (the last three writing in Greek).

The philosophical achievement of the Greek Stoics, and especially that of Chrysippus, was enormous: the invention of propositional logic, the invention of the philosophy of language, unprecedented achievements in moral psychology, distinction in areas ranging from metaphysics and epistemology to moral and political philosophy. Through an accident of history, however, all the works of all the major Greek Stoics have been lost, and we must recover their thoughts through fragments, reports (particularly the lengthy accounts in Diogenes Laertius's *Lives of the Philosophers*, in Cicero, and in Sextus Empiricus's skeptical writings, since the Stoics are his primary target), and the works of the Roman thinkers—who often are adjusting Stoic doctrines to fit Roman reality and probably contributing creative insights of their own. This also means that we know somewhat less about Stoic logic or physics than about Stoic ethics, since the Romans took a particular interest in the practical domain.

The goal of Stoic philosophy, like that of other philosophical schools of the Hellenistic era, was to give the pupil a flourishing life free from the forms of distress and moral failure that the Stoics thought ubiquitous in their societies. Unlike some of their competitor schools, however, they emphasized the need to study all parts of their threefold system—logic, physics, and ethics—in order to understand the universe and its interconnections. To the extent that a

Roman such as Cicero believed he could uphold the moral truths of Stoicism without a confident belief in a rationally ordered universe, he held a heretical position (one shared many centuries later by Immanuel Kant).

Stoic physics held that the universe is a rationally ordered whole, and that everything that happens in it happens for the best of reasons. (It is this position, in its Leibnizian incarnation, that is pilloried in Voltaire's *Candide*.) Rejecting traditional anthropomorphic religion, the Stoics gave the name Zeus to the rational and providential principle animating the universe as a whole, and they could find even in the most trivial or distressing events (such as earthquakes and thunderbolts) signs of the universe's overall good order. This order was also a moral order based on the inherent dignity and worth of the moral capacities of each and every rational being. The Stoics believed that this order was deterministic: everything happens of necessity. But they were also "compatibilists," believing that human free will is compatible with the truth of determinism. They engaged in spirited debates with "incompatibilist" Aristotelians, making lasting contributions to the free will controversy.

Stoic ethics begins from the idea of the boundless worth of the rational capacity in each and every human being. The Roman Stoics understood this capacity to be centrally practical and moral. (Thus, unlike Plato, they did not think that people who had a natural talent for mathematics were better than people who didn't, and they became more and more skeptical that even the study of logic had much practical value.) They held that all human beings are equal in worth by virtue of their possession of the precious capacity to choose and direct their lives, ranking some ends ahead of others. This, they said, was what distinguished human beings from animals: this power of selection and rejection. (Unlike most other ancient schools, they had little concern for the morality of animal treatment, since they thought that only moral capacity entitled a being to respect and good treatment.) Children, they said, come into the world like little animals, with a natural orientation toward self-preservation but no understanding of true worth. Later, however, a remarkable shift will take place, already set up by their possession of innate human nature: they will be able to appreciate the beauty of the capacity for choice and the way in which moral reason has shaped the entire universe.

This recognition, they said, should lead people to respect both self and others in an entirely new way. Stoics were serious about (human) equality: they urged the equal education of both slaves and women. Epictetus himself was a former slave.

Stoicism looks thus far like an ethical view with radical political consequences, and so it became during the Enlightenment, when its distinctive emphases were used to argue in favor of equal political rights and more nearly equal economic opportunities. However, the original Stoics maintain a claim of great significance for politics: moral capacity is the only thing that has intrinsic worth. Money, honor, power, bodily health, and even the love of friends, children, and spouse—all these are held to be things that one may reasonably pursue if nothing impedes (they are called "preferred indifferents"), but they have no true intrinsic worth. They should not even be seen as commensurate with moral worth. So when they do not arrive as one wishes, it is wrong to be distressed.

This was the context in which the Stoics introduced their famous doctrine of *apatheia*, freedom from the passions. Defining the major emotions or passions as all involving a high valuation of "external goods," they argue that the good Stoic will not have any of these disturbances of the personality. Realizing that chance events lie beyond our control, the Stoic will find it unnecessary to experience grief, anger, fear, or even hope: all these are characteristic of a mind that waits in suspense, awestruck by things indifferent. We can have a life that truly involves joy (of the right sort) if we appreciate that the most precious thing of all, and the only truly precious thing, lies within our control at all times.

Stoics do not think that it is at all easy to get rid of the cultural errors that are the basis of the rejected passions: thus a Stoic life is a constant therapeutic process in which mental exercises are devised to wean the mind from its unwise attachments. Their works depict processes of therapy through which the reader may make progress in the direction of Stoic virtue, and they often engage their reader in just such a process. Epictetus and Marcus Aurelius describe processes of repeated meditation; Seneca (in *On Anger*) describes his own nightly self-examination. Seneca's *Letters* show the role that a wiser teacher can play in such a therapeutic process, but Seneca evidently does not think that even he himself is free from erroneous attachments. The "wise man" is in that sense a distant ideal, not a worldly reality, particularly for the Roman Stoics. A large aid in the therapeutic process is the study of the horrible deformities that societies (including one's own) suffer by caring too much about external goods. If one sees the ugly face of power, honor, and even love clearly enough, this may assist one in making the progress toward true virtue. Thus Seneca's *On Anger* is an example of a genre that we know to have been common in Stoicism.

Because of their doctrine of value, the Stoics actually do not propose radical changes in the distribution of worldly goods, as one might suppose equal regard for the dignity of all human beings would require. They think that equal respect does require dignified treatment of each person; thus Seneca urges masters not to beat their slaves or use them as sexual tools. About the institution of slavery, however, there is silence, and worse than silence: Seneca argues that true freedom is internal freedom, so the external sort does not really matter. Musonius, similarly, advocates respectful treatment for women, including access to a Stoic education. But as for changes in the legal arrangements that confined women to a domestic role and gave males power of life and death over them, he too is silent, arguing that women will manifest their Stoic virtue in the domestic context. Some Roman Stoics do appear to have thought that political liberty is a part of dignity, and thus died supporting republican institutions, but whether this attention to external conditions was consistent with Stoicism remains unclear. (Certainly Cicero's profound grief over the loss of political freedom was not the attitude of a Stoic, any more than was his agonizing grief over his daughter's death.)

There was also much debate about whether the Stoic norm of *apatheia* encouraged people to detach themselves from bad political events in a way that gave aid and comfort to bad politics. Certainly Stoics were known to counsel retirement from politics (a theme in Seneca's own life as he sought Nero's permission for retirement, unsuccessfully), and they were thought to believe that upheaval is worse than lawless tyranny. Plutarch reports that Brutus (a Platonist) questioned potential coconspirators in the assassination of Julius Caesar by trying to determine whether they accepted that Stoic norm or believed, with him, that lawless tyranny is worse than civil strife; only non-Stoics were selected for the group of assassins. During Nero's reign, however, several prominent Stoics—including Seneca and his nephew Lucan—joined republican political movements aimed at overthrowing Nero and lost their lives for their efforts, by politically ordered suicide.

Stoics believed that from the moral point of view, national boundaries are as irrelevant as honor, wealth, gender, and birth. They held that we are, first and foremost, citizens of the universe as a whole. (The term *kosmou polites*, citizen of the universe, was apparently first used by Diogenes the Cynic, but the Stoics took it up and were the real forefathers of modern cosmopolitanism.) What cosmopolitanism meant in practical terms was unclear, for the reasons already given—but Cicero thinks, at any rate (in *On Duties*, a highly Stoic work), that our common human dignity entails some very strict limits on the reasons for going to war and the sort of conduct that is permissible in it. He thus adumbrated the basis of the modern law of war. Cicero denied, however, that our common humanity entails any duty to distribute material goods beyond our own borders, thus displaying the unfortunate capacity of Stoic doctrine to support the status quo. Cicero's *On Duties* has had such an enormous influence on posterity in this that it is scarcely an exaggeration to blame the Stoics for the fact that we have well-worked-out doctrines of international law in the area of war and peace, but no well-established understanding of our material duties to one another.

Stoicism's influence on the development of the entire Western intellectual tradition cannot be underestimated. Christian thought owes it a large debt. Clement of Alexandria is just one example of a Christian thinker steeped in Stoicism; even a thinker such as Augustine, who contests many Stoic theses, finds it natural to begin from Stoic positions. Even more strikingly, many philosophers of the early modern era turn to Stoicism for guidance—far more often than they turn to Aristotle or Plato. Descartes' ethical ideas are built largely on Stoic models; Spinoza is steeped in Stoicism at every point; Leibniz's teleology is essentially Stoic; Hugo Grotius bases his ideas of international morality and law on Stoic models; Adam Smith draws more from the Stoics than from other ancient schools of thought; Rousseau's ideas of education are in essence based on Stoic models; Kant finds inspiration in the Stoic ideas of human dignity and the peaceful world community; and the American founders are steeped in Stoic ideas, including the ideas of equal dignity and cosmopolitanism, which also deeply influence the American transcendentalists Emerson and Thoreau. Because the leading works of Greek Stoicism had long been lost, all these thinkers were reading the Roman Stoics. Because many of them read little Greek, they were primarily reading Cicero and Seneca.

The Stoic influence on the history of literature has also been immense. In the Roman world, all the major poets, like other educated Romans, were acquainted with Stoic ideas and alluded to them often in their work. Virgil and Lucan are perhaps particularly significant in this regard. Later European literary traditions also show marked traces of Stoic influence—in part via the influence of Roman literature, and in part through the influence of philosophers in their own time who were themselves influenced by Stoic thought, but often also through their own reading of the influential works of Cicero, Seneca, and Marcus Aurelius.

Seneca's Stoicism

Seneca identifies himself as a Stoic. He declares his allegiance by repeatedly referring to "our people" (*nostri*)—the Stoics—in his writings. Yet he exercises considerable independence in relation to other Stoics. While he is committed to upholding basic Stoic doctrines, he recasts them on the basis of his own experience as a Roman and a wide reading of other philosophers. In this respect he follows a tradition of Stoic philosophical innovation exemplified most clearly by Panaetius and Posidonius, who introduced some Platonic and Aristotelian elements while adapting Stoicism to Roman circumstances. Seneca differs from previous Stoics by welcoming some aspects of Epicurean philosophy along with other influences.

Seneca is concerned above all with applying Stoic ethical principles to his life and to the lives of others like him. The question that dominates his philosophical writings is how an individual can achieve a good life. In his eyes, the quest for virtue and happiness is a heroic endeavor that places the successful person above the assaults of fortune and on a level with god. To this end, Seneca transforms the sage into an inspirational figure who can motivate others to become like him by his gentle humanity and joyful tranquility. Key topics are how to reconcile adversity with providence, how to free oneself from passions (particularly anger and grief), how to face death, how to disengage oneself from political involvement, how to practice poverty and use wealth, and how to benefit others. All these endeavors are viewed within the context of a supreme, perfectly rational and virtuous deity who looks with favor on the efforts of humans to attain the same condition of virtue. In the field of politics, Seneca argues for clemency on the part of the supreme ruler, Nero. In human relations, he pays special attention to friendship and the position of slaves. Overall, he aims to replace social hierarchies, with their dependence on fortune, with a moral hierarchy arranged according to proximity to the goal of being a sage.

Seneca's own concerns and personality permeate his writings. The modern reader learns much about the life of an aristocrat in the time of Claudius and Nero, and much about Seneca's personal strengths and weaknesses. At the same time, there is also much in the work that transcends the immediate concerns of Seneca and his period. Some topics that resonate especially with a modern audience are his vision of humans as members of a universal community of mankind, the respect he demands for slaves, his concern with human emotions, and, in general, his insistence on looking within oneself to find happiness. What is perhaps less appealing to the modern reader is the rhetorical elaboration of his message, which features an undeniable tendency toward hyperbole. Most of all, Seneca's own character strikes many readers as problematic. From his own time onward, he was perceived by some as a hypocrite who was far from practicing what he preached. Some of Seneca's writings (in particular, his *Consolations* to Polybius and his mother Helvia, and his essay *On the Happy Life*) are obviously self-serving. As Seneca himself suggests (*Letters* 84), he has transformed the teachings he has culled, in the manner of bees, into a whole that reflects his own complex character.

The Stoics divided logic into dialectic (short argument) and rhetoric (continuous exposition). There is not much to be said on dialectic in Seneca's writings except that he shuns it, along with formal logic in general. Every so often, however, he engages in a satirical display of fine-grained Stoic-type reasoning. The point is that carrying logical precision to excess is futile: it does not make a person any better. Quibbles of all kinds should be avoided, whether they involve carrying through a minute line of argument, making overly subtle verbal distinctions, or indulging in abstruse philological interpretation. While making the point, Seneca makes sure the reader knows he could beat the quibbler at his own game if he wanted to.

We have only sparse details about how the Stoics viewed rhetoric. What is clear about Seneca, however, is that he used the full panoply of Roman rhetorical methods to persuade readers of his philosophical message. His writings are full of vivid examples, stunning metaphors, pointed sayings, ringing sound effects. He knows how to vary his tone, from casual conversation to soaring exhortation and bitter denunciation. He peoples his text with a varied cast of characters: the addressee, the implied audience, hypothetical objectors, friends, opponents, historical figures. He himself hovers over the proceedings as watchful friend and sometime foe. Following Cleanthes, he intersperses poetry into his prose to impel the reader even more forcefully toward the task of self-improvement.

Given Seneca's ethical aims, it is perhaps surprising that he devotes a large work, *Natural Questions*, to physics. Yet the entire work has an overarching ethical aim. As Seneca insists repeatedly, the mind is uplifted by venturing beyond narrowly human concerns to survey the world as a whole. The contemplation of the physical world complements moral action by showing the full context of human action: we see god in his full glory, caring for human lives as he administers the world as a whole. In the spirit of Lucretius (who championed a rival philosophy), Seneca also intersperses ethical messages throughout his physical inquiries. Thus he emphasizes that humans must confront natural events, such as death and natural disasters, with courage and gratitude to god; and he warns against human misuse of natural resources and the decadence that accompanies progress. Of all areas of inquiry, physics affords Seneca the greatest scope for making additions and corrections to Stoic doctrine. He ranges over the whole history of physical inquiries, from the Pre-Socratics to his own time, to improve on the Stoics.

Seneca writes (*Letters* 45.4) that while he believes "in the judgment of great men," he also claims something for his own judgment: previous philosophers left some things to be investigated by us, which they might indeed have discovered for themselves if they hadn't engaged in useless quibbles. Granted that Seneca shows special investigative fervor in his cosmological inquiries, his moral teachings too are a product of his own judgment and innovation. What he contributes is a new vision rather than new theories. Using certain strict Stoic distinctions as a basis, he paints a new picture of the challenges that humans face and the happiness that awaits those who practice the correct philosophy. In agreement with Stoic orthodoxy, Seneca is uncompromising about differentiating between external advantages and the good, about the need to eradicate the passions, about the perfect rationality of the wise person, about the identity of god with fate. What he adds is a moral fervor, joined by a highly poetic sensibility, that turns these distinctions into springboards for action.

The Stoic sage was generally viewed by critics as a forbidding figure, outside the reach of human capabilities and immune to human feeling. Seneca concedes, or rather emphasizes, that the sage is indeed rare; he remarks that the sage is like a phoenix, appearing perhaps every five hundred years (*Letters* 42.1). As he sees it, the sage's exceptional status is not a barrier to improvement; it inspires. Seneca gives real-life immediacy to the sage by citing the younger Cato, opponent of Julius Caesar, as an example. Cato, indeed, is not just any sage; Seneca says he is not sure whether Cato might even surpass *him* (*On Constancy* 7.1). In this he is not blurring Stoic distinctions but highlighting the indomitable moral strength of a sage. Through Cato and numerous other examples from the Roman past, Seneca fuses the Stoic sage with the traditional image of a Roman hero, thus spurring his Roman readers to fulfill their duties by emulating both at once.

Below the level of sage, Seneca outlines three stages of moral progress, demarcated according to our vulnerability to irrational emotions (*Letters* 75). There is the condition very near to that of being a sage, in which a person is not yet confident of being able to withstand irrational emotions (the so-called passions, *pathê*). Just below it is the stage in which a person is still capable of lapsing, and at the lowest level of progress a person can avoid most irrational emotions, but not all. Below these are the innumerable people who have yet to make progress. Seneca has nothing to say to them; he wants to avoid them, lest he be contaminated. What he does allow is that persons who are still struggling to become good may give way to grief initially; but he insists that this period must be brief. The Stoics talk "big words," he says, when they forbid moans and groans; he'll adopt a more gentle tone (*Letters* 23.4). Still, he insists, these words are "true"; and his aim is to lead, as much as he can, to the goal of a dispassionate attitude toward externals. Like everyone, the wise person is prone to initial shocks—reactions that look momentarily like irrational emotions—but these are involuntary responses to be succeeded immediately by the calmness of judgment. Seneca's sage is kind to others and is filled with a serene joy that has nothing to do with the ephemeral pleasure that other people take in externals.

Looking toward Roman heroism, Seneca portrays moral progress as an arduous struggle, like a military campaign or the uphill storming of an enemy's position. The enemy is fortune, viciously attacking its victim in the form of the most cruel disasters. Its opponent may succumb, but he will have conquered fortune if he resists to the end. In reality, the disasters come from other people or simply from circumstances. Seneca commonly cites death (whether one's own or that of a loved one), exile, torture, and illness. His own life is rich with examples. He goes so far as to advocate adversity as a means of making moral progress, but he also allows (with a view to his own wealth) that favorable circumstances are a help to the person who is still struggling to make progress.

To make progress, a person must not only confront externals but also, above all, look within oneself. Drawing inspiration from Plato, Seneca tells us there is a god inside; there is a soul that seeks to free itself from the dross of the body. Seneca invites the reader to withdraw into this inner self, so as to both meditate on one's particular condition and take flight in the contemplation of god. This withdrawal can occur in the press of a very active life. But it's easier when one is no longer fully caught up in politics, and so Seneca associates moral withdrawal with his own attempt to withdraw from politics toward the end of his life. He insists that he will continue to help others through his philosophical teachings, like other Stoics.

Senecan Tragedy

From Seneca's hand there survive eight tragedies (*Agamemnon*, *Thyestes*, *Oedipus*, *Medea*, *Phaedra*, *Phoenissae*, *Troades*, *Hercules Furens*), not including the spurious *Octavia* and the probably spurious *Hercules Oetaeus*; of the *Phoenissae* there remain only fragments. These dramas have undergone many vicissitudes in fortune throughout the centuries; however, they are no longer criticized as being mere flawed versions of the older Greek dramas in which much of Seneca's subject matter had already been treated. While Seneca's plays were once mined only for the light they shed on Roman Stoic philosophy, for examples of rhetorical extravagance, or for the reconstruction of missing plays by Sophocles and his fellows, the traits that once marked the dramas as unworthy of critical attention now engage us in their own right. Indeed, they are the only extant versions of any Roman tragedy, the writings of other dramatists such as Marcus Pacuvius (ca. 220–130 BCE) and Lucius Accius (ca. 170–86 BCE) having been lost to posterity. It is thus only Seneca's version of Roman drama, translated into English as the *Tenne Tragedies* in 1581, that so influenced the tragedians of the Elizabethan era.

Seneca may have turned his hand to writing drama as early as the reign of Caligula (37–41 CE), although there is no way of determining exactly when he began. Our first reference to the plays comes from a famous graffito from the *Agamemnon* preserved on a wall in Pompeii, but we can only deduce that this was written before the eruption of Vesuvius in 79 CE; it is of little actual use in trying to date the dramas. Stylistic analysis has not provided us with a sure order of composition, though scholars seem to agree that the *Thyestes* and the *Phoenissae* are late efforts. Certainly we are unable to make claims about their dating with respect to the *Essays* and *Letters*, despite the very different tones of Seneca's prose and his poetry—a difference that led some readers, including the fifth-century churchman and orator Sidonius Apollinaris and after him Erasmus and Diderot, to speculate (erroneously) that there might have been two Lucius Annaeus Senecas at work on them rather than one.

This confusion about the authorship of Seneca's writing may seem natural, given the argument that Stoicism fails as a way of life in the dramas. Whether it fails because its adherents are too weak to resist the pull of desire or emotion, because Stoicism itself is too difficult to practice successfully, because the universe is not the locus of a divine providence, or because the protagonists are so evil that they fail to see providence in action is open to argument; a metaliterary view might even suggest that plotlines inherited from mythology provide the force that condemns a Cassandra or a Polyxena to death at the hands of a Clytemnestra or a Ulysses, with Seneca taking advantage of this dramatic fact to suggest the inexorable workings of Fate and the futility of struggle against it. Consider the *Thyestes* (a topic often dramatized in the Late Republic, though Seneca's version is the only one we have). We meet the eponymous exile as he praises the pauper's life to his children—only the man who drinks out of earthenware cups can be truly happy and without fear, he reminds them—but when invited to return to the palace at Argos by his conniving brother Atreus, the source of his exile, he allows himself to be lured back after only a token hesitation about giving up his newfound equanimity. "Sequor," he says to his son, "I follow you"; but in following his appetite for the luxurious life he does the opposite of the good Stoic.

The rest is, well, the stuff of myth. Dressed in royal regalia, Thyestes sits down to enjoy a hearty stew and some fine red wine, but his satiated belches soon turn into howls of horror as the delighted Atreus informs him of his dinner's provenance: the meal is made up of the dismembered bodies of Thyestes' own sons. Is there an explicit ethical or philosophical message here? If we followed the view of another Stoic, Epictetus (ca. 55–ca. 135 CE), who defined tragedy as what happens "when chance events befall fools" (*Discourses* 2.26.31), we might conclude that the story of Thyestes precisely illustrates the folly of giving in to a desire for power (or haute cuisine). In Seneca's treatment, however, such a clear object lesson seems undermined by a number of factors: the fact that Atreus reigns triumphant as the drama ends; the undeniable echoes of Stoic exhortation in the impotent counsels of Atreus's adviser; and the fragility of civic and religious values—the hellish scene in which Atreus sacrifices the children represents precisely a travesty of sacrifice itself, while *xenia* (the ancient tradition of hospitality) fares still worse. The adviser or a nurse mouthing Stoic platitudes without effect is featured in many of the plays: Phaedra, Clytemnestra, and Medea all have nurses to counsel them against their paths of action, even though their advice is invariably distorted and thrown back in their faces. Creon plays a similar role in the *Agamemnon*.

Other Senecan protagonists have more lasting doubts than Thyestes about the value of earthly success. Oedipus asks: "Joys any man in power?" And unlike his more confident Sophoclean manifestation, he feels the answer is clearly no. From the beginning of the play, the *Oedipus* provides striking contrasts to its Greek precedent, whose emphasis on the discovery of identity yields here to the overwhelming sense of pollution affecting Oedipus. The king, anxious even as the drama opens, worries that he will not escape the prophecy of his parricide, and suspects he is responsible for the plague ravaging Thebes. Despondent, he hopes for immediate death; his emotional state is far different from that of the character at the center of Sophocles' play. Seneca's version also features Creon's report of the long necromantic invocation of Laius's ghost in a dark grove, something absent in Sophocles. Even the sense that the characters' interaction onstage fails to drive the drama makes sense in the context of Seneca's forbidding and inexorable dramatic world. Causality and *anagnorisis* (dramatic recognition) are put aside in favor of the individual's helplessness before what awaits him, and the characters' speeches react to the violence rather than motivate it.

The pollution of the heavens by humans goes against Stoic physics but finds its place in the plays. The Stoics posited a tensional relationship between the cosmos and its parts; according to this view, the *pneuma*, or vital spirit, that subtends all matter results in a cosmic sympathy of the parts with the whole. "All things are united together . . . and earthly things feel the influence of heavenly ones," as Epictetus (*Discourses* 1.4.1) puts it. But what we see in the dramas is a disquieting manifestation of this *sympatheia*: the idea that the wickedness of one or a few could disrupt the rational and harmonic logos of the entire cosmos represents a reversal of the more orthodox Stoic viewpoint that the world is accessible to understanding and to reason. Thus we see the universe trembling at Medea's words, and the law of heaven in disorder. In the *Thyestes*, the sun hides its face in response to Atreus's crime; in the *Phaedra*, the chorus notes an eclipse after Phaedra's secret passion is unveiled. Horrific portents presage what is to come in the *Troades*. In Seneca's dramas, unlike in Greek tragedy, there is no role for civic institutions or the city to intervene in this relationship. The treatment of the gods is similarly unorthodox. Although Jason calls on Medea to witness that there are no gods in the heavens, the very chariot in which she flies away is evidence of the assistance given her by her divine father. The gods are there; the problem is that they are unrecognizable.

Seneca's great antiheroes like Medea and Thyestes are troubling not only because they often triumph, but because the manner of their triumph can resemble the goal point of the aspiring Stoic: in exhorting themselves to take up a certain stance toward the world, in abandoning familial and social ties, in rejecting the moral order of the world around them, and in trying to live up to a form of self-hood they have judged to be "better," Seneca's tyrants, just like his sages, construct a private and autonomous world around themselves which nothing can penetrate. Not only do they borrow the self-exhortations and self-reproving of the Stoic's arsenal, in which the dialogue conducted with the self suggests a split between a first-order desiring self and a second-order judging self, but they also adopt the consideration of what befits or is worthy of them as a guiding principle—always with a negative outcome.

This leads in turn to a metatheatrical tinge in several of the plays. In the *Medea*, for example, Medea seems to look to prior versions of her own story to discover what exactly is appropriate for her persona, in the same way that Oedipus, after putting out his eyes, remarks, "*This* face befits (an) Oedipus" (*Oedipus* 1000) or that Atreus says of his recipe, "This is a crime that befits Thyestes—and befits Atreus" (*Thyestes* 271). Such metatheatricality seems to draw on the concern of the traditional Roman elite to perform exemplary actions for an approving audience, to generate one's ethical exemplarity by making sure that spectators for it exist.

And spectators do exist—we, the theater audience or the recitation audience. Scholars have long debated the question of whether Seneca's dramas were staged in antiquity. It is possible, as argued by the nineteenth-century German scholar Friedrich Leo, the tragedies were written for recitation only; inter alia, it would be unusual (but not impossible) to represent animal sacrifice and murder onstage. The question is unresolvable, but whether the original audiences were in the theater or in the recitation room, they shared with us the full knowledge of how the story would turn out, and in this they un-comfortably resembled some of the plotting antiheroes themselves. Indeed, our pleasure in watching Senecan tragedy unfold might seem to assimilate us to the pleasure these characters take in inflicting suffering on one another. In a famous line from the *Troades*, the messenger who brings news of Astyanax's murder reports of the scene of his death—which he has already compared to a theater—that "the greater part of the fickle crowd abhors the crime—and watches it" (1128–29). Here, in the tension between sadistic voyeurism and horror at what the drama unfolds, we can recognize the uncomfortable position of the spectator of Seneca's despairing plays.

Senecan Drama after the Classical Period

The fortunes of Senecan drama have crested twice: once during the Elizabethan period, and again in our own day. Although Seneca himself never refers to his tragedies, they were known in antiquity at least until Boethius (ca. 480–524 CE), whose *Consolation of Philosophy* draws on the themes of Seneca's choral odes. The dramas then largely dropped from sight, to reemerge in 1300 in a popular edition and commentary by Nicholas Trevet, a Dominican scholar at Oxford. Trevet's work was followed by vernacular translations in Spain, Italy, and France over the next two centuries. In Italy, an early imitator was Albertino Mussato (1261–1329), who wrote his tragic drama *Ecerinis* to alert his fellow Paduans to the danger presented by the tyrant of Verona. In England, the Jesuit priest and poet Jasper Heywood (1535–1598) produced translations of three of the plays; these were followed by Thomas Newton's *Seneca His Tenne Tragedies Translated into English* in 1581—of which one tragedy was Newton's own *Thebais*. The dramas were considered to be no mere pale shadow of their Greek predecessors: Petrarch, Salutati, and Scaliger all held Seneca inferior to none on the classical stage. In Scaliger's influential treatise on poetry, the *Poetices libri septem* (1561), he ranks Seneca as the equal of the Greek dramatists in solemnity and superior to Euripides in elegance and polish (6.6).

The Elizabethan playwrights in particular took up Seneca as a model for translation or imitation. T. S. Eliot claimed, "No author exercised a wider or deeper influence on the Elizabethan mind or on the Elizabethan form of tragedy than did Seneca," and the consensus is that he was right. It is perhaps little wonder that Seneca appealed to an age in which tragedy was seen as the correct vehicle for the representation of "haughtinesse, arrogancy, ambition, pride, iniury, anger, wrath, envy, hatred, contention, warre, murther, cruelty, rapine, incest, rovings, depredations, piracyes, spoyles, robberies, rebellions, treasons, killings, hewing, stabbing, dagger-drawing, fighting, butchery, treachery, villainy, etc., and all kind of heroyicke evils whatsoever" (John Greene, *A Refutation of the Apology for Actors*, 1615, p. 56). Kyd, Marlowe, Marston, and Shakespeare all read Seneca in Latin at school, and much of their drama shows his influence in one form or another. The itinerant players at Elsinore in Shakespeare's *Hamlet* famously opine that "Seneca cannot be too heavy nor Plautus too light" (2.2.400–401), but it is Shakespeare's *Titus Andronicus* that shows the greatest Senecan influence with its taste for revenge, rape, decapitation, human cookery, and insanity. Richard III and Macbeth, on the other hand, exemplify the presence of unrestrained, brooding ambition in the power-hungry protagonist. Similarly, in such plays as Thomas Kyd's *The Spanish Tragedy* and John Marston's *Antonio's Revenge* we see the influence of such Senecan fixtures as ghosts speaking from beyond the grave, graphic violence, obsession with revenge, and even structural features such as choruses, use of stichomythia, and division into five acts.

The bleak content of the dramas was often tied to the notion of a moral lesson. Already Trevet's preface to the *Thyestes* argued that the play taught the correction of morals by example, as well as simply offered the audience enjoyment. The Jesuit Martín Antonio Delrio (1551–1608) defended the use of Roman drama in a Christian education by suggesting that it provided a masked instruction in wisdom, as did Mussato before him. Nonetheless, after the middle of the seventeenth century Seneca's drama fell largely into disrepute. The Restoration poet John Dryden (1631–1700) took the opportunity in the preface to his own *Oedipus* to criticize both Seneca's and Corneille's versions; of the former, he wrote that "Seneca . . . is always running after pompous expression, pointed sentences, and Philosophical notions, more proper for the Study than the Stage." The French dramatist Jean Racine (1639–1699) used Seneca as a model for his *Phèdre*, but at the same time claimed that his main debt was to Euripides. Not surprisingly, the Romantics did not find much to like in Seneca. Recently, however, an efflorescence of interest in both the literary and the performance aspects of Senecan drama has produced new editions, scholarly monographs, and the staging of some of the plays. Noteworthy here are Sarah Kane's adaptation *Phaedra's Love*, performed in New York in May 1996; Michael Elliot

Rutenberg's May 2005 dramatization of a post-Holocaust *Oedipus* at Haifa University in Israel; and a 2007 Joanne Akalaitis production of the *Thyestes* at the Court Theatre in Chicago.

232A note on the translations: they are designed to be faithful to the Latin while reading idiomatically in English. The focus is on high standards of accuracy, clarity, and style in both the prose and the poetry. As such, the translations are intended to provide a basis for interpretive work rather than to convey personal interpretations. They eschew terminology that would imply a Judeo-Christian moral framework (e.g., "sin"). Where needed, notes have been supplied to explain proper names in mythology and geography.

For further information

On Seneca's life: Miriam T. Griffin, *Seneca: A Philosopher in Politics* (Oxford: 1976), and Paul Veyne, *Seneca: The Life of a Stoic*, translated from the French by David Sullivan (New York: 2003). On his philosophical thought: Brad Inwood, *Seneca: Stoic Philosophy at Rome* (Oxford: 2005), and Shadi Bartsch and David Wray, *Seneca and the Self* (Cambridge: 2009). On the dramas: A. J. Boyle, *Tragic Seneca: An Essay in the Theatrical Tradition* (New York and London: 1997); C. A. J. Littlewood, *Self-Representation and Illusion in Senecan Tragedy* (Oxford: 2004); and Thomas G. Rosenmeyer, *Senecan Drama and Stoic Cosmology* (Berkeley: 1989). On Seneca and Shakespeare: Robert S. Miola, *Shakespeare and Classical Tragedy: The Influence of Seneca* (Oxford: 1992), and Henry B. Charlton, *The Senecan Tradition in Renaissance Tragedy* (Manchester: 1946).

SENECA AND HIS WORLD

Note on Essays and Their Sequence

This volume contains all of Seneca's essays on ethical topics, with the exception of *On Benefits* (printed in a separate volume, *On Benefits*, trans. Miriam Griffin and Brad Inwood [Chicago: University of Chicago Press, 2011]), and *On Anger* and *On Clemency* (contained in the volume *Anger, Mercy, Revenge*, trans. Robert A. Kaster and Martha C. Nussbaum [Chicago: University of Chicago Press, 2010]).

All translations, except *On the Shortness of Life* and *On Leisure*, are based on the Latin texts of L. D. Reynolds, ed., *L. Annaei Senecae Dialogorum libri duodecim* (Oxford: Oxford University Press, 1977). Departures from this edition are stated in the notes. *On the Shortness of Life* and *On Leisure* are based on Gareth D. Williams, ed., *Seneca: "De Otio," "De Brevitate Vitae"* (Cambridge: Cambridge University Press, 2003).

The order of the essays in this volume is based on the chronological sequence proposed by Miriam Griffin, *Seneca: A Philosopher in Politics* (Cambridge: Cambridge University Press, 1976), 396.

Consolation to Marcia

Introduction

HARRY M. HINE

Without Seneca's *Consolation to Marcia*, we would never have heard of the woman to whom it is addressed; but her father, the historian Aulus Cremutius Cordus, appears in other ancient sources. During the reigns of Augustus and Tiberius he wrote a history of the civil wars, but during the latter's reign (in 25 CE) he was prosecuted on a charge of treason, he committed suicide, and his works were burned. After Tiberius's death in 37, Cordus's reputation was reinstated and his historical work circulated once more (though it does not survive today). Seneca refers to this rehabilitation, so the *Consolation* must have been written after the death of Tiberius, and most likely during the reign of Gaius (37–41); for Seneca seems to be in Rome at the time of writing (chapter 16.2), which rules out the years of his exile (41–49), and a date after 49 is hard to reconcile with the information Seneca gives about Marcia's age. A date of composition under Gaius would make this the earliest of Seneca's surviving prose works.

The work is a consolation, a work that offers comfort to someone who has been bereaved. Consolation had become a highly developed literary genre, drawing on various philosophical and rhetorical traditions. Two of the most influential prose consolations in antiquity no longer survive—the *On Grief* of the Academic philosopher Crantor (ca. 335–275 BCE), and Cicero's *Consolation*, written for himself after the death of his daughter Tullia in 45 BCE. In fact, Seneca's *Consolation to Marcia* is the earliest full-length consolation that survives. It may be compared with his *Consolation to Polybius* and two consolatory letters (63 and 99). All his consolations draw on traditional themes, such as praise of the deceased, exhortation not to indulge in excessive grieving, and the argument that, whether death is the end or the soul survives, for the deceased person death is better than life. Seneca simultaneously acknowledges that he is writing within an established tradition and draws attention to his own creativity when at 2.1 he says that he will depart from usual practice and begin with examples rather than advice. Stoicism is not prominent in his consolations: he repudiates the strict Stoic doctrine that the wise man will not grieve at all. He does, however, draw on the doctrine that grief, like all other emotions, is the product of false beliefs. In the case of grief, these are false beliefs about the nature of death and its effects on the deceased and the bereaved.

We do not know exactly what prompted Seneca to write this work for Marcia, for he does not claim any particular relationship or friendship with her or her family. It has been conjectured that by addressing Marcia, the daughter of one of Sejanus's victims, Seneca was attempting to distance himself from Sejanus, who had been discredited and executed under Tiberius; for Seneca's family had connections with Sejanus. But the conjecture cannot be proved. The ostensible reason for the work is that Marcia was still grieving for Metilius, her son who had died three years earlier, and Seneca wanted to persuade her to put her grief behind her. But the interval since her son's death, and the fact that in sizable sections of the work (as indicated in the notes to the translation) Marcia fades into the background as Seneca addresses a generalized male audience, show that the work is not simply a work of private, personal condolence.

Acknowledgments

I am grateful to Elizabeth Asmis and the press's reader for suggesting improvements to the translation, but I alone am responsible for remaining deficiencies.

Structure

1 Introduction

2–5 Examples: the contrasting reactions of Octavia and Livia to loss of a son

6–11 General advice about death and bereavement

12–19.3 Advice specifically related to Marcia's situation

19.3–25 Metilius's present condition does not justify continued mourning

26 Conclusion: Marcia's dead father is imagined appealing to her

Further Reading

Manning, C. E. 1981. *On Seneca's "Ad Marciam."* Mnemosyne Supplement 69. Leiden: E. J. Brill.

Olberding, A. 2005. "The 'Stout Heart': Seneca's Strategy for Dispelling Grief." *Ancient Philosophy* 25:141–54.

Shelton, J.-A. 1995. "Persuasion and Paradigm in Seneca's *Consolatio ad Marciam* 1–6." *Classica et Mediaevalia* 46:157–88.

Wilcox, A. 2006. "Exemplary Grief: Gender and Virtue in Seneca's Consolations to Women." *Helios* 33, no. 1: 73–100.

Consolation to Marcia

LUCIUS ANNAEUS SENECA

TRANSLATED BY HARRY M. HINE

(1.1) If I did not know, Marcia, that you have drawn back from the frailties of the female temperament just as much as you have from all other kinds of fault, and that people look up to your character as though it were some ancient paragon, I would not dare to attack your grief head-on—for even men readily cling to grief and brood over it—nor would I have formed the hope that at such an unfavorable time, before such a hostile judge, on such a hateful charge, I could get you to acquit the misfortune you have suffered. But your strength of character, which is already well established, and your courage, whose worth has been demonstrated under severe testing, have given me confidence.

(2) It has not gone unnoticed how you behaved in regard to your father, whom you loved just as much as your children, except that you did not wish him to outlive you. Or maybe you did wish even that; for great love sometimes allows itself to contravene normal moral rules. As far as you were able, you tried to prevent the death of your father Aulus Cremutius Cordus.[1] After it became clear to you that this was the only escape from slavery available to him when Sejanus's henchmen were closing in,[2] you did not support his intention, but you signaled acceptance of defeat; you openly shed tears,[3] and you swallowed your sighs, yet did not conceal them beneath a cheerful expression—and all this in that period when doing nothing unloving was equivalent to showing great love. (3) As soon as the changing political climate provided an opportunity,[4] you enabled the public to have access once more to your father's literary talent, which had been the target of the punishment; you rescued him from real death,[5] and restored to our public records the books that that exceptionally brave man had written in his own blood. You performed a superb service to Roman literature, for an important part of it had gone up in flames; a superb service to later generations, who will inherit a reliable, undistorted history, which cost its author dear; a superb service to him whose memory is strong and will remain strong for as long as a knowledge of Roman history is held to be valuable, for as long

as there is anyone who wants to look back to the achievements of his ancestors, for as long as there is anyone who wants to know what it is to be a Roman man, what it is to remain unflinching when everyone else is forced to bow the head and submit to the yoke of a Sejanus, what it is to be a human being with unfettered intelligence, mind, and hands. (4) The state would have suffered a great loss, by Hercules, if you had not rescued him after he had been cast into oblivion on account of two excellent characteristics, his eloquence and his outspokenness. He is being read, he is popular, he is welcomed into people's hands and hearts, and he has no fear of the passage of time. But those butchers will soon have even their crimes, the only things for which they deserved to be remembered, consigned to silence.

(5) This noble-mindedness of yours has prevented me from taking any notice of your sex, or of your face, which is still marred by so many years' continual sadness, just as it was disfigured by it at the start. And observe that I am not being underhanded with you or thinking of cheating your feelings: I have reminded you of sufferings that are long past; and so that you may realize that the present wound also needs healing, I have shown you the scar of an equally severe injury. So other people may treat you gently and soothingly, but I have decided to do battle with your grief; I shall bring your weary, exhausted eyes under control, eyes which, if you want to know the truth, flow more from habit than from longing; I shall do this, if possible, with your support for the remedies, but if not, I shall do it even against your will, even if you embrace and cling to your grief, which you have kept alive in place of your son. (6) For where will it end? Everything has been tried to no avail: the comforting words of friends and the influence of great men who are related to you have been exhausted; love of literature, a blessing you have inherited from your father, proves an ineffectual comfort, barely creating even a brief distraction, and it makes no impression on your deaf ears; nature's own remedy, time, which heals even the greatest distress, in your case alone has proved powerless. (7) Three years have now passed, and there has been no lessening of that initial shock; your mourning renews and strengthens itself each day; through the passage of time it has established squatter's rights, and has reached the point where it thinks that it would be shameful to stop. Just as every kind of fault becomes deeply embedded unless it is stamped out while it is still

growing, so these sad, wretched, self-destructive faults in the end feed on their own bitterness, and the unhappy mind finds a perverse pleasure in grief. (8) So I wish I could have begun this treatment in the early stages: a milder medicine could have been used to check the attack while it was still building up; but chronic diseases need to be fought more vigorously. For with wounds as well, healing is easy while they are fresh and still bleeding; but when they have festered and turned foully ulcerous, they must be cauterized and cut open again and must allow fingers to probe into them. As things stand, I cannot attack such a hardened grief by polite or gentle means: it has to be shattered.

(2.1) I know that everyone who wants to give advice begins with instructions and ends with examples. Sometimes it is useful to change this pattern. Different people need different treatment: some are guided by reason; some need to be confronted with famous names, with prestige that will constrain their thinking when they are captivated by superficial appearances. (2) I shall set before you two outstanding examples of your own sex and your own generation: one, a woman who let grief sweep her away, the other, someone affected by a similar misfortune but by a greater loss, who nevertheless did not allow her sufferings to control her for long but soon recovered her usual frame of mind. (3) Octavia and Livia, one the sister of Augustus, the other the wife, lost young sons, both in the sure hope that he would be emperor:[6] Octavia lost Marcellus, on whom his uncle, also his father-in-law, had begun to depend,[7] on whom the burden of imperial power had begun to weigh, a young man of mental alacrity and powerful intellect, but with a frugality and self-control that deserved no little admiration in someone of his years or wealth; doggedly hardworking, a stranger to pleasures, ready to bear whatever burdens his uncle wanted to place and, so to speak, build on him; he had carefully chosen foundations that would not buckle under any weight. (4) Throughout her entire life she never brought her weeping and lamenting to an end;[8] she would not listen to any words of helpful advice, and would not even let herself be distracted; intent on one thing, with her whole mind fixed on it, throughout her life she behaved just as she had at the funeral. I do not say she did not venture to get herself up, but she refused to be helped up, thinking that abandoning her tears would be a second bereavement.

(5) She would not keep any image of her beloved son, or allow any mention to be made of him. She hated all mothers, and was especially enraged at Livia, because the happiness that she herself had been promised seemed to have transferred to that woman's son. She was most at home with darkness and solitude; she never even thought of her brother; she rejected poems written to celebrate the memory of Marcellus, and other literary tributes;[9] and she shut her ears against any kind of comfort. Withdrawing from her official duties, and detesting the excessive brilliance of her brother's greatness and good fortune, she buried and hid herself away. When her children[10] and her grandchildren gathered around her, she did not take off her mourning clothes, an insult to all her family, for though they were alive, she thought of herself as childless.

(3.1) Livia had lost her son Drusus, who would have made a great emperor, and was already a great commander. He had entered deep into Germany and had set up Roman standards where there was scarcely any knowledge of the Romans' existence.[11] He had died on campaign; while he was ill, the enemy themselves, with intense respect, gave him safe passage, joined in observing a truce, and did not dare to pray for the outcome that suited them. At his death, which he had met in the service of the state, there was a tremendous sense of loss among the citizens, the provinces, and the whole of Italy; throughout the country, municipalities and colonies had poured out to pay their mournful respects as his funeral cortège proceeded toward the city with all the appearance of a triumph. (2) His mother had not been allowed to drink in her son's final kisses or the sweet sound of his dying words; on the long journey, as she escorted the remains of her beloved Drusus, she was upset by the many pyres blazing throughout the length and breadth of Italy, as though she were losing him all over again with each one. Nevertheless, as soon as she had placed him in the tomb,[12] she laid both him and her grief to rest, and mourned no more than was honorable or just while Caesar was still alive. And finally, she never stopped praising the name of her dear Drusus, recalling him everywhere both in private and in public, gladly speaking about him and hearing about him: she lived with his memory, something no one can preserve and revisit if it has been allowed to become a source of sadness.

(3) So choose which of these examples you think the more com-

mendable. If you want to follow the first one, you will absent yourself from the company of the living; you will avoid both other people's children and your own, and even the very child you miss; mothers will regard you as a bad omen when you encounter them; you will spurn pleasures that are honorable and permissible, as though inappropriate to your misfortune; you will hate the light in which you linger, and will bitterly detest your age, because it does not instantly strike you down and bring your life to an end; and—something most shameful and quite out of keeping with your character, which is very highly regarded—you will demonstrate that you do not want to live and yet are incapable of dying. (4) But if you devote yourself to the other more self-controlled, more humane example set by a truly great woman, you will not be distressed and will not endure agonies of torment; for in heaven's name, what madness it is to punish oneself for one's misfortune, and to add to one's own miseries![13] The same virtue and the same reserve as you have maintained throughout your life will be on display in your present circumstances too; for even grieving has its own form of modesty. As for the young man, he thoroughly deserves to make you happy with every mention or thought of him, and you will do him greater honor if he continues to be just as cheerful and joyful in his mother's presence as he was during his lifetime.

(4.1) I shall not steer you toward instructions of a more rigorous sort, ordering you to endure human experience in an inhuman way, or drying a mother's eyes on the very day of the funeral.[14] I shall go to arbitration with you: the dispute between us will be whether grief should be great or unending. (2) I have no doubt that the example of Julia Augusta, with whom you were on friendly terms, pleases you more.[15] She now beckons you to join in a conversation: in her initial turmoil, when a person's misery is at its most recalcitrant and extreme, she let Areus, her husband's philosopher,[16] console her, and acknowledged that she had benefited greatly from that course of action: more than from the Roman people, whom she did not want to sadden with her own sadness; more than from Augustus, who was reeling from the loss of one of his two supports,[17] and must not be thrown off balance by his family's grief; more than from her son Tiberius, whose love ensured that at that untimely funeral, which made the nations weep, the only loss she suffered was to the number of her children.

(3) This, I imagine, was how he approached her, this was how he began to address a woman who carefully protected her reputation: "Down to this day, Julia,[18] as far as I know—and I have been a constant companion of your husband; I have known not only what was said in public but all the inmost feelings of both your hearts—you have been at pains to ensure that there was nothing for which anyone could reproach you; not only in more important matters but in the most trivial ones, you have been careful not to do anything that you would want public opinion, that most outspoken critic of emperors, to forgive. (4) I think there is nothing more glorious than when those who are at the pinnacle of society grant pardon for many actions, but seek pardon for none; so in the present circumstances too you need to stick to your usual practice, and do nothing that you might wish you had not done at all or had done differently.

(5.1) "Then I beg and implore you not to present a difficult and intractable face to your friends. For you should be aware that all of them are at a loss how to behave, whether to speak about Drusus in your presence, lest either failure to recall the outstanding young man should hurt him, or mention of him should hurt you. (2) When we have left your presence and have gathered together, we celebrate his deeds and words with the respect that he deserves; in your presence we maintain total silence about him. So you are missing out on a supreme pleasure, the praises of your son—for which, I have no doubt, you would ensure everlasting survival, if the opportunity arose, even at the cost of your own life. (3) So permit, or rather invite, conversations where he is the topic, and keep your ears open to the name and memory of your son; do not think this depressing, as others do who in similar misfortune regard listening to words of comfort as a part of their suffering. (4) As things are, you have gone to the one extreme: forgetting the better times, you are focusing on the worse aspects of your fortune. You are not turning your attention to the life you shared with your son and the enjoyable times you spent with him, or his boyish, adorable charms, or the progress of his education; you dwell on that final scene, and add as much as you can to its horror, as though it were not horrid enough already. Do not, I beg you, long for a most perverse kind of glory, that of being regarded as the most unfortunate of women. (5) At the same time remember that it is no great achievement to behave bravely when conditions are favorable, when life is proceeding smoothly: a calm sea and following wind do not display the steersman's skill either; some challenge must arise to test his courage. **(6)** So do not be dejected, but rather stand firm, and bear whatever burdens fall on you without being terrified, once the initial disturbance is past.[19] Nothing shows greater contempt for fortune than a calm mind." After saying this, he drew her attention to her surviving son, he drew her attention to her grandchildren from the son she had lost.[20]

(6.1) Your own circumstances were addressed on that occasion, Marcia, it was you that Areus sat beside; change the cast list, and he offered comfort to you. Still, Marcia, suppose that you have been robbed of more than any other mother has ever lost—I am not trying to mollify you, nor am I making light of your misfortune: **(2)** if fate can be overcome by weeping, let us resort to weeping; let every day be spent in grieving, let sleepless misery consume the night; let our hands pummel our bruised breasts, let our very faces come under attack, and let sorrow, to advance its cause, employ every kind of cruelty. But if no breast-beating can bring back the dead, if fate, unchanging and fixed for eternity, is not altered by any distress, and death keeps whatever it has taken, let there be an end to a grief that is just being wasted. **(3)** So let us keep control of ourselves and not allow that force to drive us off course. It is shameful when a ship's helmsman has the rudder wrested from his grasp by the waves, when he abandons the sails as they flap wildly, and leaves his vessel at the mercy of the storm; but even in a shipwreck, praise is due to a helmsman who is overwhelmed by the sea as he is still clinging to the rudder and struggling.

(7.1) "But grieving for one's relatives is natural." Who can disagree, as long as it is done in moderation? For when we are merely separated from our dear ones, never mind when we lose them, there is an unavoidable stab of pain, and a contraction even in the most resolute minds.[21] But what imagination adds goes beyond what nature commands. **(2)** In the case of mute animals, see how agitated their grieving is, and yet how short lived: with cows, their bellowing is heard for one or two days, and with mares, their erratic, demented charging around lasts no longer; when wild animals have followed the tracks of their cubs and wandered all through the forests, when they have returned repeatedly to their ransacked lairs, they extinguish their rage within a short time; birds squawk around their empty nests with loud shrieks, but in a moment they fall silent and resume their flight. No animals mourn their offspring for long, apart from human beings; they encourage their own grief, and the duration of their affliction depends not on what they feel but on what they decide.

(3) You can tell it is not natural to be broken by grief because, first of all, the same bereavement wounds women more than men, barbarians more than people of peaceful, cultured races, and the uneducated more than the educated. Yet things that derive their force from nature maintain the same force in every instance: if something shows variation, evidently it is not based on nature. (4) Fire will burn people of every age, citizens of every city, men as well as women; steel will display its ability to cut in bodies of every kind. Why? Because they get their power from nature, which does not discriminate among persons. Different people have different reactions to poverty, grief, and ambition, depending on the habits that have become ingrained in them; and they are rendered weak and unable to endure by a preformed belief in the frightfulness of things that should not be feared.

(8.1) Second, what is natural does not diminish with time: but the passing days eventually exhaust grief. No matter how stubborn it is, reviving every day and fervently resisting any remedies, nevertheless time, the most effective tamer of fierce emotions, robs it of its strength. (2) You, Marcia, still suffer enormous sorrow, and it now seems to have developed a callus: it is not the keen sorrow it was at the beginning, but a stubborn, recalcitrant one. However, the passage of time will gradually free you even from this: whenever your attention is elsewhere, your mind will relax. (3) At the moment you are keeping yourself under surveillance; but there is an important difference between allowing yourself to grieve and ordering yourself to. It suits the excellence of your character much better to impose an end on your mourning rather than wait for its end, and to refuse to hold out until the day when, against your wishes, grief will fade away. You should renounce it yourself!

(9.1) "So what is the origin of the great stubbornness with which we lament our loved ones, if it does not occur at nature's command?" It is because we do not anticipate suffering until it happens; rather, as though we ourselves were exempt and had set out on a more tranquil journey than other people, we fail to learn from the misfortunes of others that they are common to all. **(2)** So many funeral processions pass our house: yet we do not think about death. There are so many untimely deaths: yet we plan for our children getting their toga,[22] for their military service, for their inheriting their father's estate. We are confronted by so many wealthy people who suddenly face poverty: and yet it never occurs to us that our own wealth is equally precarious. This makes our fall all the greater: it is as if we are struck out of the blue. But when things have long been anticipated, their attack has less power. **(3)** You[23] must realize that you stand exposed to every kind of blow, and that the weapons that have struck others have been whizzing past you. Just as if, with poor equipment, you were climbing up to attack some city wall or a high point occupied by a large enemy force, you should expect to be wounded, and should reckon that your body is the target of the rocks that are raining down, and of the arrows and the spears. Whenever someone falls beside you or behind you, cry out: "You will not deceive me, fortune, or find me complacent or heedless when you destroy me. I know what you are up to: you struck somebody else, but you were aiming at me." **(4)** Who has ever examined his life in the recognition that he is going to die? Which of you has ever ventured to think about exile, poverty, grief? Who would not, if he were advised to think about them, spit out the advice like words of ill omen, and bid the curse fall on his enemies, or on the unwelcome adviser himself? **(5)** "I didn't think it would happen." How can you think that anything is not going to happen when you know that it can happen, and you see that it has happened to many people? What a fine line of poetry this is, deserving better than to have come from the stage:

"What can happen to one person can happen to anyone"![24]

That man lost his children: you too can lose yours. That man was condemned: your innocence too is within range. This delusion deceives and unmans us, when we suffer what we never foresaw that we could suffer. Those who have anticipated the occurrence of suffering rob it of its force when it arrives.

(10.1) All the extraneous, glittering things that surround us, Marcia—children, honors, wealth, large atria, forecourts packed with a crowd of clients who are kept at bay, a famous name, a noble or beautiful wife, and all the other things that depend on uncertain, fickle chance—these are paraphernalia that do not belong to us but are on loan; not one of them is a gift. The stage is furnished with borrowed props that will revert to their owners; some things will be returned on day one, others on day two, a few will remain right up to the end. (2) So we should not be proud of ourselves as though it were our own possessions that surround us: we have received them on loan. We may enjoy the use of them, but the giver manages his gift and sets the time limit.[25] We must ensure that what has been granted for an unspecified period is always available, and when we are summoned, we must hand it back without complaint: it is a very poor kind of debtor who starts lashing out at his creditor. (3) So we must love all our relatives, both those who, in accordance with the laws of birth, we want to outlive us, and those who, with complete justification, we pray will predecease us; but we must love them in the knowledge that we have received no promise that their lives will be endless, indeed no promise that they will be long. Our minds need frequent prompting to love things on the understanding that we are sure to lose them, or rather that we are already losing them: you should treat all of fortune's gifts as coming without a guarantee. (4) So seize the pleasures afforded by your children,[26] let your children enjoy you in turn, and extract all the joy you can without delay: no promise has been made about the coming night; I have granted too long an extension—no promise has been made about the next hour. You must hurry, you are being hotly pursued: soon your unit will be scattered; soon, as the battle cry goes up, all that camaraderie will be destroyed. Nothing escapes the looting: wretched people, you do not know how to live on the run!

(5) If you are grieving because your son is dead,[27] it is the moment of his birth that should be in the dock; for notice of death was served on him as he was being born; he came into being under this regulation; this fate started to accompany him as soon as he left the womb. (6) We have arrived in the kingdom of fortune, a harsh and intransigent place, and we shall suffer deservedly and undeservedly at its will. It will subject our bodies to reckless, humiliating, cruel mistreatment: it will burn some of them with fire, deployed either as a punishment or as a remedy; others it will bind in chains—sometimes letting enemies do this, sometimes fellow citizens; others it will toss

up and down, naked, on the treacherous seas, and after they have wrestled with the waves it will not even throw them up onto sand or shore, but will bury them in the stomach of some huge sea creature; others, after they have been utterly debilitated by various kinds of illness, it will keep long poised between life and death. Like a temperamental, capricious owner who neglects her slaves, it will veer between punishments and rewards.

(II.I) What need is there to shed tears over life's individual stages? For the whole of life requires tears. New misfortunes will assail you before you have dealt with the old. So you women, who show no restraint in your suffering, must be especially restrained, and must share out the resources of the human spirit among many griefs. And then, why this forgetfulness about your own condition, about the universal human condition? You were born a mortal and you have given birth to mortals:[28] though you yourself are a decaying, feeble body, repeatedly targeted by diseases, did you hope that from such weak material you had carried in your womb something robust and everlasting? (2) Your son has died, that is, he has completed the course and reached the finish line which those you think more fortunate than your own offspring are fast approaching. The entire multitude that goes to law in the forum, that <claps> in the theater, that prays in the temples, is advancing at different speeds toward this point: what you love and honor, and what you despise, will be reduced to the same ashes. (3) Plainly that <saying> attributed to the Pythian oracle, "Know yourself," <is relevant> here.[29] What is a human being? A pot that can be broken by the slightest knock, the slightest jolt. There is no need of a great storm to cause destruction: in any collision, a person will break into pieces. What is a human being? A weak, fragile body, naked and, in its natural state, unprotected, requiring external help, exposed to all the humiliations of fortune, and, even when it has built up its muscles, a meal for any wild beast, a sacrificial victim for any; formed from weak, impermanent constituents, handsome only in its external features; unable to endure cold, heat, or hard work, yet prone to sink into decay through idleness and inactivity; fearful about the things it eats, one moment <passing away> for lack of them, <the next> being destroyed <by excess>; a body anxious and troubled about its own protection, whose breathing is fragile and insecure, which is shaken by a sudden fright or by the sound of an unexpected noise assailing its ears, constantly feeding its own anxiety, sick and useless. (4) In such a body are we surprised to discover death, which can be caused by a single hiccough? For the body to drop dead, is great exertion required? A smell, a taste, tiredness, insomnia, liquid, food, and all the essentials of life can be deadly. Wherever the body travels, it is immediately aware of its vulnerability, being unable to tolerate some climates: unfamiliar kinds of water, a breath of an unaccustomed breeze, the slightest causes and upsets make it ill. It is sickly, an invalid, and inaugurates its life with tears. Yet what a commotion is incessantly created by this despicable creature, what grand thoughts it harbors when it forgets its own condition! (5) People entertain ideas of immortality and eternity, and make provision for grandchildren and great-grandchildren, yet while they are planning for the long term, death is destroying them; and what is called old age is the passing of only very few years.

(12.1) Is your grief, if it has any rational basis at all, focused on its own sufferings, or on those of the deceased? In the loss of your son, are you swayed by the thought that you derived no pleasure from him, or that you could have enjoyed greater pleasure if he had lived longer? (2) If you say you have enjoyed no pleasure, you will make your loss more bearable; for human beings do not miss very greatly things from which they derived no joy or happiness. If you admit that you did derive great pleasure from him, you must not complain about what has been withheld, but must give thanks for what has been granted; for you have obtained sufficient reward for your labors from your involvement in his upbringing, unless perhaps those who devotedly nurture puppies and birds and faddish sorts of pet gain some pleasure from the sight and touch and fond adoration of dumb animals, whereas those who nurture children do not find the process of bringing them up to be a reward in itself. So even if you have derived no benefit from his hard work, no protection from his attentiveness, no guidance from his wisdom, the very fact that you have had him and have loved him is reward enough. (3) "But it could have been longer lasting and greater." Yet you were better off than if you had never had a son, since, if faced with the choice between being happy for a limited time or not at all, it is better for us to receive blessings that will evaporate than none at all. Would you rather have had a worthless son, one who counts as a son in name only, or one with the great talents that your own son had, a young man who swiftly displayed wisdom, swiftly displayed love, swiftly became a husband, swiftly became a father, swiftly took all his duties seriously, swiftly became a priest—and constantly gave the impression of being in a hurry? Virtually no one receives blessings that are both great and long lasting; only slow-maturing happiness endures and reaches the finish line. The immortal gods were not going to give you a son for long, so they gave you one who immediately displayed qualities that people <struggle to> develop even over a long period of time.

(4) And you cannot say that you were singled out by the gods to be refused the chance to enjoy your son: cast your eyes over the whole multitude of people known and unknown, and everywhere you will find those who have been through greater sufferings. Great commanders have experienced them, so have emperors; in mythology, not even the gods have been left unscathed, in order, I think, that our bereavements should be lightened by the realization that even the divine can suffer ruin.[30] Look around at everyone, I tell you: you will not be able to name a single family <so> wretched that it cannot draw comfort from one more wretched. (5) But, by Hercules, I do not take so poor a view of your character as to think you can bear your misfortune more easily if I parade a huge number of mourners before you: a mass of wretched people is a cruel form of consolation. But I shall produce some examples, not to show you that human beings have often been bereaved—for it would be ridiculous to accumulate examples of our mortality—but to show you that many people have softened a harsh blow by bearing it with composure.

(6) I shall begin with a most fortunate man.[31] Lucius Sulla lost his son, but that neither blunted the malevolence and the intense courage he showed toward enemies and fellow citizens, nor made it look as though he was wrong to assume that cognomen of his. He adopted it after the loss of his son, fearing neither the hatred of humans, for whom his excessive good fortune meant suffering, nor the ill will of the gods, who stood accused of being responsible for Sulla's good fortune. But let us treat the character of Sulla as something on which final judgment has yet to be passed—even his enemies will admit that he was right to take up arms, and right to lay them down again:[32] there will be agreement on the point here at

stake, that a suffering that affects even the most fortunate is not the most extreme kind.

(**13.1**) Pulvillus the pontifex ensured that Greece should not be overproud of the father who, when news of the death of his son reached him as he was in the middle of a sacrifice, simply told the piper to stop playing, removed the garland from his head, and then completed the rest of the ritual;[33] for Pulvillus, when he received news of the death of his son as he was holding on to the doorpost during the dedication of the Capitol,[34] pretended he had not heard, and chanted the traditional words of the pontifex's hymn; not a single groan interrupted his prayers, and just after hearing his son's name he was seeking Jupiter's favor. (**2**) Do you think such a grief ought to have an end point, when its first day and first shock could not tear a father away from the public altars and the proper performance of the ceremony? By Hercules, he deserved to make a dedication that went down in history, he deserved a most exalted priesthood, for he did not stop worshipping the gods even when they were angry with him. However, when he got home, his eyes did fill with tears and he did utter some cries of grief; but when he had done what custom required for the deceased, he resumed the expression he had maintained on the Capitol.

(**3**) Paulus, around the time of that celebrated triumph in which he made Perses walk in front of his chariot in chains, gave away two sons to be adopted, and buried <the two> he had kept for himself. What do you reckon was the caliber of the ones he kept when one of those he parted with was Scipio?[35] The Roman people were full of emotion as they watched Paulus's empty chariot.[36] He still made a speech, and he thanked the gods for granting his prayer; for he had asked that if the envy aroused by his great victory demanded any payment, the debt should be settled at his own expense, not the state's. (**4**) You see what courage he showed? He regarded his bereavement as a blessing. And who could have been more deeply affected by so great a reversal of fortune? At a single stroke he lost his sources of both comfort and support. Yet Perses was not allowed to see Paulus sorrowful.

(**14.1**) Now, why should I take you through innumerable examples of great men and look for the ones who were wretched, as though it were not harder to find ones who were fortunate? For how few families have remained intact right up to the end, without any tragedy striking! Pick any year you want and make a roll call of its magistrates—Lucius Bibulus and Gaius Caesar, if you like: you will observe that those colleagues, despite their mutual hostility, were as one in their misfortune.[37] **(2)** Lucius Bibulus, a good man but not a courageous one, had two sons who were killed at the same time, after enduring humiliating treatment at the hands of Egyptian soldiers; so the circumstances of the loss called for tears just as much as the loss itself. Throughout his year of office Bibulus had insulted his colleague by lurking at home, yet the day after he received the news of the double death, he resumed his normal duties as commander.[38] Who could devote less than one day to two sons? That was how quickly he stopped mourning his children, though he had mourned his consulship for a year. **(3)** When Gaius Caesar was campaigning across Britain, being incapable of allowing the ocean to limit his good fortune,[39] he heard that his daughter had died, taking the fate of the nation with her.[40] He could see clearly that Gnaeus Pompeius would not take kindly to anyone else in the state being great,[41] and would seek to limit his advancement, which he felt was threatening, even though it was of general benefit. Nevertheless, within three days Caesar resumed his duties as commander, and conquered his grief as quickly as he always conquered everything else.

(15.1) Do I need to remind you of the bereavements of other Caesars? I think that fortune sometimes attacks them in order that they may confer on the human race the further benefit of demonstrating that even those who are reputedly born of the gods and destined to father gods[42] do not have the same control over their own fortune as they have over other people's. **(2)** The deified Augustus, after he had lost his children and grandchildren and the supply of Caesars was exhausted, used adoption to shore up his abandoned house:[43] he bore all this with the bravery of someone who was already directly concerned and had a personal stake in ensuring that no one should complain about the gods.[44] **(3)** Tiberius Caesar lost both the son he had fathered and the one he had adopted.[45] Yet he himself spoke in praise of his son before the Rostra; he stood with the corpse placed in full view, save that a curtain was hung up to shield the pontifex's eyes from the dead body.[46] While the Roman people wept, his face showed no emotion; he demonstrated to Sejanus, who was standing next to him, how resolutely he could endure losing those closest to him.[47]

(4) Do you see what a large number of men of great distinction were not exempted from the misfortune that strikes everything down, men on whom were showered so many good qualities of mind, so many honors both public and private? But of course this storm circles around and around, randomly destroying everything, or carrying it off as though it owned it. Get everyone to examine their accounts: no one has managed to be born without incurring a cost.

(16.1) I know what you are saying: "You have forgotten that you are offering comfort to a woman: you are giving examples of men." Who says that nature has been stingy in its treatment of women's characters, and has imposed narrow restrictions on their virtues? Believe me, they have just as much strength, and just as much potential for moral goodness, <so long as> they want it; they endure grief and hardship just as effectively, if they have developed the habit. (2) In which city are we talking like this, good gods? The one in which Lucretia and Brutus overthrew a king who was oppressing the citizens of Rome: we are indebted to Brutus for liberty, to Lucretia for Brutus;[48] the one in which Cloelia ignored the enemy and the river, and for her outstanding courage we have virtually treated her as a man: for, seated on horseback in her statue at a busy spot on the Sacred Way, as our young men climb into their cushioned litters, Cloelia rebukes them for traveling in that manner in a city in which we have awarded horses even to women.[49] (3) But if you want examples of women who were brave when they lost relatives, I shall not go from door to door searching for them; I shall offer you two Cornelias from one household. First the daughter of Scipio, mother of the Gracchi:[50] she recalled twelve births with as many funerals; the others, who made no impact on the city at their birth or their demise, are of no significance, but Tiberius and Gaius, who will be acknowledged as great men even by those who deny that they were good, those she saw murdered and then denied burial. But to those who consoled her and called her wretched she said, "I shall never stop saying that I am fortunate, I who gave birth to the Gracchi."[51] (4) Cornelia, the wife of Livius Drusus, had lost a most eminent young man of exceptional ability; he was marching on in the footsteps of the Gracchi, and left numerous bills still in progress when he was murdered in his own home, and it was uncertain who was responsible for the killing.[52] Still, she bore the untimely and unpunished death of her son with as much courage as he had shown in proposing his laws. (5) Now, will you make your peace with fortune, Marcia, if, after hurling its weapons at the Scipios and the mothers and daughters of the Scipios, after aiming them at the Caesars, it has not pointed them away from you either?

Life is filled and plagued with a variety of misfortunes, which grant no one a lasting peace, scarcely even a truce. You had brought four children into the world, Marcia. They say that no missile falls ineffectively when it is thrown at a densely packed army on the march: is it surprising that such a large group could not pass on its way unscathed by spite or harm? (6) "But fortune was more unjust because it didn't merely take my sons away but picked them out." But you should never talk of injustice when you get the same share as someone more powerful: it left you two daughters and grandchildren from them. And it has not removed all trace of the son for whom you grieve the most, forgetting the one you lost earlier: you have two daughters of his, great burdens, if your attitude is wrong, great comforts, if your attitude is right. Make this your aim, that when you see them, you should be reminded of your son, not of your sorrow. (7) When trees are toppled either because a wind has torn them up by the roots or because the sudden blast of a twisting tornado has snapped their trunks, the farmer nurtures the shoots they leave behind, and in <place> of the lost trees he at once plants out seeds and cuttings; and in an instant (for as with losses, so with gains, time moves rapidly and swiftly) the new growth is more luxuriant than what was lost. (8) So let these daughters of your Metilius be a substitute for him, let them fill the void; relieve your grief for one person with the comfort you get from two. This is human nature, that nothing is dearer to us than what we have lost; we are very unfair toward what remains, because of our longing for what has been taken from us. But if you care to assess how very lenient fortune has been with you, even when it was in a rage, you will realize that you have something more than consolations: look at your many grandchildren, and at your two daughters. You should also say this to yourself, Marcia: "I would be upset if everyone's fortune were determined by their character, and bad things never happened to good people: as it is, I can see that bad and good people are afflicted in the same way, without distinction."

(17.1) "But it is hard to lose a young man whom you have raised, just when he was beginning to lend help and distinction to his mother and his father." Who would deny it is hard? But it is human. You were born for this,[53] to suffer loss, to perish, to hope and to fear, to upset others and yourself, to dread death and yet also desire it, and, worst of all, never to understand your true condition.

(2) If someone said to a man who was heading for Syracuse: "Find out beforehand about all the disadvantages and all the delights of your intended journey, and only then set sail. These are the things you might marvel at: first of all you will see the island itself, separated from Italy by a narrow channel, but once, so it is thought, joined to the mainland; suddenly the sea burst in and 'split Hesperia's flank from Sicily's.'[54] Then you will see the Charybdis of mythology (for you will be able to skirt the edge of that voracious whirlpool); it stays calm while it is unaffected by the south wind, but if a strong gale blows from that direction, it swallows ships in its broad, deep mouth.[55] (3) You will see the spring of Arethusa, famed in poetry, with its sparkling pool, transparent right to the bottom, pouring out ice-cold waters, whether it finds them rising up there for the first time, or it restores a river that has flowed undiminished belowground, beneath all those seas, preserved from contamination with the tainted water.[56] (4) You will see a harbor that is the calmest of all that have been formed by nature or improved by human hands for the protection of fleets, so safe that there is no access even for the raging of the mightiest storms. You will see where the power of Athens was broken, where that natural prison, carved out of the rocks to an immeasurable depth, incarcerated all those thousands of captives.[57] You will see the immense city itself, whose layout covers a greater area than the entire territory controlled by many another city. You will see very mild winters, and never a day without some sunshine. (5) But when you have made all those discoveries, the oppressive, unhealthy summer will spoil the advantages of the winter climate. There you will find the tyrant Dionysius, the destroyer of liberty, justice, and law, a man greedy for absolute power even after Plato, for life even after exile;[58] he will burn some people, he will beat others, he will order others to be beheaded for some trivial offense, he

will send for males and females to serve his lust, and for the disgusting devotees of the palace's licentiousness it will not be enough to couple with just two people at the same time. You have heard what could attract you, and what could put you off: so either set sail or stop right here." (6) After this advice, if someone still said that he wanted to enter Syracuse, the only person he could fairly complain to would be himself, given that he had not just stumbled into the situation but had arrived with eyes open, and fully informed.

Nature says to all of us:[59] "I deceive no one. If you bring up children, you may have attractive ones and you may have ugly ones. Perhaps many will be born to you: one of them could be the savior of his country, or equally its betrayer. (7) Do not abandon the hope that they will gain such a good reputation that no one will dare to reproach you on their account; but also imagine them incurring such disgrace that they become bywords for evil. There is nothing to prevent their being the ones who perform your funeral rites and your children being the ones who deliver your eulogy; but be prepared for the possibility of placing a boy, perhaps, on the pyre, or a young man, or an old man—for the age is irrelevant, since any funeral procession that includes a parent is untimely." After these terms have been set out, if you still bring up children, you free the gods from any reproach, for they have given you no guarantees.

(18.1) Come on, now, picture your entry into the whole of your life in the same terms. I have explained what could entice you and what could put you off if you were wondering whether to visit Syracuse: imagine me coming to give you advice as you were being born: (2) "You are about to enter a city shared by gods and men,[60] one that embraces everything, is bound by fixed, eternal laws, and ensures that the revolving heavenly bodies carry out their duties untiringly. There you will see countless stars twinkling; you will see the universe filled with the light of a single star, the sun on its daily course marking out the periods of day and night, and on its annual course demarcating summers and winters more evenly.[61] You will see the moon taking over at night, borrowing a gentle, reflected light from her encounters with her brother, at one time hidden, at another looming over the earth with her face full,[62] changing as she waxes and wanes, always different from the previous night. (3) You will see the five planets following different courses and straining against the motion of the hurtling world;[63] the fortunes of nations depend on their slightest movements, and the greatest and the smallest things are shaped by the arrival of a favorable or an unfavorable star. You will marvel at gathering clouds and falling rainwater and zigzagging lightning and the heavens filled with thunder. **(4)** When you have had your fill of the spectacle of the world above and turn your gaze down to earth, you will be welcomed by a different kind of world with different marvels: here sprawling, level plains that stretch out endlessly, here the high-soaring summits of mountains rising up with huge, snowy ridges; streams tumbling down, and vast rivers flowing east and west from a single source; woodlands with their treetops swaying, and enormous forests with their wildlife and the dissonant choiring of birds; **(5)** cities in varied locations, nations cut off by difficult terrain, some retreating up precipitous mountains, others fearfully encircling themselves with the shores of lakes and with marshes;[64] crops promoted by cultivation, and trees with no one to cultivate their wildness; streams gently flowing through meadows, pleasant bays, and shores receding to form a harbor; and all those islands scattered across the empty waters, adorning the seas where they emerge. **(6)** What about the brilliance of stones and gems, the gold that flows mingled with the sand of swift torrents, bursts of blazing fire in the middle of the land and also in the middle of the sea,[65] and the ocean encircling the land, interrupting the continuity of the nations with its trio of gulfs[66] as its tides surge with complete abandon? **(7)** Here you will see, swimming in waters that are restless and billowing even when there is no wind, creatures of a size exceeding land animals, some of them ponderous, moving under another's control,[67] some swift, faster than rowers at full stretch, some sucking in water and breathing it out, causing grave danger to passing sailors. Here you will see ships looking for unknown lands. You will not see anything left unattempted by human boldness, and you will be both a spectator of, and a partner in, great endeavors: you will learn and teach skills, some that sustain life, some that enhance it, some that guide it. **(8)** But in that same place there will be thousands of afflictions of body and mind, wars, robberies, poisons, shipwrecks, climatic and bodily disorders, bitter grief for those dearest to you, and death, which may be easy or may result from punishment and torture. Think it over and weigh up what you want: to reach the one set of experiences you must run the gauntlet of the other." You will reply that you want to live, of course. (Or on second thought, I suppose, you will not put yourself in a position where any curtailment causes you grief!) So live on the terms agreed. "No one consulted us," you say. But our parents were consulted about us when, knowing life's terms, they raised us to live by them.

(19.1) But let me move on to sources of consolation: let us first see where treatment is needed, then what kind of treatment. A person who is grieving is affected by longing for the loved one. That in itself seems to be bearable; for while they are still alive we do not weep for people who are absent or are going to be absent, even though we lose all contact with them when we lose sight of them. So it is our belief that tortures us, and evils are only ever as great as our valuation of them. We have the remedy in our own hands: let us think of the deceased as absent, let us deceive ourselves; we have sent them on their way, or rather we have sent them on ahead and are going to follow. (2) A person who is grieving is also swayed by this thought: "There will be no one to protect me, to save me from being treated with disrespect." I offer a consolation that is far from commendable, but it is true: in our city bereavement creates more goodwill than it destroys, and loneliness, which used to be the curse of old age, gives it such power that some people pretend to dislike their sons, and disown their offspring, deliberately making themselves childless.[68]

(3) I know what you will say: "I am not troubled by my own losses; for people do not deserve consolation if they are upset by the death of a son in the same way as by that of a servant, if in their son's case they find time to think of anything except the son himself." So what is troubling you, Marcia? That your son has died, or that he did not live long? If it is that he has died, you ought to have grieved for him all along; for you knew all along that he was going to die. (4) You must realize that a dead person is not afflicted by any sufferings, that the things that make the underworld seem terrifying are just myths, that no darkness looms over the dead, no prison, no rivers blazing with fire, no river of Oblivion,[69] no law courts and defendants, nor in that state of utter freedom are there tyrants all over again.[70] Poets have indulged in these fantasies and have hounded us with empty terrors. (5) Death is a release from every pain, a boundary that our sufferings cannot cross; death restores us to the state of peace in which we lay before our birth. Anyone who feels pity for the dead

should also feel pity for the unborn. Death is neither a good nor an evil; for only a something can be a good or an evil; but what is itself nothing, and reduces everything to nothing, does not leave us at the mercy of fortune. For evil and good subsist in some material object: fortune cannot get a grip on what nature has released; a nonexistent person cannot be wretched. **(6)** Your son has crossed the frontier, leaving behind this place of slavery; immense and everlasting peace has welcomed him. He is not attacked by fear of poverty, or by anxiety over wealth, or by stabs of the lust that corrodes the mind with pleasure; he is not affected by envy of other people's prosperity or oppressed by others' envy of his own, and his sensitive ears are not assailed by insults of any sort; he anticipates no disasters, either public or personal; he is not anxious about the future, hanging on results that always lead to greater uncertainty.[71] He has finally come to a halt where nothing can force him out, nothing can terrify him.

(20.1) O, how lacking in awareness of their sufferings are those who do not praise death and do not look forward to it as nature's finest discovery, whether it sets a seal on our happiness, or keeps disaster at bay, or ends the old man's jadedness and weariness, or cuts a young life short in its prime when even better things are expected, or calls a halt to childhood before the more difficult stages are reached: for everybody death is an end, for many a cure, for some an answer to prayer; and it does no one a greater favor than those to whom it comes without waiting to be asked. **(2)** It brings freedom from slavery against the owner's wishes; it removes the chains from captives; it lets out of prison those to whom unbridled power had denied release; it shows exiles who are always straining their minds and eyes toward their homeland that it does not matter beneath whose soil one is buried; when fortune has shared out common possessions unfairly, and has given one person ownership of another even though they were born with equal rights, death is the great equalizer. After death, no one any longer acts at the whim of another; it lets no one feel inferior; it is available to all; it is what your father longed for, Marcia; it is, I tell you, what ensures that birth is not a punishment, what ensures that I do not fall when faced with fortune's threats, that I can keep my mind sound and in control of itself: for I have something to which I can make a final appeal. **(3)** Here I see crosses, not all of the same kind but constructed differently by different people: some hang their victims upside down with their heads toward the ground, others drive a stake through their private parts, others stretch out their arms on the gibbet; I see racks, I see scourges, and instruments of torture specially tailored to each joint[72]—but I also see death. Here are cruel enemies, arrogant fellow citizens: but here I also see death. It is no problem being a slave if, when you grow tired of being someone else's property, you can cross over to freedom with a single step. Life, you are dear to me, thanks to death!

(4) Think what a blessing a timely death can be, and how many people have been disadvantaged by living too long. If Gnaeus Pompeius, the glory and the mainstay of the empire, had been carried off by ill health when he was at Naples, he would have departed as the undisputed leader of the Roman people; but as it turned out, a brief extension toppled him from his pinnacle. He saw legions slaughtered before his eyes, and from that battle in which the senate formed the front line he saw (what a pitiful remnant!) the commander emerge alive;[73] he saw the Egyptian butcher, and he surrendered to an underling the body that the victors held sacrosanct. Even if he had been left unharmed he would have regretted being spared; for what was more shameful than for Pompey's life to depend on the generosity of a king?[74] (5) If Marcus Cicero had fallen at the time when he evaded Catiline's daggers, directed at him and at his country alike, when he was the savior of the state he had liberated, or even if he had died soon after his daughter, he could still have died happy. He would not have seen swords drawn against the lives of fellow citizens, or assassins carving up the possessions of the murdered so that they might actually meet the expenses of their own deaths, or the auction of consular spoils, or slaughter put out to public tender, or robbery, war, plunder, and so many more Catilines.[75] (6) If the sea had swallowed up Marcus Cato when he was on his way back from Cyprus and from administering the king's inheritance, even if it had also swallowed up the money he was bringing home to pay for the civil wars, would that not have been a blessing? He would certainly have died believing that no one would dare to do wrong in the presence of Cato; but an extension of just a few years compelled a man born for the sake of freedom—not just his own but also his country's—to flee Caesar and to follow Pompey.[76]

So an early death caused him no suffering, and it actually spared him suffering of all kinds.[77]

(21.1) "But he died too soon and too young." First of all, suppose he could have looked forward to . . . think of the longest time that a human being can keep going: how long is that? Born for a very short period, soon to make way for others, we see each new arrival assigned to these temporary lodgings. Am I talking just about our own lives, which <we know> roll forward with incredible speed?[78] Count up the centuries that cities have lasted: you will see how even those that boast of their antiquity have not been standing for long. All human affairs are brief and transient and occupy a negligible fraction of infinite time. (2) This earth, with its cities and peoples and rivers and its encircling sea, we count as a pinprick in comparison with the universe; our life span occupies a smaller portion than a pinprick if it is compared with all of time, whose duration exceeds that of the world, since the latter repeats itself over and over again within the course of time.[79] So what is the point of prolonging something that, however great the increase, will still be next to nothing? The only way our life can be long is if we find it sufficient. (3) You may give me the names of long-lived men whose length of years has passed into history, you may count up the hundred and ten years of each one: when you let your mind focus on the whole of time, the difference between the shortest and the longest life will be as nothing, if you examine the length of time a person lived and then compare the length of time he did not live.

(4) Furthermore, from his own viewpoint his death was well timed; for he lived as long as he had to, and there was nothing more left for him to do. There is no single measure of old age for humans, no more than there is for animals, for it exhausts some of them within fourteen years, and their maximum life span is just the first stage of a human being's; each creature is given a different potential for living. No one dies too soon, because he was not going to live any longer than he did live. (5) A boundary stone has been firmly fixed in place for each of us: it will always remain where it has been set up, and no effort or influence will move it farther away. Realize this, that your losing him was planned: he reached his allotted span "and arrived at the goal of the life assigned to him."[80] (6) So you should not make yourself depressed by thinking, "He could have lived lon-

ger." His life was not cut short, nor does chance ever intervene in a person's years. Each person is paid what he was promised; the fates go their own way and do not add to or subtract from what has once been promised. Prayer and effort are futile: each person will get what was allocated to him on his first day. From the moment he first saw the light, he started on the journey toward death and drew closer to his fate, and the years that were added to his adolescence were subtracted from his life. (7) We are all prone to the mistake of thinking that only the elderly and those getting on in years are heading toward death, despite the fact that right from the start infancy, and youth, and every stage of life, are taking us in that direction. The fates are doing their job; they make sure we are not conscious of our execution, and so that it may creep up on us more easily, death lurks beneath the very word *life*: infancy metamorphoses into childhood, childhood into puberty, and the old man does away with the young one. The stages of growth, if you calculate correctly, are actually losses.

(22.1) Are you complaining, Marcia, that your son did not live as long as he could have? So how do you know whether he would have gained from living longer, or whether this death was to his advantage? Can you find anyone today whose circumstances are so firmly rooted and grounded that he has nothing to fear from the passage of time? Human affairs are slippery and fluid, and no stage of our life is as exposed and vulnerable as the one that gives the most pleasure; so we should wish for death when we are at our happiest, because amid all the instability and turmoil of life nothing is certain except what is past. (2) Your son's handsome body attracted the gaze of the degenerate city, but he kept it pure by vigilantly guarding his honor; however, who can guarantee you that his body could have escaped every illness and preserved its fine appearance unblemished into old age? Think of the thousands of faults that affect the mind: upright, talented individuals who show promise in their youth do not always maintain it until old age, but are often driven off course; either degeneracy attacks later in life, hence all the more shamefully, and starts to bring discredit on honorable beginnings; or they sink to the level of cafés and bellies, and all they care about is what they eat and what they drink. (3) Think too of fires, collapsing buildings, shipwrecks, and the butchery inflicted by doctors who remove bones from the living, force their entire hands into their intestines, and cause all sorts of pain as they treat their private parts. Next think of exile (your son was no more blameless than Rutilius), of prison (he was no wiser than Socrates), of a breast pierced by a self-inflicted wound (he was no more saintly than Cato):[81] when you have digested all this, you will realize that the people who have been best treated are the ones whom nature quickly pulled back to safety, for this was the kind of campaign in which they could expect to serve during their lives. Nothing is as deceptive as human life, nothing as treacherous: by Hercules, nobody would have accepted it were they not unaware of being offered it. So, if the most fortunate thing is not to be born, second best, I think, is to enjoy a brief life and be quickly restored to our original state.

(4) Picture to yourself that period which caused you such pain, when Sejanus made a gift of your father to his client Satrius Secundus.[82] He was angry with him for his outspokenness on one or two occasions, for he had not been able to endure in silence when Sejanus was not just being foisted on us but was clambering over us. There was a proposal that a statue of him be set up in the theater of Pompey, which Caesar was rebuilding after a fire:[83] Cordus exclaimed that this would really ruin the theater. (5) Well, why should he not have been bursting with indignation at the prospect of Sejanus standing on the ashes of Gnaeus Pompeius, of a treacherous soldier being glorified in the memorial to a very great general? An indictment was patched together,[84] and the fierce dogs, which he used to feed on human blood to make them obedient to himself alone and savage toward everyone else, began to howl around the man ***.[85] (6) What was he to do? If he wanted to live, he had to plead with Sejanus; if to die, he had to plead with his daughter, and both of them would refuse to listen: he decided to deceive his daughter. So after bathing, to use up more of his strength, he retired to his bedroom as if to take a meal, and dismissing his slaves, he threw some food out the window, to create the impression that he had eaten it; then he missed dinner, pretending he had already had enough to eat in his bedroom. On the second and third days he did the same; on the fourth day his physical deterioration gave the game away. So he embraced you and said, "My dearest daughter, this is the only thing I have kept from you in my entire life: I have started the journey to death and now I am about halfway; you neither should nor can call me back." Then he ordered all the day-

light to be shut out, and he buried himself in darkness. **(7)** When his intentions became known there was public delight, because the prey was being snatched from the jaws of the greedy wolves. The accusers, at Sejanus's bidding, went to the consuls' court and complained that Cordus was dying so that they could intervene in what they had forced him to do; they really felt that Cordus was escaping from them. It was a major issue at the hearing, whether plaintiffs lost the <right> to die; while this was being debated, while the accusers came to court a second time, he had secured his own acquittal. **(8)** Do you see, Marcia, what reversals threaten us unexpectedly in evil times? Are you weeping because one of your family had to die? He almost lost the right to do so.

(23.1) Quite apart from the fact that the whole of the future is uncertain, and fairly certain to get worse, minds that are released quickly from human society have the easiest journey to the world above; for they drag very little impurity or baggage with them. Liberated before they could become desensitized and too deeply infected with earthly affairs, they fly back to their place of origin with greater agility, and more easily wash away any trace of dirt and grime. **(2)** Great intellects never enjoy lingering in the body: they long to leave and break away, they resent these restrictions, for they are used to roaming through the universe far above and looking down on human affairs from on high. That is the basis for what Plato proclaims:[86] the wise man's mind is entirely oriented toward death; this is what it wants, this is what it thinks about; it is constantly motivated by this desire in its striving toward the transcendent.

(3) Tell me, Marcia, when you saw in that young man an old man's wisdom, a mind that had overcome every kind of pleasure, that was flawless, free from faults, seeking wealth without greed, honors without self-interest, pleasure without excess, did you think you could enjoy him unscathed for long? Whatever reaches its climax is close to its end; perfect virtue escapes and vanishes from our sight, and things that ripen early do not keep till the end of the season. **(4)** The brighter a fire blazes, the sooner it goes out: it is longer lived when it wrestles with slow-burning, tough fuel, enveloped in smoke and gleaming through the murk; for the source that feeds it grudgingly also makes it last. In the same way, the brighter that human intellects shine, the shorter lived they are; for when there is no room for growth, decline is close at hand. **(5)** Fabianus says[87]—something our parents saw as well—that at Rome there was a boy with the physique of an enormous man; but he quickly passed away, and sensible people all predicted he would die soon;[88] for he could not live to the age that he had anticipated prematurely. That is how it is: precociousness is a sign of an imminent demise; the end is approaching when potential for growth is all used up.

(24.1) If you start to value him in terms of his virtues, not his years, then he lived sufficiently long. He was left as a ward in the care of guardians until he was fourteen, and was always under his mother's guardianship. Although he had his own home, he did not want to leave yours, and he was still living with his mother at an age when children can barely stand living with their father. His stature, his fine appearance, and his robust physical strength made him a young man born for military service, but he refused to go into the army so as not to leave you. **(2)** Work out, Marcia, how rarely mothers who live in separate houses see their children; consider how all the years during which mothers have sons in the army are lost to them, and spent in anxiety: you will realize that you had an extended period of which you lost nothing. He never left your sight; under your eyes he developed the intellectual pursuits for which he had an outstanding talent, one that would have matched his grandfather's, had he not been inhibited by modesty, which keeps many people's achievements in obscurity. **(3)** As a young man of exceptionally handsome appearance, surrounded by such a host of seductive women, he gave none of them what they hoped for, and when some of them were brazen enough to try to flirt with him, he blushed as though it were his fault that he was attractive to them. This purity of character meant he was thought worthy of a priesthood while still a child; no doubt he had his mother's backing, but not even his mother could have exerted much influence except in support of a good candidate. **(4)** While you contemplate these virtues, hold your son in your embrace, as it were. Now he has more time for you, now there is nothing to call him away; he will never cause you anxiety, never grief. You have already been through the only kind of sorrow that could be occasioned by such a good son; the future is free from the clutches of chance and is filled with pleasure, provided that you know how to enjoy your son, provided that you understand what was most valuable about him.

(5) It is merely an image of your son that has perished, a likeness that was not very close; he himself is eternal, and is now in a better state, stripped of external baggage and left with just himself. What you see enveloping us—bones, muscles, the covering of skin, the face, our servants the hands, and the other things in which we are swathed—for our minds these are chains and darkness; the mind is smothered, choked, and poisoned by them, it is cut off from what is real, from where it truly belongs, and is plunged into what is unreal. It is in perpetual conflict with this burdensome flesh, to save itself from being dragged back and sinking; it struggles up toward the place from which it was banished. There eternal rest awaits it, and it will see purity and brightness instead of chaos and gloom. **(25.1)** So there is no reason to rush to your son's tomb: in it lie the most worthless bits of him, which caused him the greatest trouble, his bones and ashes, no more parts of him than were his clothes and the other things that covered his body. He has escaped intact, leaving nothing of himself on earth; the whole of him has departed; after lingering for a short while just above us while he was being purified and was getting rid of any remaining faults and all the encrustation of mortal life, he was then raised up high and hurried to join the souls of the blessed. **(2)** He has been welcomed by a sacred entourage, by Scipios and Catos, and, among those who despised life and are free thanks to <death>, by your own father, Marcia. He takes his grandson under his wing—even though everything is interrelated there—as he rejoices in the unfamiliar light; he teaches him about the paths of the neighboring stars, and gladly initiates him into nature's secrets, relying not on hypothesis but on his experience of everything as it truly is. And as a visitor is grateful to have a guide in an unfamiliar city, so he, all eager to understand the causes of celestial events, is grateful to have someone from his own family to explain things. He also <tells> him to direct his gaze toward the earth far below; for it is good to look down from on high at what you have left behind. **(3)** So, Marcia, behave as though you are in full view of your father and your son, who are not as you knew them, but far nobler, living in the highest heaven. You should feel ashamed of <entertaining> humble, commonplace <thoughts>, and of weeping for your relatives when they have been transformed into something better. They have <gained possession of> eternity and <have been> set free to wander in vast, open spaces;[89]

no intervening seas or high mountains or pathless valleys or shallows of the treacherous Syrtes bar their way;[90] they can reach everything easily,[91] and they move about readily, unencumbered; they are accessible to each other and they mingle with the stars.

(26.1) So imagine, Marcia, that your father, who had as much influence over you as you had over your son, is speaking from that heavenly citadel—not with the eloquence he employed to lament the civil wars and to proscribe forever those responsible for the proscriptions, but with an eloquence far superior to that, as he himself is now more exalted: (2) "Why, my daughter, are you in the grip of such long lasting grief? Why do you persist in such ignorance of the truth that you think your son has been unjustly treated because he has gone to join his ancestors at a time when his family circumstances were undiminished and he himself was undiminished? Do you not realize with what storms fortune convulses everything, how it treats no one kindly and indulgently except those who have had least to do with it? Should I give you the names of kings who would have been supremely happy if death had rescued them sooner from the ills that threatened them? Or the names of Roman generals whose greatness will be undiminished if you subtract a little from their life span? Or the names of the noblest and most famous men resolutely awaiting the stroke of a soldier's sword on their unflinching neck? (3) Look at your father and your grandfather: he fell into the clutches of a foreign assassin;[92] I let no one have any power over me, and depriving myself of food, I showed that the bravery of my writing reflected the bravery of my living. Why, in our family, is the person whose death was the most fortunate being lamented the longest? We are all united, and no longer surrounded by deep night, we see that nothing in your world is, as you suppose, desirable, nothing is sublime, nothing is glorious, but everything is insignificant, oppressive, anxious, and aware of only a tiny fraction of the light we enjoy! (4) Need I say that here no armies charge at each other in a frenzy, fleets are not shattered against fleets, family murders are not planned or even contemplated, and the marketplaces do not buzz with court cases all day and every day? Need I say that nothing is kept secret, minds are laid bare, hearts are transparent, life is lived in public and in the open, and all of history is visible, together with events to come? (5) I gained pleasure from writing about the deeds of a single generation, unfolding in the remotest part of the universe and among a tiny number of people: but now it is possible to see many generations and the interplay and succession of many eras throughout the whole of time; it is possible to look at kingdoms about to rise or fall, at the collapse of great cities, and at new inroads made by the sea. **(6)** If the universality of fate can be of any comfort to you in your bereavement, realize that nothing will remain standing where it now stands, that old age will topple everything and sweep it away. It will toy not just with human beings (for what a tiny fraction of the power of fortune they represent) but with places, with countries, with whole sections of the world. It will flatten entire mountains and in other places will force up new cliffs; it will swallow seas, divert rivers, disrupt communication between nations, and undo the partnership and cohesion of the human race; elsewhere it will make cities disappear into huge chasms, shake them with earthquakes, send plague-ridden air from deep below, cover all habitation with floods, kill every living creature as it drowns the earth, and scorch and burn all that is mortal in huge fires. And when the time comes for the world to extinguish and renew itself, everything will destroy itself by its own strength, stars will collide with stars; and as all matter goes up in flames, the bodies that now shine in an orderly configuration will all burn in a single fire. **(7)** We also, the blessed souls destined for eternity, when god decides to recreate the world, as everything else collapses, we too shall be a small appendage to the wholesale destruction, and we shall be returned to our original elements."

How fortunate is your son, Marcia, who already knows all this!

Notes

1. Cremutius Cordus was a historian who wrote under Augustus and Tiberius. His history of the civil wars (which does not survive) celebrated the republican side, and was the basis for the charges that Seneca refers to.

2. Lucius Aelius Seianus was prefect of the praetorian guard under Tiberius, and became the most powerful man in Rome from 26 CE, when Tiberius retired to Capri, until his fall from power and execution in 31.

3. Some translate this as "you openly routed [i.e., defeated] your tears," but this is a strained translation. However, the sequence of ideas is puzzling.

4. After the accession of Caligula in 37.

5. The Romans regarded a person's writings as giving him immortality.

6. Octavia, Augustus's sister, was first married to C. Claudius Marcellus; upon his death in 40 BCE she was soon married to Mark Antony. The Marcellus Seneca talks about was the child of her first marriage. Livia, born 58 BCE, first married Ti. Claudius Nero, and they had two sons: the future emperor Tiberius, and Drusus, who died in 9 BCE. In 39 BCE she divorced, and married Octavian, the future Augustus. She outlived him and died in 29 CE.

7. M. Claudius Marcellus, born in 42 BCE, married Augustus's daughter Julia in 25 BCE (so Augustus was both his uncle and his father-in-law). He died in 23 BCE.

8. Octavia died in 11 BCE.

9. In extant poetry, Marcellus is praised in Virgil *Aeneid* 6.861–83; Propertius 3.18.

10. Octavia had four daughters.

11. Drusus led the Roman campaigns in Germany from 12 BCE until his death in 9 BCE.

12. He was buried in the Mausoleum of Augustus.

13. Reading *mala sua augere.*

14. Seneca alludes to the strict Stoic view that any kind of grieving is wrong.

15. After Augustus's death in 14 CE, under his will, Livia was adopted into his family with the names Julia Augusta.

16. The philosopher Areus (or Arius) Didymus, originally from Alexandria, was closely associated with Augustus.

17. His other support was Tiberius, mentioned below.

18. Livia acquired the name Julia only after Augustus's death, so here in Areus's speech it is anachronistic. Some manuscripts read "Livia," but it is unnecessary to follow them, for such anachronisms are not unknown in Seneca.

19. Seneca alludes to the Stoic doctrine of *propatheiai*: even the wise man will at first be shaken by a sudden misfortune, but in his case reason will swiftly take control and prevent fear or grief or other damaging emotions from developing. See also 7.1.

20. Livia's surviving son was Tiberius; Drusus had two sons, Germanicus and Claudius (who became emperor, 41–54 CE), and a daughter, Livia.

21. The Stoics said that bereavement produced a physical contraction in the mind or soul, a *propatheia* (see 5.6).

22. Roman boys started to wear the adult toga around the age of sixteen.

23. The "you" of the rest of this chapter is a generalized masculine "you," not Marcia specifically.

24. A line of the mime-writer Publilius Syrus (C34 Meyer). (Roman mime was a popular form of comedy that, unlike modern mime, used dialogue.)

25. The masculine suggests that Seneca is here thinking of god as the giver, though elsewhere in this section it is (feminine) fortune.

26. Seneca here switches to second-person plurals.

27. Seneca returns to the second-person singular.

28. Seneca again addresses Marcia individually.

29. Reading *uidelicet <pertinet>*.

30. Hercules and Achilles were familiar examples of offspring of the gods who were mortal.

31. L. Cornelius Sulla Felix (ca. 138–78 BCE), one of the most prominent military and political figures of the early first century BCE; his ruthlessness and cruelty in the civil wars of the eighties was long remembered. *Felicissimo*, "most fortunate," is a play on Sulla's cognomen Felix, "fortunate," to which Seneca alludes in what follows.

32. In 88 Sulla was appointed commander in the war against Mithradates but then deprived of the command, whereupon he marched on Rome with his army to reclaim it. Later, in 79, he voluntarily laid down his powers and returned to private life.

33. This refers to the behavior of Xenophon, Greek soldier and writer (ca. 430–354 BCE), upon hearing of the death of his son Gryllos in 362.

34. The temple of Jupiter on the Capitol was dedicated in the late sixth century BCE. Other ancient sources say that Pulvillus was consul at the time, not pontifex. Holding the doorpost was an essential part of the dedication ritual.

35. L. Aemilius Paulus defeated Perses, king of Macedonia, at the battle of Pydna in 168 BCE, and celebrated the triumph in the following year. The sons given in adoption were sons of an earlier marriage, and the adoptions probably occurred some years earlier. Seneca refers to the one who became P. Cornelius Scipio Aemilianus Africanus, the conqueror of Carthage.

36. The young sons of a triumphing general regularly rode with him in his chariot.

37. Marcus (Seneca's "Lucius" is a mistake) Calpurnius Bibulus and Gaius Julius Caesar were the consuls of 59 BCE. In an attempt to block Caesar's legislation, Bibulus refused to leave his home, declaring that he was watching for omens.

38. The sons were killed in 50, while Bibulus was proconsul of Syria. Other sources say they were killed by Roman soldiers stationed in Egypt.

39. Britain was regarded as lying across the ocean, and attempting to cross the ocean was commonly represented as a sign of reckless ambition. (The Greeks and Romans believed that the landmass of Europe, Asia, and Africa was encircled by the ocean.)

40. Caesar's daughter Julia died in 54 BCE. Her marriage to Pompey in 59 had strengthened the alliance between Caesar and Pompey, which was widely thought to have been weakened by her death.

41. Pompey's cognomen was Magnus, "Great."

42. The Julii traced their ancestry to Venus; Julius Caesar and Augustus had already been deified after death; and, Seneca implies, subsequent members of the family could be deified in the future.

43. Seneca's terse statements gloss over details: Augustus had only one child, his daughter Julia, who was sent into exile but outlived him; however, "children" might include his son-in-law Marcellus (see 2.3); two grandsons, Gaius and Lucius, both predeceased him, but other grandsons survived (although Augustus did not think they deserved to succeed him); the adoption referred to is that of Tiberius (although Augustus had also adopted Gaius and Lucius as sons).

44. Augustus was deified after his death, and during his lifetime was already called a god by poets.

45. Tiberius's son Drusus died in 23 CE, his adopted son Germanicus in 19.

46. Tiberius was pontifex maximus, so he had to avoid the pollution of seeing a corpse.

47. In Latin the verb *perdere* can mean "destroying" as well as "losing"; on Sejanus see 1.2.

48. The legend was that Lucretia was forced to commit adultery by a son of Tarquin, the last king of Rome. After revealing what had happened to her husband and father, she killed herself. Her death prompted Brutus to lead the revolt that expelled the king and established the republic in 509 BCE.

49. The legend was that in the early years of the republic, Cloelia was given as a hostage to Lars Porsenna, king of Clusium, but she managed to escape across the river Tiber.

50. This Cornelia was the daughter of Scipio Africanus (see 13.3).

40

51. Tiberius and Gaius Gracchus, whose programs of reform were controversial both during their lifetimes and subsequently, died violent deaths. Their corpses were thrown into the Tiber in 133 and 121 BCE respectively.

52. Cornelia's husband was M. Livius Drusus, tribune in 122 BCE; her son of the same name was murdered while tribune in 91 (or, according to another, less reliable account, he committed suicide).

53. Again Seneca addresses a generalized masculine "you."

54. Virgil *Aeneid* 3.418. Hesperia is a poetic name for Italy.

55. The Homeric sea monster Charybdis was identified with a whirlpool between Italy and Sicily.

56. The river Alpheus was said to disappear underground in mainland Greece, flow beneath the sea, and reemerge as the freshwater spring of Arethusa in Syracuse. "Tainted" water is here salt water.

57. The Athenian expedition against Sicily in 415–413 BCE ended in disaster, and many Athenians were taken prisoner.

58. Dionysius II was tyrant of Syracuse in 367–357 BCE. Then he was ousted, and following an unsuccessful attempt at a comeback (346–344), he retired to Corinth. Plato twice visited his court.

59. This speech, and Seneca's speech in chapter 18, address a generalized male audience.

60. The Stoics regarded the whole world as a city-state of which all human beings are citizens.

61. Seneca's point is that the length of day and night varies constantly with the season of the year. Sometimes the day is longer than the night, sometimes vice versa, but the length of summer and winter is always the same.

62. The "looming" moon echoes Horace *Odes* 1.4.5.

63. The five planets then known were Mercury, Venus, Mars, Jupiter, and Saturn. The phrase "straining against the motion of the hurtling world" refers to their apparent gradual eastward movement through the zodiac as it and the other fixed stars move westward.

64. "others fearfully . . . marshes": the Latin text is incurably corrupt; I have translated Madvig's tentative suggestion *aliae ripis lacuum paludibusque pauidae circumfunduntur*.

65. The word translated as "blazing" is corrupt, but the reference to volcanic eruptions is clear.

66. Referring to the Mediterranean, the Caspian, and the Red Seas, which were regarded as breaking up a single landmass.

67. It was believed that some whales had poor eyesight and were guided by smaller fish.

68. Seneca alludes to the way in which wealthy childless people attracted the attentions of legacy hunters.

69. *Lēthē* in Greek.

70. Compare Lucretius's denunciation of the traditional underworld in 3.978–1023, and Seneca *Letter* 24.18.

71. Reading *incertiora reponenti*.

72. The Latin of this clause is incurably corrupt, but the general sense is clear.

73. I.e., he, the commander, would rather have been killed in battle.

74. After his army was defeated at Pharsalus, Pompey fled to Egypt, but was killed by a local commander as he landed (48 BCE).

75. Cicero died in the proscriptions in 43 BCE. The conspiracy of Catiline was in 63, his daughter's death in 45.

76. The younger Cato committed suicide in 46 BCE rather than seek pardon from Caesar after the defeat of Pompey's forces. He had supervised the annexation of Cyprus in 58.

77. Seneca, suddenly, is once more talking about Marcia's son.

78. Reading *quas <scimus> incredibili celeritate conuolui*.

79. An allusion to the Stoic doctrine of repeated, identical world cycles.

80. Virgil *Aeneid* 10.472.

81. P. Rutilius Rufus, consul of 105 BCE, was prosecuted for extortion and exiled in 92, though generally acknowledged to be innocent; Socrates was condemned by an Athenian court in 399, and refused to go into exile to avoid execution; on Cato see 20.3.

82. Satrius Secundus was one of Cremutius Cordus's prosecutors.

83. "Caesar" is here Tiberius.

84. Reading *consarcinatur*.

85. A few hopelessly corrupt words are left untranslated. The "dogs" are Sejanus's henchmen.

86. *Phaedo* 64a, 67d.

87. Papirius Fabianus was a declaimer and philosopher of the early imperial period who deeply influenced Seneca.

88. Transposing *ante* to before *dixit*.

89. Reading *aeternarum rerum <potiti> per libera et uasta spatia dimissi <sunt>*.

90. The Syrtes were dangerous areas of shallow sea off the coast of North Africa.

91. Reading *omnia plano adeunt*.

92. We know nothing more about Marcia's grandfather.

Consolation to Helvia

Introduction

GARETH D. WILLIAMS

In this treatise Seneca strives to ease his mother's sorrow over his banishment to Corsica in 41 CE, apparently on the charge of adultery with Julia Livilla, the emperor Gaius's sister (cf. Dio 60.8.5); given the time that Seneca lets pass before offering this consolation (cf. 1.1–2), the work can plausibly be dated to 42/43. The paradoxical novelty that he, the lamented, offers comfort to his lamenter (cf. 1.2) gives an idiosyncratic stamp to this Senecan variation on that subgenre of the ancient consolatory tradition, the consolation on exile, examples of which survive (in part or whole) in Greek from the Cynic Teles (third century BCE), the Stoic Musonius Rufus (ca. 30–100 CE), Dio Chrysostom (Musonius's pupil), Plutarch (ca. 45–after 120 CE), and Favorinus (ca. 85–155 CE). A familiar Stoic emphasis in that tradition is that to be excluded from one's homeland is no great hardship: as citizens of the universe, exile deprives us not of our true fatherland (*patris*) but only of our given *polis* (Musonius Rufus, *That Exile Is Not an Evil* p. 42.1–6 Hense). Elsewhere, Seneca himself urges: "Live in this belief: I am born for no one corner of the universe; this whole world is my country" (*Letters* 28.4).

Seneca duly invokes this familiar emphasis in his *Consolation* for Helvia: "Wherever we go, the two finest attributes will go with us— universal nature and individual virtue" (8.2). He builds on this core point, however, to analyze the exilic condition from a perspective that is less visible in the Greek tradition. If our existence is centered not in localized place but in the universal whole, and if the mind is directed away from the narrowness of petty preoccupation with earthly matters (*terrena*, 9.2) to engage instead with the universal immensity, the very idea of exile takes on a paradoxical quality: who is more truly the exile, one banished from the localized state, or one alienated from, or blind to, the higher claims of cosmic citizenship? On this figurative approach, Seneca's exile as represented in this *Consolation* marks a homecoming of sorts. In concluding the treatise with a rapturous vision of his mind soaring from ground level and ascending unfettered to the celestial heights, where it finally luxuriates in "the most beautiful sight of things divine" (20.2), Seneca truly arrives: far from merely ending on a climactic note of good cheer to console Helvia, his flight of mind amounts to a journey *from* exile, and from all the everyday involvements and distractions that he associates with our alienation from the cosmic viewpoint. Already, the sage who keeps his distance from the crowd and from the dubious attractions of external goods (cf. 5.1) is a figurative exile from everyday values, while the masses are themselves estranged from what Seneca portrays as the favorable conditions of our birth ("We are born in circumstances that would be favorable if we didn't abandon them," 5.1). The gluttons who crave ever more exotic foodstuffs from distant parts of the world (10.2–11) give extreme expression to this estrangement, hopelessly alienated as they are from the simple life in accordance with nature. The endemic moral corruption of Rome in the present alienates it, Seneca asserts, from the standards of Rome past (cf. 12.5–7); in comparison with what he further portrays as the vices to which Roman womanhood routinely succumbs in his day (16.3–5), Helvia is truly an exile of sorts from contemporary degradation, and more at home in the company of such republican role models as Cornelia, mother of the Gracchi (16.6).

In these various ways Seneca on Corsica offers in his *Consolation* to Helvia a wide-ranging literary-philosophical disquisition on many different modes, versions, and connotations of exilic alienation; his theme is not so much his own exile as the exilic condition itself, both literal and figurative. Helvia may find ample comfort for her loss of Seneca to exile in the support of her family (18.2–19.7), but philosophy beckons as the source of greatest solace (17.3–5). Yet the self-reliance that Seneca inculcates in her by detaching her from vulnerability to external circumstance suggestively extends the exilic theme in yet another, fortifying direction, with self-retreat figured as inner exile; and the protections offered by Helvia's mode of self-reliance may extend, in turn, the relevance of Seneca's message from the particular case of his mother's grief to his prescription of a way of life, a way of coping, for *any* reader in parallel distress. In this respect, his *Consolation* to Helvia constitutes no special, intimately personal case within his philosophical oeuvre but amounts to another stage or aspect of the therapeutic program that his prose corpus cumulatively represents.

As part of his critique of the nature of exile itself, moreover, Rome herself is characterized as a city crowded with exiles, and as a place whose identity is founded on *dis*placement: Rome too is explicitly implicated in Seneca's roving survey in chapter 7 of peoples displaced over the ages, and cities founded, by colonization or migration. Roman power, however unprecedented, ubiquitous, and influential in one way (cf. 7.7: "Wherever the Romans have conquered, there they settle"), is "normalized" by its integration within this larger pattern of human experience—an aspect of the *Consolation* that gently interrogates the underpinnings of Roman self-assurance by suggesting that "being Roman" is no fixed commodity but an ongoing process, or a state of negotiation, in a fluid world. The cosmic viewpoint thus functions not just to bring alleviation from trauma at the personal level; by locating Roman power within a macrovision of human development and transition across time, Seneca also asserts a form of detachment from the very authority that exiled him in the first place. The individual may be controlled and sentenced by imperial edict, but Seneca rises above such confinement and vulnerability in Claudius's Rome in the 40s BCE by exercising primary citizenship in the cosmic whole. The paradoxical end result is that the exile is empowered by his punishment, liberated as he is by cosmic release in the *Consolation* to Helvia to view afresh Rome's place in the world.

Further Reading

Fantham, E. 2007. "Dialogues of Displacement: Seneca's Consolations to Helvia and Polybius." In *Writing Exile: The Discourse of Displacement in Greco-Roman Antiquity and Beyond*, ed. J. F. Gaertner (Leiden: Brill), 173–92.

Williams, G. D. 2006. "States of Exile, States of Mind: Paradox and Reversal in Seneca's Consolatio ad Heluiam." In *Seeing Seneca Whole: Perspectives on Philosophy, Poetry and Politics*, ed. K. Volk and G. D. Williams, Columbia Studies in the Classical Tradition (Leiden: Brill), 147–73.

Consolation to Helvia

LUCIUS ANNAEUS SENECA

TRANSLATED BY GARETH D. WILLIAMS

(**1.1**) Often by now, dearest mother, I have felt the urge to send you consolation, and as often restrained it. The considerations that prompted me to dare the attempt were many. First, I imagined that I would lay aside all my troubles when I'd wiped your tears away at least for a while, even if I couldn't stop them altogether; second, I was sure that I would have more power to raise you up if I'd first arisen myself; and, further, I was afraid that fortune, though conquered by me, might still conquer someone close to me. And so, placing my hand over my own gash, I tried as best I could to crawl forward to bandage your wounds. (**2**) On the other hand, there were factors to delay this purpose of mine. I realized that your grief should not be confronted while it was fresh and violently felt, in case the consolations themselves aggravated and inflamed it; for in diseases as well, nothing is more harmful than overhasty treatment.[1] And so I was waiting until your grief tempered its own strength by itself, and softened by time to submit to remedies, it allowed itself to be touched and handled. Moreover, although I read through all the works composed by the most distinguished authors for the purpose of controlling and tempering grief, I found no example of someone who had consoled his own relatives when he himself was the object of their lamentation. In this novel situation, therefore, I was undecided, fearing that my efforts would bring not consolation but exacerbation. (**3**) Besides, a person raising his head from the very funeral pyre to console his own dear ones needs words that are different, and not drawn from conventional, everyday consolation. But every grief that is surpassing in scale necessarily takes away our ability to choose words, since it often chokes the voice itself. (**4**) In any event, I'll try as best I can, not with confidence in my abilities but because I can offer the most effective consolation by myself being the consoler. You never refused me anything; and so I hope you won't refuse me at least this much, even though grief is always unyielding: your consent for me to set a limit to your sense of loss.

(**2.1**) See how much I've promised myself from your love for me:

I don't doubt that I shall have more power over you than your grief will, though there's nothing that has more power over the wretched. So in order not to join battle with it immediately, I'll first take its side and heap on encouragement for its growth; I'll expose and split open all the wounds that have already been covered over. (2) The objection will be: "What kind of consolation is this, to recall forgotten woes and to set the mind in full view of all its hardships when it can scarcely endure one of them?" But let him reflect: whatever diseases are so destructive as to gather strength against their remedies can generally be treated by opposite methods. And so I'll set before the mind all its sorrows and all its bereavements: this will not be to apply a gentle approach to healing, but to cauterize and cut. What shall I achieve? That the mind that has overcome so many miseries is ashamed to be distressed by one more wound on a body already so scarred. (3) So let those whose long prosperity has weakened their pampered minds carry on weeping and lamenting, and let them fall faint at the disturbance caused by the slightest injuries; but let those who have spent all their years in a succession of disasters endure even the heaviest blows with brave and steadfast resolve. The one benefit of continual misfortune is that it eventually hardens those whom it always afflicts.

(4) Fortune has given you no respite from the heaviest sorrows, and made no exception even for the day of your birth. You lost your mother as soon as you were born, or rather while you were being born, and you entered life as, in a sense, a child exposed. You grew up in the care of a stepmother, but by showing all the obedience and devotion which can be observed even in a daughter, you made her become a real mother; nevertheless, even a good stepmother comes at a great cost to any child. Your uncle, the kindest, finest and most courageous of men, you lost just when you were awaiting his arrival; and lest fortune should alleviate its harshness by separating out its blows, within a month you buried your dearest husband, who made you the mother of three children.[2] (5) This blow was announced to you when you were already grieving, and when in fact your children were all elsewhere, as if your misfortunes were purposely concentrated within that time period so that your grief would have nowhere to find solace. I pass over the multiple dangers, the multiple fears, which you endured as they assailed you without ceasing. Just re-

cently you took back the bones of three grandchildren into the same lap from which you'd sent forth three grandchildren;[3] and less than twenty days after you'd buried my son, who died in your arms as you kissed him, you heard that I'd been snatched away.[4] This alone you had lacked before—to mourn the living.

(3.1) Of all the wounds that have ever penetrated your body, this latest one is, I admit, the most severe: it hasn't just broken the skin but split apart your breast and innermost organs. But just as new recruits cry out even though they are only superficially wounded, and tremble more at the hands of doctors than they do at the sword, whereas veterans, even though they are pierced through, patiently and without a groan allow their bodies to be cleansed as if they were not their own, so you must now bravely submit to treatment. (2) Away with wailings and lamentations and the rest of the commotion that usually accompanies a woman's grief; for you've wasted so many sorrows if you've not yet learned how to be wretched. My treatment of you hardly seems timid, does it? Not one of your misfortunes have I withheld from you, but I've piled them all up and set them before you.

(4.1) I've taken this bold approach because I've resolved to conquer your grief, not limit it. And I shall conquer it, I think, first if I show that I am experiencing nothing that could cause me to be called wretched, let alone make my relatives wretched on my account; and, second, if I turn to you and demonstrate that your lot, which is completely dependent on mine, is not hard to bear either. (2) I shall deal first with what your devotion to me eagerly wants to hear: that I'm suffering no distress. If I can, I shall make it clear that those very conditions which you think are weighing me down are not unbearable. But if you find that unbelievable, at least I'll be better pleased with myself for being content in circumstances which usually make people wretched. (3) There's no reason for you to take the word of others about me; to protect you from the distress of not knowing what to think, I myself declare to you that I am not unhappy. And to reassure you still more, I'll add that I cannot even be made unhappy.

(5.1) We are born in circumstances that would be favorable if we didn't abandon them. It was nature's design that no great equipment is needed for living well; each and every individual is capable of making himself happy. External goods have trivial importance and exert little influence in one direction or the other: the sage is neither carried away by prosperity nor cast down by adversity, for he has always striven to rely to the fullest extent on himself, and to derive all his joy from within himself. (2) So what? Am I saying that I'm a sage? Not at all; for if I could claim as much, I wouldn't just be denying that I am unhappy but proclaiming that I'm the most fortunate of all mankind, and that I've been brought close to god. But as things are, I've placed myself in the hands of wise men, which is sufficient for alleviating every distress; and since I'm not yet robust enough to help myself, I've sought refuge in the camp of others,[5] who protect themselves and their followers with ease. (3) They have ordered me to keep watch constantly, as if a soldier on guard, and to anticipate every attempted blow of fortune, every attack, long before they strike. Fortune falls heavily on those it suddenly surprises; the person who always awaits its attack easily withstands it. For an enemy's approach also confounds only those it takes by surprise; but those who have prepared themselves for the coming war before it arrives are well organized and equipped, and they easily absorb the first blow, which is the most violent. (4) Never have I placed trust in fortune, even when it seemed to be at peace. All that it very generously bestowed on me—money, high office, influence—I stored in a place from which it could reclaim them without causing me any disturbance. I have kept a great distance between them and me; and so fortune has taken them from me, not wrenched them away. No one is shattered by hostile fortune unless first beguiled by its favor. (5) Those who loved its gifts as if they were theirs forever, and who wanted to be admired because of them, lie prostrate with grief when those false and fickle delights abandon their empty and childish minds, ignorant as they are of all lasting pleasure. But the person who isn't puffed up by prosperity is not diminished when circumstances change; his strength of purpose is already tested, and he maintains a mindset that is unassailable in the face of either condition; for in the midst of prosperity, he has tested his ability to cope with bad. (6) Consequently, I've never thought that there is any real good in the things everyone prays for. Besides, I've found them to be all show, decorated as they are with appealing but deceptive colors, but with nothing within that resembles their outward appearance. And in my present circumstances, these so-called hardships, I find nothing as fearful and oppressive as was threatened by common opinion. The very term *exile* now falls more harshly on the ear because of a certain conviction and common feeling, and it strikes listeners as something bleak and detestable. For so the masses have ordained, but sages in large part disregard the people's decrees.

(**6.1**) Therefore, disregarding the judgment of the majority, who are carried away by the outward appearance of things, whatever the grounds for trusting it, let's consider what exile really is. Of course, a change of location. To avoid any impression that I'm diminishing its force and removing its worst properties, certain inconveniences accompany this change of place: poverty, disgrace, contempt. I'll take issue with these factors later;[6] meanwhile, the first question I want to consider is what distress is entailed in the actual change of location.

(**2**) "To be deprived of your homeland is unbearable." Come now! Look on this vast throng,[7] which the buildings of the enormous city can scarcely accommodate: most of that crowd are separated from their homeland. They've gathered together from their towns and colonies, from the whole wide world in fact, some drawn by ambition, some by the requirements of public duty, some because they are charged with diplomatic business, some by self-indulgence in quest of a place favorably rich in vice, some by a longing for higher learning, some because of public shows. Some are attracted by friendship, some by their appetite for work, seeing ample scope for displaying their special qualities; some have brought their good looks to sell, others their eloquence for sale. (**3**) Every conceivable type of person has flocked to the city, which sets high prices on both virtues and vices. Have them all summoned by name, and ask each of them: "Where are you from?" You'll find that the majority of them have left their own homes to come to this city, which is very great and most beautiful to be sure, but not their own. (**4**) Then move on from this city, which can be said in a way to belong to all, and visit every city: there's none that doesn't have a large proportion of foreigners. Pass on from those cities whose delightful setting and convenient situation draw large numbers, and run your mind over desolate places and the most rugged islands, Sciathus and Seriphus, Gyara and Cossura:[8] you'll find no place of exile where someone doesn't stay for his own gratification. (**5**) What could be found as bare as this rock,[9] what as precipitous on all sides? If you consider its resources, what could be more barren? If its people, what more savage? If the very topography of the place, what more rugged? If the climate, what more extreme? Yet here live more foreigners than natives. In itself, therefore, a change of place is so far from being a hardship that even this place has drawn some people away from their homeland. (6) I find some[10] who say that innate to our minds is a certain incitement to change abode and to move from one place to another; for mankind was given a mind that is shifting and restless. It never stays put but goes in all directions, projecting its thoughts to all places, known and unknown—a wanderer which cannot tolerate being at rest and takes the greatest delight in encountering the new and different. (7) This will cause you no surprise if you consider its earliest origin. It was not composed of heavy, earthy substance but descended from the lofty, heavenly breath.[11] But heavenly entities are by nature always on the move, speeding away and driven on with the swiftest motion. Consider the planets that illuminate the world: none of them remains stationary. The sun glides on continuously and shifts from place to place, and though it revolves with the universe, it nevertheless moves in a direction contrary to the heavens themselves:[12] it runs through all the signs of the zodiac and never comes to a halt; its movement is ceaseless as it migrates from one place to another. (8) All the planets are always traveling in their orbits and passing by, and in accordance with the incontrovertible law of nature, they are carried from place to place; when in the course of fixed spans of years they've completed their circuits, they will again proceed along the paths they took before. How absurd, then, to imagine that the human mind, which is composed of the same elements as divine beings, is distressed by its travels and changes of abode, while god naturally finds pleasure and even self-preservation in incessant and extremely rapid movement!

(7.1) Turn now from heavenly to human affairs, and you'll see that whole tribes and peoples have changed their abode. What's the meaning of Greek cities in the heart of barbarian territories? Why is the Macedonian tongue heard among Indians and Persians?[13] Scythia and that whole region of wild and unconquered tribes show Achaean cities established on the shores of the Black Sea; neither the harshness of the perpetual winter nor the character of the inhabitants, savage like their climate, deterred migrants from settling there. **(2)** There is a mass of Athenians in Asia;[14] Miletus has sent forth in different directions enough people to fill seventy-five cities; the entire coast of Italy that is washed by the Lower Sea[15] became Greater Greece; Asia claims the Etruscans as her own;[16] Tyrians have settled in Africa, Carthaginians in Spain; Greeks have forced their way into Gaul, Gauls into Greece;[17] the Pyrenees did not prevent the Germans from crossing.[18] Through pathless regions and unknown parts, the restlessness of mankind has made its way. **(3)** Children and wives and parents heavy with age were dragged along. Some peoples, driven to and fro in their long wandering, did not deliberately choose their destination but wearily settled on the land that was nearest; others established their right in a foreign country by force of arms. Some tribes were engulfed by the sea when they were going in quest of unknown lands, while some settled at the place where they were stranded because their supplies had run out. **(4)** Nor did they all have the same motive for leaving and seeking a new homeland. The destruction of their cities by enemy attack forced some to escape to foreign lands when they were robbed of their own; some were dislodged by political discord at home; some were sent out to relieve the burden caused by the overcrowding of an excessive population; some were driven out by disease, by frequent earthquakes, or by some unbearable deficiencies in the unproductive soil; some were beguiled by overblown reports of a fertile shore. **(5)** Different peoples have been led by different causes to leave their homes, but this at least is clear: nothing has stayed where it came into being. The human race is constantly running this way and that, and in a world so vast something changes every day: the foundations of new cities are laid and new names of nations emerge, while older powers are obliterated or transformed into a subsidiary of a stronger power. But all these migrations of peoples—what are they but states of communal exile? **(6)** Why drag you through so lengthy a cycle? Why bother to mention Antenor, the founder of Padua, and Evander, who established the Arcadian kingdom on the banks of the Tiber? Why mention Diomedes and others, conquered as well as conquerors, who were scattered over foreign lands by the Trojan War? **(7)** To be sure, the Roman Empire itself looks back to an exile[19] as its founder—a refugee from his captured city who, taking with him its few survivors, was forced by fear of the conqueror to make for distant parts and was brought to Italy. In turn, this people—how many colonies has it sent to every province! Wherever the Romans have conquered, there they settle. People willingly put their names down for this kind of migration, and even old men left their altars and followed the colonists overseas. (8) The point needs no listing of further instances, but I'll nevertheless add one that forces itself on my attention: this very island has often changed its population. To pass over its earlier history, which the long passage of time has obscured, the Greeks who left Phocis and now inhabit Massilia first settled on this island.[20] What caused them to leave it is unclear, whether the harshness of the climate, or their close-up view of Italy's outstanding power, or the shortage of harbors. For the cause was evidently not the savagery of the native inhabitants, given that they settled among the most fierce and uncivilized peoples of Gaul at that time. (9) Subsequently the Ligurians crossed to the island, and also the Spanish, as is plain from their similar customs: the islanders wear the same head coverings and the same kind of shoes as the Cantabrians, and certain words are the same—but some only, because their language as a whole has lost its original character through association with the Greeks and Ligurians.[21] Later, two colonies of Roman citizens were founded, one by Marius, another by Sulla:[22] so often has the population of this barren and thorny rock been changed! (10) To sum up, you'll scarcely find any land which is still lived in by its original inhabitants; every population consists of mixed and foreign stock. One people has come after another, what one people has viewed with disdain another has ardently desired, and one people has expelled another only to be driven out itself. So it is by decree of fate that nothing remains where it is in the same condition forever.

(8.1) To offset the actual change of place, and barring the other disadvantages that attach to exile, Varro, the most learned of Romans,[23] holds that this is remedy enough, that wherever we come, we inevitably experience the same order of nature. Marcus Brutus[24] thinks it a sufficient compensation that exiles can take with them their own virtues. (2) Even if anyone judges these two considerations, taken individually, inadequate to comfort the exile, he'll admit that they are extremely effective in combination. For how little it is that we actually lose! Wherever we go, the two finest attributes will go with us—universal nature and individual virtue. (3) So it was intended, believe me, by whoever fashioned the universe, whether that was an all-powerful god, or incorporeal reason capable of producing vast works, or a divine breath pervading all things from the greatest to the smallest with uniform tension, or fate and the unalterable sequence of causes that are interconnected[25]—so it was intended, I say, that none but the most worthless of our possessions should fall under anyone else's control. (4) Whatever is best for mankind lies beyond human control, and can be neither given nor taken away. This world, which is nature's greatest and best-endowed creation, and the human mind, which surveys the world and marvels at it, and is the most glorious part of it—these are our own possessions, lasting indefinitely and set to remain with us as long as we ourselves remain alive. (5) So, enthusiastic and confident, let us hasten with undaunted step wherever circumstances lead us, let us travel over any lands whatsoever: no place of exile [can] be found in the world, [since nothing in the world] is alien to mankind.[26] From any point on earth you raise your eyes to the heavens on an equal basis: there is always the same distance between all things divine and all things human. (6) Accordingly, so long as my eyes are not directed away from that spectacle, which they can never look on enough; so long as I may watch the sun and the moon and fix my gaze on the other planets; so long as I may track their risings and settings, the intervals between occurrences, and the reasons for their moving faster or slower; so long as I may observe so many stars gleaming throughout the night—some fixed, others not voyaging forth over a great distance but circling around their own given area, some suddenly bursting forth, others dazzling our eyes with spreading fire as if they were falling, or flying by with a long trail of brilliant light; so long as I may commune with these and, so far as a human can, mingle with things divine, and so long as I may keep my mind always striving to contemplate the kindred objects on high—what difference does it make to me what ground I tread?

(9.1) "But this land produces no trees rich in fruit or foliage, it isn't irrigated by the channels of any great or navigable rivers, it produces nothing that other nations want, and it's scarcely fertile enough to support its inhabitants; no valuable stone is quarried here, and no veins of gold and silver are mined." (2) Narrow is the mind that takes delight in earthly matters; it should be directed instead to those objects that are equally visible from any vantage point, and from any vantage point equally radiant. And another consideration should be borne in mind: earthly objects block our view of true goods through our perverse belief in false goods. The further people extend their colonnades, the higher they raise their towers, the wider they stretch their country seats, the deeper they dig their summer caves,[27] the more massive the structures raising the roofs of their banquet halls— so much more will there be to obscure the heavens from their sight. (3) Misfortune has cast you into a region where the most sumptuous shelter is a mere hut. truly you show a narrow-mindedness that consoles itself cheaply if you put up with this bravely only because you know of Romulus's hut.[28] Rather, say to yourself: "This lowly shack has room, I take it, for the virtues? Soon it will be more beautiful than every temple, when justice will be seen there, and forbearance, and wisdom, and righteousness, and a system for properly apportioning all duties, and knowledge of things human and divine. No place is confining which can accommodate this multitude of such great virtues; no exile is hard to bear when you can enter it in this company."

(4) Brutus says, in the book that he wrote on virtue,[29] that he saw Marcellus in exile at Mytilene, living as happily as human nature permits and never more devoted to liberal studies than at that time.[30] And so he adds that when he was set to return without Marcellus, he felt that he himself was going into exile rather than leaving Marcellus in exile. (5) How much more fortunate was Marcellus at that moment when he won Brutus's applause for his exile, than when he won the state's applause for his consulship! How great a man that was who made someone feel like an exile because he was parting from an exile! What a man that was who drew the admiration of one admired even by Cato, his kinsman![31] (6) Brutus also says that Gaius Caesar[32] had sailed past Mytilene because he couldn't bear to see a great man marred by disgrace. The senate did indeed secure his recall by public petition, and in so anxious and mournful a mood that all seemed to have the same feelings as Brutus did on that day, and to be making their entreaty not on Marcellus's behalf but their own, for fear that they would be exiles if they had to do without him. But he achieved much more on that day when Brutus couldn't bear to leave him, and Caesar to see him, in exile. For he received the testimony of both: Brutus grieved that he was returning without Marcellus, and Caesar

blushed. **(7)** Can you doubt that that great and distinguished man often encouraged himself to bear his exile with equanimity in terms such as these? "The loss of your country is no cause of sorrow. Thoroughly steeped in your studies as you are, you know that to the wise man every place is his homeland. Besides, wasn't the man who banished you himself without his country for ten successive years?[33] The reason was doubtless to enlarge the empire; but he was still without his country. **(8)** Look! Now he's being pulled toward Africa, which is teeming with threats of renewed war; pulled toward Spain, which is reviving the strength of the broken and shattered opposition; pulled toward treacherous Egypt,[34] and in short toward the whole world, which is watching closely for an opportunity against the weakened empire. Which problem will he meet first? Against which part of the world will he first make a stand? He'll be driven through every land by his own victorious course. Let nations admire and worship him; live yourself content to have an admirer in Brutus!"

(10.1) Marcellus endured his exile well, then, and his change of place caused no change at all in his mind, although poverty went with him. But there's nothing disastrous in poverty, as anyone knows who has not yet been driven to the madness of greed and extravagant indulgence, which ruin everything. For how little is the amount needed to support a man! And who can lack this much if he possesses any virtue whatsoever? **(2)** As far as my own case is concerned, I know that I've lost not wealth but my preoccupations. The needs of the body are slight: it wants the cold to be kept off, and to allay hunger and thirst with basic provisions; if we crave anything more, we exert ourselves for our vices, not our needs. There's no need to scour every ocean and to burden the stomach with the carnage of animals, or to pluck shellfish from the uncharted shore of the remotest sea. May gods and goddesses destroy those whose luxurious tastes overstep the boundaries of an empire that already arouses such envy! **(3)** They want game from beyond the Phasis[35] to supply their ostentatious kitchen, and they feel no shame at trying to get fowl from the Parthians, from whom we have yet to exact vengeance.[36] From all parts they gather up everything known to the finicky palate, and from the ends of the ocean food is transported which their stomachs, weakened by their luxurious living, can scarcely take in. They vomit to eat, eat to vomit, and the feasts which they search out from the world over they don't deign even to digest. If a man disdains such things, how can poverty harm him? If a man yearns for them, poverty even benefits him; for he's healed despite himself, and if he doesn't swallow his medicine even under compulsion, at least for a time his inability to get such things resembles a lack of desire for them. (4) Gaius Caesar,[37] whom nature produced, it seems to me, to show what supreme vice can do in combination with supreme power, dined one day at a cost of ten million sesterces; and though everyone used their ingenuity to help him to this end, he could scarcely find how to spend the tribute from three provinces on a single dinner. (5) How wretched are the people whose appetite is stimulated only by costly foods! But what makes them costly is not their exquisite flavor or some pleasant sensation in the throat but their rarity and the difficulty of obtaining them. Otherwise, if these people would willingly return to sanity, what need of so many professional skills that serve the belly? What need of imports, or of devastating forests, or of scouring the sea? All about us lie the foods which nature has made available in every place; but these people pass them by as if blind, and they roam through every country, they cross the seas, and though they could allay their hunger at a trifling cost, they excite it at great expense. (6) I feel like saying to them: "Why do you launch your ships? Why do you take up the sword against both beasts and humans? Why do you rush about with so much commotion? Why do you heap riches on riches? Won't you consider how small your bodies are? Isn't it madness and the wildest derangement to desire so much when you have room for so little? And so, though you may increase your worth and extend your lands, you'll never enlarge the capacity of your bodies. Though your business has thrived, though your military service has brought you much, though you've tracked down and gathered in foods from all parts, you'll have nowhere to store those sumptuous supplies of yours. (7) Why do you hunt down so many things? I ask you! Our ancestors, whose virtue even to this day props up our vices, were doubtless unhappy because they provided food for themselves with their own hands, because the ground was their bed, because their houses weren't yet gleaming with gold, and because their temples had yet to shine with precious stones—and so in those days oaths would solemnly be sworn by gods of clay,[38] and those who'd invoked the gods would return to the enemy, even though they were certain to die, rather than break their word.[39] **(8)** Doubtless our dictator,[40] who listened to the envoys of the Samnites as he himself cooked at the hearth the simplest kind of food with his own hand (the hand which had already frequently routed the enemy and placed a triumphal laurel branch on the lap of Capitoline Jupiter)—this man doubtless lived less happily than did Apicius[41] within our own memory, who lectured on cookery in the very city from which philosophers were once expelled[42] on the grounds of corrupting youth, and who defiled his age by his teaching." It's worth knowing Apicius's end. **(9)** After he'd poured a hundred million sesterces into his kitchen, and after he'd swallowed up at every one of his revels the equivalent of so many imperial gratuities and the enormous state revenue of the Capitol, he was overwhelmed by debt and then forced for the first time to look carefully into his accounts. He calculated that he would have ten million sesterces left over; and as if doomed to live in extreme starvation if he existed on ten million sesterces, he took his life by poison. **(10)** What luxury, if ten million counted as poverty for him! What folly to think that what matters is the amount of money, not wealth of mind! Someone shuddered at ten million sesterces, and he escaped by poison what others pray for! In truth, for a man of such a perverse mindset, that last drink was most healthy. It was when he was not simply enjoying his boundless banquets but boasting of them, when he was ostentatiously displaying his own vices, when he was drawing the city's attention to his own luxurious ways, when he was rousing the young to imitate him (even without corrupt examples they are naturally impressionable)—it was then that he was truly eating and drinking poisons. **(11)** Such an end is what befalls people who measure their wealth not by the standard of reason, which has fixed limits, but by that of a corrupt disposition whose sway is boundless and illimitable. Nothing is ever enough for greed, but for nature even too little is enough. The poverty of an exile therefore involves no hardship; for no place of exile is so lacking in resources that it cannot amply support a person.

(11.1) "But the exile is going to feel the loss of his clothes and his home." These too he will miss only to the extent that he needs them—and he will lack neither shelter nor basic clothing, for it takes as little to protect the body as it is does to feed it. Nothing that nature made a necessity for mankind did it make hard to get. **(2)** But he longs for garments deep-dyed in purple, embroidered with gold, and spangled with different colors and designs: it's not fortune's fault but his own if he feels poor. Even if you give him back whatever he's lost, you'll achieve nothing; for his desires will make him feel more deprived, now he's restored, than his possessions made him feel when in exile. (3) But he longs for sideboards gleaming with golden vessels, and silver plate distinguished by the names of its old master craftsmen, and bronze that is made costly by the frenzied collecting of a few, and a mass of slaves that would crowd any house, however large, and draft animals whose bodies are stuffed and fattened through forced feeding, and marbles from every country: though all these things are amassed, they'll never satisfy his insatiable soul, just as no amount of fluid will be enough to satisfy the man whose craving arises not from a lack of water but from the heat that scorches his insides; for that isn't thirst but disease. (4) Nor does this apply only to money or food. Every desire, provided that it arises not from need but from vice, has a like character: however much you heap up for it, it will serve not as the end of the desire but only as a stage in it. So the person who keeps himself within the bounds set by nature will not feel poverty, while the man who goes beyond those bounds will be pursued by poverty even amid the greatest wealth. Even places of exile are adequate for essentials, but not even kingdoms for superfluities. (5) It's the mind that makes us rich; it follows us into exile, and in the harshest wildernesses, when it has found enough there to support the body, it takes delight in its own plentiful goods. Money is of no concern to the mind, any more than it is to the immortal gods. (6) All those things that win the admiration of untutored intellects which are too attached to their bodies—marbles, gold, silver, and polished tables, round and huge—all are earthly burdens that cannot be loved by the mind which is unsullied and conscious of its true nature, since it is light and unencumbered and set to dart upward to the highest heavens at whatever time it's freed from the body. In the meantime, so far as it is unimpeded by our limbs and by the heavy burden of flesh that surrounds it, it ranges over things divine in swift flights of thought. (7) And so the mind cannot ever be exiled, liberated as it is and akin to the gods and equal to all the world and all ages; for its thought moves around the entire heavens and is granted access to the whole of time, past and future.[43] This mere body, the soul's prison and chain, is tossed this way and that; punishments are inflicted on it, and villainies and diseases. But the mind itself is sacred and eternal, and no violent hand can be laid on it.

(**12.1**) In case you think I'm using the teachings of philosophers only to belittle the hardships of poverty, which no one feels to be burdensome unless he thinks it so, consider first that the proportion of poor people is so much greater; and yet you'll notice that they're not a bit more unhappy or troubled than the rich. Rather, I'm inclined to think that the fewer the claims that distract their minds, the happier they are. (**2**) Let's pass on to the wealthy: how many are the occasions when they look just like paupers! When they travel abroad, their baggage is limited; and whenever the constraints of their journey force them to hurry on, they dismiss their crowd of attendants. When they're on active military service, how small a part of their belongings do they keep with them, since camp discipline prohibits all luxurious paraphernalia! (**3**) And it's not just the special circumstances of time and place that put them on a par with the needy: when they're in the grip of boredom with their riches, they pick certain days on which to dine on the ground and, laying aside their gold and silver plate, to use earthenware dishes. What madmen! They always dread this state of poverty that they sometimes crave! What darkness of mind, what ignorance of truth [blinds those who are troubled by fear of the poverty][44] that they take pleasure in simulating! (**4**) In my own case, whenever I look back to the models of times long past, I'm ashamed to find any consolations for poverty, since the extravagance of the times has degenerated to the point where an exile's traveling allowance is more than the inheritance left by the leading citizens of old. It's well known that Homer had one slave, Plato three, and Zeno, the founder of the stern and manly Stoic philosophy, none. Will anyone therefore suggest that they lived wretched lives without himself thereby seeming thoroughly wretched to all? (**5**) Menenius Agrippa,[45] who acted as mediator between the patricians and the plebeians to keep the state at peace, was buried by public donation. Atilius Regulus,[46] when he was routing the Carthaginians in Africa, wrote to the senate that his hired hand had gone, leaving his farm abandoned; the senate decreed that in Regulus's absence, his farm would be managed at public expense. Wasn't being without a slave a price worth paying, so that the Roman people would become his tenant-farmer? **(6)** Scipio's[47] daughters received a dowry from the public treasury because their father had left them nothing: it was utterly reasonable for the Roman people to pay Scipio tribute just once, since he was always exacting it from Carthage. Lucky were the girls' husbands, to have the Roman people as their father-in-law! Do you think those fathers whose pantomime-actress daughters wed with a dowry of a million sesterces are happier than Scipio, whose daughters received from the senate, their guardian, a weight of copper as a dowry? **(7)** Can anyone feel contempt for poverty when it shows such distinguished models? Can an exile be aggrieved that he lacks anything when Scipio lacked a dowry, Regulus a hired hand, Menenius a funeral? And when in all those cases their need was met all the more honorably precisely because they were in need? And so, with advocates such as these to plead for her, poverty is not only assured of acquittal but even attractive.

(13.1) To this the response might be: "Why do you unnaturally separate the factors you mention, which can be endured individually, but not in combination? A change of place is endurable if you change only the place; poverty is endurable if it involves no disgrace, which even on its own is enough to crush the spirit." **(2)** In reply to anyone who'll try to frighten me with a mass of troubles, this needs to be said: "If you're sufficiently fortified against any one aspect of fortune, the same will apply against all aspects. Once virtue has toughened the mind, it makes it invulnerable on every front. If greed, the most powerful pestilence of the human race, has loosened its hold on you, ambition won't detain you. If you look on your last day not as a punishment but as a law of nature, no fear of anything will dare enter the breast from which you've banished all fear of death. **(3)** If you believe that sexual desire was given to man not for pleasure's sake but for the continuation of the human race, once you've escaped this hidden plague that is embedded in our very vitals, every other desire will leave you untouched. Reason doesn't strike down the vices one by one but all of them together; the victory is total and final." **(4)** Do you think that any sage who relies entirely on himself and keeps his distance from popular opinion can be distressed by disgrace? A disgraceful death is worse even than disgrace. Yet Socrates entered prison with the same expression that he wore when he alone once cut the thirty tyrants down to size,[48] and he was set to remove all disgrace even from prison;⁴⁹ for no place where Socrates was could seem a prison. **(5)** Who is so blind to the truth that he thinks that Marcus Cato's double defeat in his bid for the praetorship and the consulship⁵⁰ was a disgrace to him? That disgrace fell on the praetorship and the consulship, which gained distinction from Cato's candidacy. **(6)** No one is despised by another unless first despised by himself. A submissive and groveling mind may lend itself to the insult of others, but the person who lifts himself to face the cruelest misfortunes and to overcome the evils that overwhelm others wears his very sorrows as a mark of distinction; for our disposition is such that nothing commands our admiration as much as a man who is brave amid adversity. **(7)** When, at Athens, Aristides⁵¹ was being led to execution, everyone who met him cast down his eyes and groaned, as if it was not merely a just man but justice itself that was sentenced to death. The base exception, however, was someone who spat in his face. Aristides might have reacted with annoyance, knowing that only a foulmouthed creature would dare such a thing. Instead, he wiped his face clean and, smiling, said to the magistrate accompanying him: "Warn that fellow not to open his mouth so offensively in the future." This was to put insult on insult itself. **(8)** I know some people say that there's nothing harder to bear than contempt, and that they find death preferable. My response to them will be that exile too is often free of any contempt. If a great man has fallen and remains great as he lies prostrate, he is no more despised than the ruins of a temple are trampled underfoot—a temple which the devout treat as reverently as when it still stood.

(14.1) Since you have no reason, dearest mother, to be driven to endless tears on my account, it follows that you are moved to weep for reasons of your own. There are two possibilities: you are distressed either because you appear to have lost some protection, or because you find your longing for me unendurable in itself.

(2) I must touch on the first point only lightly, for I know that at heart you love your dear ones for nothing more than themselves. Let those mothers take note who exploit their children's power with a woman's weakness; who, because women are not allowed to hold office, are eager for advancement through their children; who both swallow up their sons' inheritances and try to be their heirs; and who wear out their sons' eloquence by lending it to others. **(3)** But you've taken the greatest joy in your sons' strengths, and exploited them to the least extent. You've always set limits on our generosity, though not on yours. Though your father was still alive,[52] you actually bestowed gifts on your wealthy sons. You managed our inheritances as if you were taking diligent care of your own inheritance and dealing scrupulously with a stranger's. You made sparing use of our influence, as if it belonged to someone else, and our times in office brought you nothing except pleasure and expense. Never did your kindness look toward self interest. And so, now that your son has been snatched away, you can't feel the absence of those things that you never considered a concern to you when he was safely at home.

(15.1) It is to the other point that I must entirely direct my consolation—the source from which the real force of a mother's grief arises. "So I've lost my dearest son's embrace," you say, "and I cannot delight in seeing him and conversing with him. When he appeared, my face relaxed its sad expression, and to him I entrusted all my anxieties: where is he? Where are the talks that always left me wanting more? Where are his studies, in which I participated with more than a woman's willingness, and with an intimacy beyond our maternal relationship? Where are those meetings of ours? Where that boyish sense of glee whenever he saw his mother?" (2) To all this you can add the actual places where we celebrated together and spent time with each other, and the reminders of the close association that we lately shared—reminders that inevitably cause the greatest anguish. For this blow too, fortune cruelly contrived against you: it willed that only two days before I was struck down, you should depart from me[53] with easy mind and unafraid of any such disaster. (3) It was a good thing that we had been living far apart from each other, and good that my absence from you for several years had prepared you for this blow; the effect of your return to Rome was not that you gained the pleasure of seeing your son, but that you lost the habit of longing for him. Had you departed long before my exile, you would have endured the loss more bravely, since distance would have eased your longing; had you not gone back, you would at least have gained the final benefit of seeing your son for two days longer. But as it is, cruel fate so arranged matters that you could neither be with me when disaster struck nor get used to being away from me. (4) But the harder those circumstances, the greater the courage you must call on and the more bitterly you must fight, as if against a known enemy who has often been defeated in the past. It's not from an undamaged body that this blood has flowed; you've been struck through your very scars.

(**16.1**) You must not plead the excuse that consists in being a woman, who has been granted a virtual license for immoderate weeping—but not for limitless tears. This is why our forebears allowed widows to lament their husbands for a period of ten months, thereby reaching a settlement by public decree with the persistence of female grief. They didn't forbid their mourning but set a limit to it; for when you've lost someone very close to you, to be endlessly stricken with grief is foolish self-indulgence, and to feel no grief is to be inhumanly insensitive. The best balance between dutiful affection and reason is both to feel a sense of loss and to crush it. (**2**) You must pay no heed to certain women whose grief, once assumed, was ended only by their death (you know some who've never taken off the mourning garb they donned when they lost their sons⁵⁴); your life, braver from the outset, demands more from you, and the excuse of being a woman cannot apply to one who has shown no trace of any womanly weakness. (**3**) The greatest scourge of our age, unchastity, has exempted you from the majority of women. Precious gems have not diverted you, nor have pearls; the gleam of riches has not made them seem to you the greatest good of the human race. Well brought up as you were in an old-fashioned and strict household, you've not been led astray by imitation of worse women, a danger even for upright characters. You were never ashamed of your fertility, as if it brought reproach on the age in which you live; and unlike other women who rely for their attractiveness solely on their beauty, never did you hide your pregnancy as if it were an unsightly burden, nor did you abort your hopes of children after they were conceived within you. (**4**) You didn't defile your face with paints and cosmetics, and never did you favor the kind of clothing that exposed no more flesh when it was taken off. In you has been seen that singular ornament, that most splendid form of beauty that lasts to any age, that greatest distinction: your modesty. (**5**) So you can't put forward your womanhood as an excuse to justify your grief, for your virtues set you apart from womanhood; you ought to be as far removed from female tears as you are from female vices. Not even women will permit you to wither away from your wound, but they will order you quickly to be done with your necessary mourning and then to rise again with less heavy heart[55]—if only you're willing to look to those women whose striking courage has placed them in the ranks of great men. (6) Cornelia[56] had twelve children, but fortune reduced them to two. If you wanted to reckon Cornelia's losses by number, she had lost ten; if by their value, she had lost the Gracchi. Nonetheless, when her companions were weeping around her and cursing her fate, she forbade them to censure fortune, since fortune had given her the Gracchi as her sons. From this woman could only be born the kind of man who exclaimed in public: "Would you speak ill of the mother who gave birth to me?" But to me the mother's utterance seems much more spirited: the son placed great value on the parentage of the Gracchi, but the mother on their deaths as well. (7) Rutilia[57] followed her son Cotta into exile, and was so bound up in her devotion that she preferred to endure exile than her longing for him, and she didn't come home until he did. After his return he distinguished himself in public life; when he died, she endured his loss as bravely as she had followed him into exile, and after her son's burial no one ever saw any tears. When he was exiled she showed courage, wisdom when she lost him; for in the first case nothing discouraged her from her loving duty, while in the second nothing made her persist in unnecessary and misguided sorrow. I want you to be counted with women such as these. In your efforts to control and suppress your anguish, you'll best follow the example of those women whose lives you have always imitated.

(17.1) I know that this is not a matter that is in our power, and that no strong feeling is under our control,[58] least of all that born of grief; for it is violent and stubbornly resistant to every remedy. At times we want to suppress it and swallow down our cries of pain, but our tears stream forth through the false mask of composure on our faces. Sometimes we distract the mind with public games or gladiators, but amid the very spectacles that are meant to divert it, it's undone by some slight reminder of its loss. (2) It's therefore better to defeat our sorrow than to cheat it; for grief that has been beguiled and distracted by pleasures or preoccupations rises again, and from its very rest it gathers force to rage once more. But the grief that submits to reason is quelled permanently. And so I'm not going to prescribe for you those remedies which I know many have adopted—that you should occupy or cheer yourself with travel to places either distant or charming, use up much of your time in diligently scrutinizing your accounts and managing your property, or constantly engage yourself in some new activity. All such initiatives are helpful only for a brief span; they are not a cure for grief, but they hinder it. But I'd rather end it than cheat it. **(3)** And so I'm guiding you to the refuge that's to be sought by all who are escaping fortune: liberal studies. They will heal your wound, they will root out all your sadness. Even if you'd never been familiar with them, you would need to make use of them now; but to the degree that my father's old-fashioned strictness allowed you, you have touched on all the liberal arts, even if you have yet to master them. **(4)** How I wish that my father, the best of men, had been less attached to ancestral custom, and willing for you to receive a thorough grounding in philosophical doctrine rather than just initial instruction! You'd now have no need to acquire protection against fortune, but merely to apply it. He was less inclined to let you devote yourself to philosophical study because of those women who use books not to gain wisdom but as equipment for the display of luxury. Nevertheless, thanks to your quick and voracious intellect, you took in a great deal for the amount of time you had; the foundations for every branch of philosophical study have been laid. Return to those studies now, and they will keep you safe. **(5)** They will bring you comfort, they will give you pleasure. If they truly enter your mind, never again will grief gain entry, and never will anxiety, and never the unnecessary distress caused by suffering that is pointless. Your heart will be open to none of these; for it has long been closed to all other moral failings. These studies are your surest form of protection, and the only resource that can rescue you from fortune's power.

(18.1) But because you need supports to lean on until you reach that haven which philosophy guarantees you, I want in the meantime to show you the consolations that are yours already. **(2)** Think of my brothers:[59] while they live, you have no right to find fault with fortune. In their different kinds of excellence, you have in each of them good reason for delight. One of them has achieved high office by diligent effort, while the other has despised it in his philosophical wisdom. Take comfort in the high standing of one son, the retirement of the other, the devotion of both. I know the deepest feelings of both my brothers. One seeks to improve his standing in order to bring you luster, while the other has withdrawn to a life of restful tranquility to have leisure for you. (3) Fortune has favorably arranged for your children to bring you both help and delight: you can be protected by one son's standing, enjoy the other's leisure. They will compete in their services to you, and the devotion of two sons will make up for your longing for one son. I can confidently promise that you'll lack nothing except the full number of your sons.

(4) After these, think also of your grandchildren—of Marcus, a most charming boy.[60] No one can look at him and still feel sad; no distress in anyone's heart can be so great and so freshly felt that it cannot be soothed by his embrace. (5) Whose tears would his cheerfulness not check? What mind that is tight with anxiety could fail to be relaxed by his witty chatter? Who won't be lured into merriment by his playfulness? What person, though concentrating on his own thoughts, will not be diverted and captivated by that talkativeness of his, which can never weary anyone? I pray to the gods that we die before he does! (6) May all the cruelty of fate be exhausted and extend no further than me. Whatever grief you were destined to suffer as a mother, whatever as a grandmother—may it be transferred to me, and may the rest of my family flourish unharmed. I shall make no complaint about my childlessness, and none about my present circumstances; let me only serve as the scapegoat for a family that will have no more cause of grief. (7) Fondly embrace Novatilla,[61] who will soon give you great-grandchildren. I had so brought her into my care and adopted her as my own[62] that in losing me she could seem an orphan, even though her father still lives. Cherish her for me as well! Fortune recently snatched her mother from her, but by your devotion you can see to it that she grieves only for the loss of her mother without being deeply affected by it as well. (8) Now is the time for you to arrange and mold her character; instruction leaves a deeper mark when it is stamped on impressionable minds. Let her grow accustomed to conversation with you and be shaped as you see fit; you'll give her much even if you give her only your example. Such a solemn duty as this will serve as a remedy for you; for only philosophy or a respectable form of occupation can distract from its anguish a mind that grieves for a loved one.

(9) Among your great consolations I would count your father as well, were he not away from you.[63] As it is, however, imagine his love for you, given your love for him, and you'll understand how

much more proper it is for you to preserve yourself for him than to expend yourself for me. Whenever unrestrained grief assails you and bids you to yield to it, think of your father. By giving him so many grandchildren and great-grandchildren, you've made it that you're not his only child; but for him the crowning fulfillment of a life lived happily nevertheless depends on you. As long as he lives, it is wrong to complain of your life.

(19.1) So far I've said nothing of your greatest source of comfort, your sister[64]—that heart which is so very devoted to you, receiving all the worries that you unreservedly convey to it, and that sensibility which is motherly to all of us. You blended your tears with hers, and you first began to breathe again in her embrace. (2) She always shares your feelings, but in my case she grieves not just for your sake. I was carried to Rome in her arms,[65] and it was by her devoted and motherly nursing that I recovered from my long period of illness. She exerted her influence on my behalf when I stood for the quaestorship,[66] and though she lacked the confidence of voice even for conversation or a loud greeting, on my behalf her love conquered her shyness. Neither her secluded way of life nor her modesty, which is so old-fashioned in comparison with the boorish forwardness of today's women, nor her quietness, nor her reserved character with its disposition to retirement—none of these prevented her from becoming ambitious on my behalf. (3) She, dearest mother, is the source of comfort by which you can recover your strength: attach yourself to her as closely as you can, cling to her with the tightest embraces. Mourners tend to avoid the things they love most and to seek freedom to indulge their grief; but you must share your every thought with her. Whether you'll want to persist in that state of feeling or lay it aside, you'll find in her either the end of your grief or a companion for it. (4) But if I rightly know the wisdom of this most complete of women, she won't allow you to be worn down by pointless grief, and she'll recount to you a telling experience of her own which I too witnessed.

In the very midst of a sea voyage[67] she had lost her beloved husband, my uncle, whom she had married as a virgin. She nevertheless bore the weight of both her grief and her fear simultaneously, and though shipwrecked, she overcame the storm and brought his body ashore. (5) How many women are there whose glorious deeds lie hidden in darkness! If it had been her lot to live in past times when people were straightforward in their admiration of great deeds, how much competition would there have been among gifted artists to sing the praises of a wife who forgot her physical weakness and forgot the sea, which even the boldest must fear; who placed her own life in danger in order to bury her husband; and who had no fears at all about her own funeral while she thought about his! She who was ready to give her life in place of her husband[68] has won fame through all the poets. But this is a greater achievement—for a wife to seek burial for her husband at the risk of her own life: that love is greater which gains a lesser return from an equal danger.

(6) After this, no one can be surprised that throughout the sixteen years when her husband was governor of Egypt, she was never seen in public, she never allowed any native inhabitant to enter her home, she sought no political favors from her husband and allowed none to be sought from her. So a province that was fond of gossip and talented at insulting its governors, where even those who steered clear of any wrongdoing didn't escape ill repute, looked up to her as a singular model of integrity; and—a very difficult thing for a people given to witticisms, even when risky—it curbed its freely wagging tongue, and to this day it keeps praying for, though it never expects to see, another like her. It would have been a considerable achievement if she had won the province's approval for sixteen years; but more remarkable is that she remained unknown there. (7) I mention these things, not for the purpose of enumerating her praiseworthy qualities (to run through them so sparingly is to treat them unfairly), but for you to recognize the high-mindedness of a woman who has succumbed to neither ambition nor greed, scourges that always accompany power; who, when her boat was disabled and she was watching her own shipwreck, was not deterred by fear of death from clinging to her lifeless husband; and who sought not a way to escape from the ship but a way to secure his burial. You must show courage equal to hers, and withdraw your mind from grief; and thereby ensure that no one thinks you're sorry you had children.

(20.1) But despite all your measures, your thoughts must inevitably return to me constantly, and under the circumstances it must be that none of your children enters your mind more often—not because the others are any less dear to you, but because it is natural to keep on touching the place that hurts. You must therefore think of me as follows—happy and energetic as if in the best of circumstances. For best they are, since my mind is free of all preoccupation and with time for all its own concerns, now delighting itself with lighter studies, and now, in its eagerness for the truth, rising to the contemplation of its own nature and that of the universe. (2) It first seeks to know about the lands and their position,[69] and then the nature of the sea that surrounds them, and its alternating ebb and flow. Then it investigates the expanse, full of frightening phenomena, that lies between the heavens and earth—this near space that is turbulent with thunder, lightning, wind blasts, and downfalls of rain and snow and hail. Finally, after traversing the lower reaches, it breaks through to the heights above and delights in the most beautiful sight of things divine; and mindful of its own immortality, it moves freely over all that has been and will come to be in every age across time.

Notes

Abbreviation

OLD   *Oxford Latin Dictionary*, ed. P. G. W. Glare, 2nd ed. (Oxford: Clarendon Press, 2012).

1. In keeping with Chrysippus's preference not to apply treatment while "the mind's swelling is still fresh" (cf. Cicero *Tusculan Disputations* 4.63).

2. Besides our Seneca, Helvia bore to the elder Seneca two other sons, Novatus (later Gallio, after adoption by L. Junius Gallio in his will) and Mela (cf. n. 59 below).

3. Their identities are unknown, and it is unclear if they include Seneca's own son (immediately below).

4. *Raptum me*, as if to (living) death in exile (cf. *OLD rapio* 5, of death, fate, etc., "to carry off").

5. The Stoic school; but for the charge of desertion to the rival, Epicurean camp, cf. *On Leisure* 1.4.

6. Chapters 10–13 below.

7. At Rome, as if Seneca were still there to visualize the scene.

8. Places of exile; the first three are Aegean. "Barren" Cossura (cf. Ovid *Fasti* 3.567) is now Pantellaria, between Sicily and North Africa.

9. Corsica, here portrayed with exaggerated grimness.

10. Stoics; this in anticipation of the soul drawn as part of the Stoic *pneuma* in 6.7.

11. See *On Leisure* 5.5 and n. 10.

12. Relative to the earth, the sun, moon, and planets orbit from east to west, as do the fixed stars; but the sun, moon, and planets orbit more slowly than the fixed stars, relative to which they move from west to east in an "opposite" direction (cf. *On the Constancy of the Wise Person* 14.4, *Consolation to Marcia* 18.3).

13. A consequence of Alexander the Great's eastern campaigns.

14. I.e., Ionia, the western part of Asia Minor.

15. The Tuscan or Tyrrhenian Sea, as opposed to the *mare superum* or Adriatic.

16. According to tradition, the Etruscans were Lydian in origin (cf. Herodotus 1.94).

17. Greeks: presumably the Phocaeans, apparently founders of Marseilles via Corsica after most citizens chose emigration during the Persian siege of 540 BCE (cf. Herodotus 1.163–7, and see n. 20 below). Gauls: the Celts, of whom one group apparently reached Delphi in 229 BCE while another crossed the Hellespont and settled in Asia Minor, giving their Celtic name to Galatia.

18. Possible confusion of Germans with Celts, early invaders of Spain who merged with the Iberians to form the Celtiberians.

19. Aeneas. In the vast history of migrations drawn in chapter 7, the Roman foundation legend is itself "normalized" by association with many such journeys: see my introduction to this essay.

20. *Phocide relicta* is surely in error for *Phocaea* in Asia Minor (Massilia/Marseilles was founded by the Phocaeans; cf. n. 17 above)—unless usage in fact allowed *Phocis* to be applied erroneously for *Phocaea* (cf. *OLD Phocis* 1b).

21. The implication is that the Corsican language was markedly Cantabrian/Spanish and was eroded over time by Phocaean and Ligurian influence. If so, despite the apparent temporal sequence meant in "Subsequently the Ligurians . . . and also the Spanish" above, Seneca seemingly posits Cantabrian settlement and influence before the Phocaean and Ligurian interventions.

22. The *colonia Mariana* in ca. 100 BCE, the Sullan *Aleria* ca. 82–80.

23. M. Terentius Varro (116–27 BCE), the most distinguished and prolific scholar of his time. The statement attributed to him here belongs to a lost work.

24. M. Junius Brutus (ca. 85–42 BCE), conspirator against Julius Caesar; his statement here is perhaps from his lost *On Virtue* (cf. 9.4 below).

25. Different Stoic designations of the power shaping the cosmos; cf. *On Favors* 4.7–8, *Natural Questions* 2.45.

26. Reading (with Reynolds) Vahlen's supplement to fill the lacuna in *nullum inueniri exilium intra mundum <potest; nihil enim quod intra mundum> est alienum homini est.*

27. Artificial grottoes offering escape from the sun, such as Vatia's at *Letters* 55.6.

28. One of two modest huts of straw with thatched roofs, known as *casae Romuli*, was on the Palatine, the other on the Capitol; they were carefully preserved as ancient relics symbolizing Rome's humble beginnings.

29. See 8.1 and n. 24 above.

30. M. Claudius Marcellus, consul in 51 BCE, was a vigorous opponent of Julius Caesar who retired to Mytilene after fighting on Pompey's losing side at Pharsalus in 48. Caesar had approved his return to Rome, but he was murdered at Piraeus in 45.

31. Brutus was son-in-law of M. Porcius Cato (95–46 BCE), doctrinaire Stoic and paragon of republicanism.

32. Here Julius Caesar, but Caligula is so designated at 10.4 below.

33. 58–49 BCE, the period of Caesar's Gallic Wars.

34. Caesar in Egypt: 48–47 BCE ("treacherous" Egypt because of Pompey's fate; cf. *On the Shortness of Life* 13.7 and n. 28). Africa: at Thapsus in 46, against the surviving Pompeians; and thereafter in Spain, at Munda in 45 (cf. *On the Shortness of Life* 5.2 and n. 9).

35. A river in Colchis flowing into the eastern Black Sea; the delicacy in question is pheasant (*phasiana*, derived from *Phasis*).

36. After Crassus's infamous defeat at Carrhae in 53 BCE.

37. Caligula; cf. 9.6.

38. For this symbol of simplicity, cf. *Letters* 31.11.

39. An allusion to M. Atilius Regulus, hero of the First Punic War: captured by the Carthaginians, he was sent on parole to Rome in 250 BCE to negotiate either a peace or an exchange of prisoners, but he urged the Roman senate to reject either proposal. Honoring the terms of his parole, he returned to Carthage, where he was tortured to death (see also 12.5).

40. M.' Curius Dentatus; cf. *On the Shortness of Life* 13.3 and n. 22.

41. M. Gavius Apicius, a notorious connoisseur in the Tiberian period (cf. *On the Happy Life* 11.4) whose name became a byword for gluttonous indulgence.

42. In 161 BCE.

43. Cf. *On the Shortness of Life* 15.5.

44. Reading Vahlen's supplement *excaecat, quos timor paupertatis*.

45. Consul in 503 BCE, he apparently persuaded the plebeians of the futility of their secession from Rome in 494.

46. See 10.7 and n. 39 above.

47. See *On the Shortness of Life* 17.6 and n. 44.

48. "The thirty tyrants" refers to the oligarchy that seized power at the end of the Peloponnesian War (404–403 BCE); for Socrates' defiance see Plato *Apology* 32c–d; Xenophon *Memorabilia* 1.2.32.

49. After his condemnation in 399 BCE; cf. *On Leisure* 8.2.

50. In 55 and 51 BCE respectively. For Cato see 9.5 and n. 31 above.

51. Athenian politician of the fifth century, nicknamed "the Just" (d. ca. 467). He is possibly given here in error for Phocion (ca. 402–318), the Athenian statesman and general of whom the same story is told by Plutarch (*The Life of Phocion* 36.1–2).

52. I.e., before she could draw on her inheritance.

53. Presumably to set out homeward to Spain from Rome.

54. Notably Augustus's sister Octavia, after losing her son Marcellus (cf. *Consolation to Marcia* 2.3–4).

55. Reading *sed leuiorem . . . exsurgere*, but there is no sure emendation for *leuis* or *leuiter* in the MSS.

56. Second daughter of Scipio Africanus (cf. 12.6 above) and mother of Tiberius and Gaius Gracchus, the famous tribunes.

57. Mother of the distinguished orator C. Aurelius Cotta, who was exiled in 90 BCE on the charge of inciting the Italians to revolt; recalled in 82, he was consul in 75.

58. Cf. *On the Shortness of Life* 14.2 and n. 36.

59. Novatus (Gallio) and Mela (cf. 2.4 and n. 2 above). The former rose to become proconsul of Achaia in ca. 52, suffect consul in 55 or 56; the latter is cast by the elder Seneca (*Controversiae* 2 pref. 3–4) as the cleverest of the three brothers, and also the least ambitious politically.

60. Probably the poet Lucan, Mela's son (39–65 CE).

61. Daughter of Novatus (Gallio).

62. Not formally, but in the sense of a special affection for her.

63. Presumably Helvius is in Spain, Helvia having journeyed back to Rome (cf. 15.2–3) after news of Seneca's exile reached her.

64. Apparently Helvia's stepsister, given the reference to Helvia as an only child in 18.9. The wife of Gaius Galerius, prefect of Egypt 16–31 CE, she presumably nursed Seneca back to health in Egypt (19.2) in the later part of this period.

65. As a child, from Corduba in Spain; his parents were presumably already at Rome.

66. Shortly after (33 CE?) his aunt's return from Egypt in 31.

67. Perhaps en route back from Egypt in 31 CE.

68. In Greek myth Alcestis, wife of Admetus.

69. For the ensuing distinction between *terrena*, *sublimia*, and *caelestia*, cf. (albeit in reverse order) *Natural Questions* 2.1.1–2.

Consolation to Polybius

Introduction

HARRY M. HINE

From internal references we know that this dialogue was written during the reign of the emperor Claudius while Seneca was in exile on Corsica—that is, between 41 and 49 CE. Seneca expresses the wish (13.2) that Claudius may open up Britain and celebrate triumphs, which implies that he was writing before the conquest of Britain and Claudius's subsequent triumph in 43 CE (or possibly very soon after, on the assumption that the news may have taken a little while to reach Seneca). The addressee, Polybius, was one of the freedmen who played an important role in the imperial palace during Claudius's reign—others were Marcus Antonius Pallas and Narcissus. Polybius held the post of *a libellis*, in charge of documents, particularly petitions; and he may also have been *a studiis*, in charge of literary matters. His role as imperial freedman is well attested by other ancient writers on the period, but only from Seneca do we know that he was also a literary man, and had translated Homer into Latin prose and Virgil into Greek prose.

The death of Polybius's brother prompted Seneca to write this work of consolation. The start of the work is lost, and we do not know how much is missing; but in what we have, Seneca covers a number of the standard themes of ancient consolatory literature (see the translator's introduction to the *Consolation to Marcia*). Little of the content is specifically Stoic, and in fact Seneca in passing repudiates, without naming its protagonists, the strict Stoic view that the wise man will feel no grief at all. But the arguments are tailored to Polybius's own circumstances: Seneca suggests that he use his literary talents to write about his brother and preserve his memory for posterity; and he appeals to the close relationship Polybius has with Claudius, imagining the emperor making a consolatory speech to the freedman, and telling him that the mere presence of the emperor, and the demands of his service to him, should distract him from his grief.

Yet the work is not just a consolatory treatise for Polybius but also an appeal to Claudius to recall Seneca from exile. Seneca's praises of the emperor can seem hollow and hypocritical, and some have thought them deliberately ironic. There is certainly a strong contrast between what Seneca says about Claudius in this treatise and what he later says about him in the *Apocolocyntosis*, the vicious and hilarious satire on the deification of Claudius written early in Nero's reign: the treatise praises Claudius for his justice, fairness, and eloquence, whereas the satire exposes his injustice, arbitrariness, cruelty, and incoherence; the treatise looks forward to his gaining a well-deserved place in heaven after his death, but the satire has him ejected from Olympus and consigned to a menial, bathetic fate in the underworld. However, we should perhaps not overstress the conflict, real though it is. Most of the praises of Claudius in the dialogue fit firmly within the conventions of imperial panegyric that had been established since Augustus's reign; and the criticisms, found in historical sources as well as in the *Apocolocyntosis*, may have been amplified after Claudius's death.

The structure of the work, so far as it survives, is clear and straightforward: chapters 1–11 offer advice of various traditional sorts; chapters 12–13 tell Polybius to think of the comfort he can get from his surviving relatives and from the emperor (and Seneca expresses the hope that Claudius will recall him from exile); chapters 14–17 give various examples for Polybius to emulate (14.2–16.3 is put into Claudius's mouth, and 17 offers the negative example of Caligula); and chapter 18 is the conclusion.

Acknowledgments

I am grateful to Elizabeth Asmis and the press's reader for suggesting improvements to the translation, but I alone am responsible for any remaining deficiencies.

Further Reading

Atkinson, J. E. 1985. "Seneca's *Consolatio ad Polybium.*" *Aufstieg und Niedergang der römischen Welt* II.32.2:860–84.
Kurth, T. 1994. *Senecas Trostschrift an Polybius: Dialog 11; Ein Kommentar.* Beiträge zur Altertumskunde 59. Stuttgart: B. G. Teubner.
Olberding, A. 2005. "The 'Stout Heart': Seneca's Strategy for Dispelling Grief." *Ancient Philosophy* 25:141–54.

Consolation to Polybius

LUCIUS ANNAEUS SENECA

TRANSLATED BY HARRY M. HINE

(1.1) *** \<Cities, and monuments of stone, if> you compare them to our human \<lives>,[1] are robust; if you apply the standards of nature, which destroys everything and recalls it to its origins, they are perishable. For what made by mortal hands is immortal? Those seven wonders,[2] and anything far more wonderful than them that the ambition of subsequent years has constructed, visitors will one day see leveled to the ground. Yes: nothing is everlasting, and few things are long lasting; things are fragile in different ways, their destruction takes various forms, but everything that has a beginning will also have an end. (2) Some people threaten the whole world with destruction, and this universe, which embraces everything divine and human—if you think it not blasphemous to believe it—will one day disintegrate and be sunk into its original chaos and darkness:[3] so there is no point in bewailing individual souls, or in lamenting the ashes of Carthage, Numantia, and Corinth,[4] and any other place that has fallen from a greater height, when even what has nowhere to fall is going to perish.[5] If the fates will one day go so far as to perpetrate such a great evil, there is no point in any individual's complaining that he has not been spared by them. (3) Who is so arrogantly and recklessly presumptuous as to want solely himself and his family to be exempted from the necessity imposed by nature, which summons everything to the same ending? or so presumptuous as to try to rescue a single household from the destruction that threatens the world itself? (4) So it is immensely comforting to reflect that what has happened to oneself is what everyone up till now has suffered and everyone is going to suffer; and it seems to me that nature has taken the most grievous thing it had made and has made it universal, in order that fate's equal treatment of all should be some consolation for fate's cruelty.

(2.1) It will also help you considerably if you reflect that your grief will do no good, either to him whom you sorely miss or to yourself; for you will not want what is pointless to be prolonged. If we are going to achieve anything by being despondent, I have no objection to shedding any tears left over from my own misfortune for yours;[6] right now I shall find something that can flow from these eyes already drained dry by private weeping, if only it will do you some good. (2) What are you waiting for? Let us complain together, or rather, I myself shall be the prosecutor: "Fortune, regarded by everyone as most unjust, up till now you seemed to have embraced this man[7] who, thanks to you, had won such veneration that his success attracted no envy—something that rarely happens to anyone. Look, you have inflicted on him the greatest grief he could experience while Caesar remains alive; and after careful reconnaissance from every angle, you realized that only at this point was he exposed to your blows. (3) For what else could you have done to him? Robbed him of his money? He was never a slave to it; even now he distances himself from it as far as possible, and although it is so easy for him to make money, the greatest benefit he seeks from it is to despise it. (4) Should you have robbed him of his friends? You knew that he is so lovable[8] that he could easily replace those he had lost with others; for of those I have seen exercising power in the imperial palace, I think there is no one else of whom I have found it true that, though self-interest drives people to seek his friendship, desire drives them more strongly. (5) Should you have robbed him of his good reputation? In his case it is too firm to be shaken even by you. Should you have robbed him of his good health? You knew that his mind was so well grounded in liberal studies[9]—by which he was surrounded not just during his upbringing but at birth—that it towered above all bodily pain. (6) Should you have robbed him of his breath? How little harm you would have done him! Fame promised him a very long life for his literary talent; he himself did everything to ensure that he would endure with the better part of himself,[10] and that he would protect himself from mortality through the outstanding works of literature that he had written. As long as any honor is paid to literature, as long as either the power of the Latin language or the elegance of the Greek survives, he will flourish alongside the giants whose talents he either has matched himself against or, if his modesty rejects that description, has devoted himself to. (7) Therefore you devised this as the only way in which you could do him severe harm; for the better a person is, the more regularly he has trained himself to endure you when you rage blindly, provoking fear even with your generosity. How little it would have cost you to grant immunity from such hurt to a man on whom your kindness seemed to have settled by deliberate policy, and not to have stumbled randomly in your usual fashion."

(3.1) Let us add to these complaints, if you like, that the young man's talents were cut short just as they were starting to develop. He deserved to have you for a brother: and certainly you thoroughly deserved not to suffer any grief even for an undeserving brother. He receives the same commendation from everyone; people mourn him as a compliment to you, they praise him as a compliment to the man himself. (2) There was nothing in him you would not be glad to acknowledge; you would have been good even to a less good brother, but in him your love had the right sort of material and was exercised much more readily. No one experienced his power to their detriment; he never used the fact you were his brother to threaten anyone. He had modeled himself on the example of your restraint, and he used to reflect on the way you brought your family not just great distinction but also a great burden of responsibility: he was strong enough to bear the load. (3) O cruel fates, who never treat virtue fairly! Your brother was snatched away before he could learn of his good fortune. I know my protests are too weak; for nothing is more difficult than finding words to match great grief. Still, if it will do any good, let us once again complain, (4) "What were you up to, fortune, so unjust, so violent? Did you so quickly come to regret your kindness? What cruelty is this, to launch a direct attack on brothers, and reduce the size of such a close-knit group with such a savage abduction? Did you want to disrupt a household so full of the finest young men, in which none of the brothers let the family down, did you want to reduce its size for no reason at all? (5) So, is innocence, as judged by every law, of no use? Is old-fashioned frugality of no use, or <moderation> in good fortune, <or> the highest self-restraint maintained while holding the highest power, or a genuine, secure love of literature,[11] or a mind free from any kind of fault? Polybius is mourning, and being warned by the case of one brother about what he can fear for the others, he is afraid for the very people who provide comfort for his grief. What a terrible thing, that Polybius should be mourning and suffering from grief while Caesar looks on him favorably! This without doubt is what you were up to, reckless fortune—a demonstration that no one can be protected against you, not even by Caesar."

(4.1) We can go on accusing the fates, but we cannot alter them: they remain harsh and inexorable; no one can influence them by abuse, not by weeping, not by arguing his case; they never spare anyone, never let them off. So let us spare ourselves tears, which achieve nothing; for this grief will more easily add us to the number of the dead than bring them back to us; if it torments us without helping, we must set it aside immediately, and our minds must be rescued from empty comforts and from a distressing desire for grief. For if reason does not put an end to our tears, fortune will not either. (2) Come on, survey the whole of humanity, and everywhere you find abundant, constant grounds for tears: hardworking poverty summons one person to the daily task; another is tormented by an ambition that never rests; another fears for the riches for which he had prayed, and is oppressed by what he had longed for; another is tortured by anxiety, another by work, another by the crowd that constantly lays siege to his forecourt; this man grieves because he has children, this one because he has lost them. Our tears will be exhausted sooner than our reasons for grieving. (3) Do you not see what sort of life nature promised us, when it decided that the first thing human beings do at their birth should be to cry?[12] This is our starting point when we come into the world, and the entire sequence of succeeding years follows the pattern. We live our lives on these terms, and so we should exercise moderation when doing what we have to do so often; and as we glance behind us at all the forms of sorrow that are at our backs, threatening us, we ought, if not to put a complete stop to our tears, at least to hold them in reserve. There is nothing we should use more sparingly than what we need so frequently.

(5.1) You will also be helped considerably by the reflection that no one finds your grief less pleasing than the person for whose sake it appears you are indulging in it: either he does not wish you to be in anguish, or he is unaware that you are. So there is no reason to perform a service that, as far as the beneficiary is concerned, if he is unaware of it, is superfluous, and if he is aware, is displeasing. (2) I would boldly assert that there is no one in the entire world who enjoys your tears. So, then, do you think your brother adopts an attitude toward you that no one else does, harming you by torturing you, and wanting to distract you from your occupation, that is, from your studies and from Caesar? That is not likely; for he showed you the love appropriate to a brother, the devotion appropriate to a parent, the respect appropriate to a superior; he wants you to miss him, but he does not want to cause you anguish. So what is the use of wasting away with a grief that, if the dead have any consciousness, your brother wants to be ended? (3) Were I dealing with another brother whose goodwill might seem questionable, I would treat all this as doubtful and would say, "If your brother wants you to be tormented by tears that never end, he does not deserve this affection of yours; but if he does not want that, let go of the grief that is haunting you both; an unloving brother ought not to be mourned in this way, and a loving one would not want to be." But in his case, since his love has been so clearly demonstrated, we should be certain that nothing can distress him more than seeing that this misfortune of his distresses you, that he makes you suffer in any way, that he causes your eyes, which are totally undeserving of this pain, to be disfigured and drained dry, without any end to their weeping.

(4) Nothing will divert your love from such fruitless tears as effectively as the consideration that you ought to give your brothers an example of how to bear bravely this injury that fortune has inflicted. Great generals, when things are going badly, deliberately pretend to be cheerful, and conceal bad news with a show of happiness, lest, if the soldiers see their general's spirits crushed, their morale also should collapse. That is what you too must do now. (5) Put on an expression that belies your state of mind, and if you can, get rid completely of all your grief, or if not, keep it hidden inside you, so that it is not visible; and take care to ensure that your brothers imitate you, for they will think that whatever behavior they observe in you is correct, and they will take courage from your expression. You should be both their comfort and their comforter; but you will not be able to prevent their laments if you give free rein to your own.

(6.1) Another thing that can keep you from excessive mourning is reminding yourself that nothing you do can be hidden from view. Public opinion has given you an important role: you must stick to it. Around you there stands a great throng of people offering comfort; they scrutinize your mind and observe how much strength it has when confronted with grief, and whether you are good at handling only favorable circumstances, or can also face adverse ones like a man. They are watching your eyes. (2) Those whose feelings can be concealed enjoy greater freedom: you are not free to have any secrets. Fortune has placed you in a bright light: everyone will know how you behaved after this wound, whether you laid down your weapons as soon as you were hit, or stood your ground. Caesar's love has long since elevated you, and your literary pursuits have promoted you to a higher level; nothing ordinary, nothing common is appropriate for you; and yet what is so vulgar and womanish as letting yourself be consumed by grief? (3) You are not allowed to behave in the same way as your brothers, though your loss is equal; there are many things that the reputation you have gained from your writing and from your character will not let you do; people demand much from you, they expect much. If you wanted to be allowed to behave as you liked, you should not have turned everyone's attention toward yourself: as things are, you must deliver on what you have promised. All those who praise the products of your literary talent, who make copies of them, who, though they do not want your fortune, do want your ability, they keep your mind under surveillance. You can never do anything unworthy of your claim to be a highly educated, learned man without many people regretting their admiration for you. (4) You are not allowed to weep unrestrainedly, and that is not the only thing you are not allowed to do: you are not even allowed to sleep in for part of the morning; or to escape from the hubbub of business to the leisure of a quiet country retreat; or, when your body is exhausted with constantly being on guard duty in your demanding post, to restore it with an enjoyable holiday abroad; or to seek mental diversion at shows of various kinds; or to organize your day as you please. You are not allowed to do many things that even the humblest people in obscure circumstances are allowed to: great fortune is great slavery. (5) You are not allowed to do anything as you please: you must listen to so many thousands of people, must organize so many documents; you must examine such an accumulation of business, gathered in from across the whole world, so that it can be brought to the attention of our outstanding emperor in the appropriate order. You are not allowed to weep, I tell you: you need to listen to many people who are weeping, to listen to the <requests> of many people standing trial and longing to gain access to the mercy of our most kindly Caesar, and to do all that you must dry your own tears.

(7.1) So far I have dealt with milder remedies, though they will still help: but when you want to forget everything else, think of Caesar. See what great loyalty, what great industry you owe in return for his favor toward you: you will realize that you may no more be bowed down by your burden than he on whose shoulders the world rests—or so the myths say.[13] (2) Caesar himself too is allowed to do everything; and yet, for this very reason, there are many things he is not allowed to do: his wakefulness protects everyone else's sleep, his hard work everyone else's leisure, his industry everyone else's pleasures, his ceaseless activity everyone else's free time. Ever since Caesar devoted himself to the world, he has robbed himself of himself; and like the stars, which constantly trace out their courses without resting, he is never allowed to stop or do anything for himself. (3) So to a certain extent the same necessity is imposed on you as well: you may not consider your own interests or your own studies. While Caesar controls the world you cannot devote any part of yourself to pleasure or pain or anything else: you owe your whole being to Caesar. (4) In addition, since you constantly declare that Caesar is dearer to you than your own breath, it is not right for you to complain about fortune while Caesar lives: so long as he is unharmed, your relatives are safe and sound, you have lost nothing, your eyes must be not just dry but joyful; in him you have everything, he takes the place of everything. You are not grateful enough for your good fortune— behavior that is quite alien to your very wise and loyal feelings—if you allow yourself to grieve over anything while he is alive.

(8.1) I shall go on to prescribe for you not a stronger remedy but a more personal one. Whenever you go home, at that point you will have to be on your guard against sadness. For it will be unable to gain access to you as long as you can look at your divinity; Caesar will occupy you totally. But when you leave him, then grief, as though handed an opportunity, will lay siege to your loneliness and will gradually creep up on your mind as it relaxes. (2) So you must not allow any moment to be unoccupied by your studies: during that time let the literature you have loved so long and so faithfully return the favor, during that time let it protect you, its priest and worshipper;

during that time let Homer and Virgil—they have served the human race as well as you have served both them and everyone else, when you wanted them to be known to a larger readership than they had written for[14]—let them linger long in your company: all the time that you entrust to their safekeeping will be safe. During that time write as well as you possibly can about the achievements of your Caesar, so that they may be passed on down through the ages by a herald from within his own household; for when it comes to shaping and writing a history, he himself will be the best person to give you both a subject and a model.[15] **(3)** I do not venture to get you to compose, in your usual agreeable style, fables and stories from Aesop, a genre not attempted by Roman talents.[16] It is certainly hard for your mind to find a way to embark on these lighter forms of literature so soon after it has received such a severe shock; but take it as proof that your mind has already been strengthened and restored, if it can proceed from more serious forms of writing to these more informal ones. **(4)** With the first kind, the very somberness of the subject matter will distract your mind, however much it is still ailing and struggling with itself; but your mind will not tolerate works whose composition requires a relaxed expression until it is completely at one with itself. So you will need first of all to exercise it on sterner subject matter, and later to switch to a gentler regime with something lighter.

(9.1) You will also find it a great relief if you frequently ask yourself, "Am I grieving on my own account or on the deceased's account? If on my own, my display of devotion is meaningless; grief is only justified when it is honorable, so it begins to part company with love when it takes self-interest into consideration; and when it comes to mourning for a brother, nothing suits a good man less than being calculating. **(2)** If I grieve on his account, I must necessarily judge one of the following alternatives to be the case. If the dead no longer have any sensation, my brother has now escaped all the disadvantages of life, he has been restored to the state he was in before he was born, and free from all evil, he fears nothing, desires nothing, suffers nothing. What madness is this, never to stop grieving for someone who is never going to grieve? **(3)** But if the dead do have some sensation, now my brother's mind is exulting as though released from a lengthy prison sentence and at last its own master and judge, enjoying the contemplation of the universe, and looking down on the whole human world from a higher place; best of all, it is looking from closer quarters at the divine, which for so long it had sought in vain to understand.[17] So why am I wasting away with longing for someone who is either happy or nonexistent? To weep for a happy man is envy, to weep for a nonexistent man is madness."

(4) Does it weigh with you that he seems to have lost out on great blessings just at the point when they were showering down on him? When you reflect that there are many things he has missed out on, reflect that there are more things he is not afraid of: anger will not torment him, disease will not strike him down, suspicion will not plague him; gnawing envy, always the enemy of other people's successes, will not pursue him; fear will not trouble him; the fickleness of fortune, which swiftly redirects its gifts elsewhere, will not unsettle him. If you do the sums properly, he has been let off more than he has been deprived of. (5) He will enjoy neither wealth nor influence, either yours or his own; he will not receive favors, nor will he grant them. Do you think him unhappy because he has lost all that, or blessed because he does not miss it? Believe me: the person to whom good fortune is unnecessary is more blessed than the person who has it in his grasp. All those good things that delight us with an appealing but deceptive pleasure—money, honor, power, and many other things by which the blind greed of the human race is entranced—they bring trouble to their possessor, they are viewed with envy, and, finally, they oppress the very people to whom they bring distinction; they are more a threat than a benefit; they are slippery and unreliable, one's hold on them is never secure; for even supposing that there is no fear about the future, safeguarding great prosperity is itself an anxious business. (6) If you would believe those who have a more profound insight into the truth, all life is a punishment. We are thrown into this deep, restless sea, whose tides flow back and forth, which at one moment lifts us up with sudden gains, at the next hurls us down with greater losses, constantly tossing us about; and we never settle in a stable position, but we teeter, surge to and fro, and collide with one another; occasionally we suffer shipwreck, and we are constantly afraid of it; as we sail on this squally sea, exposed to every storm, there is no harbor except that of death. (7) So do not begrudge your brother his condition: he is at rest. At last he is free, at last secure, at last eternal. He is survived by Caesar and all his progeny,[18] and he is

survived by you, together with the brothers you share. Before fortune could withdraw any part of its favor, he took his leave of it while it was still standing beside him, heaping up gifts with bountiful hands. **(8)** Now he enjoys an open, free sky; from this low, sunken spot he has soared upward to that place, whatever it is, that welcomes souls freed from their chains into its blessed embrace; now he roams there freely, and with supreme pleasure explores all of nature's goodness. You are mistaken: your brother has not been robbed of the light but has gained a purer light. **(9)** We all participate in the journey there: so why do we weep over death? He did not leave us, but went on ahead. Believe me, there is great happiness in the inevitability of death. We can be certain of nothing, not even for the rest of today. When the truth is so obscure and shrouded, who can guess whether death resented your brother or had his interests at heart?

(10.1) Your actions always proceed from a strong sense of justice, so you are bound to gain further comfort from this thought: that you suffered no injustice when you lost such a brother, but were granted a favor when you were permitted to enjoy the benefit of his love for so long. **(2)** It is unjust not to let the giver keep control of the gift; and it is greedy not to count what has been received as gain, but to count what has been handed back as loss. It is an ungrateful person who calls the termination of a pleasure an injustice; and it is a foolish person who thinks that good things are of no benefit except when they are present, and who derives no further satisfaction from them when they are past, failing to realize that things we no longer have are more dependable, because in their case there is no need to fear that they will come to an end. **(3)** Anyone who thinks he benefits only from something that he has and sees, and who regards having had it as worthless, is taking an over-restricted view of his joys; for pleasures all quickly desert us, they ebb and fade and are swept away almost before they arrive. So our mind must be focused on the past, and everything that has ever delighted us must be recalled and frequently revisited in our thoughts; the memory of pleasures is longer lasting and more dependable than their presence. **(4)** So count the fact that you had such a fine brother as one of your greatest blessings: you should think not of how much longer you could have had him, but of how long you did have him. Just as with other people and their brothers, nature did not give you ownership of him but lent him to you;[19] then when it seemed appropriate it asked for him back, being guided not by the sufficiency of your enjoyment of him but by its own laws. **(5)** If someone got annoyed about repaying money lent to him, particularly money he was able to use without interest, would he not be considered unjust? Nature gave your brother life, it gave it to you too: if it, exercising its rights, wanted to call in someone's debt rather early, it is not to blame, for its terms were well known; the blame lies with the mortal mind's greedy hopes, which repeatedly forget what nature is, and never remember their own status except when they receive a reminder. **(6)** So rejoice that you had such a good brother, and be content with your enjoyment of him, although it was briefer than you wanted. Count the fact that you had him as a great delight, the fact that you lost him as human; for there is nothing more inconsistent than for someone to be upset because he was granted such a brother for too short a time, and yet not rejoice that at any rate he was granted him.

(11.1) "But he was snatched away when I was not expecting it." People are all deceived through their own gullibility, and in the case of those they love there is a deliberate forgetfulness about their mortality: nature has testified that it will grant no one a dispensation from its requirements. Daily there pass before our eyes the funerals of people known and unknown; but we pay no attention, and we regard as unexpected what throughout our lives we have been told was going to happen. So this is not the unfairness of fate but the perverseness of the human mind with its insatiable desire for everything, which complains about departing from a place to which it was admitted as a favor. **(2)** How much more fair-minded was the person who, when he got the news of his son's death, uttered words worthy of a great man: "When I fathered him, I knew then that he would die." You would not be at all surprised that this man had a son who was able to die bravely. He did not treat his son's death as unexpected news; for what is unexpected about a human being dying, when his whole life is merely a journey toward death? **(3)** "When I fathered him, I knew then that he would die." Then he added something that showed even greater wisdom and courage: "And it was for this I lifted him up."[20] It is for this we are all lifted up; whoever is brought into life is earmarked for death. Let us rejoice in what is given to us, and let us return it when we are asked to. The fates will seize hold of different people at different times, but they will not miss anybody out; let the mind stand at the ready, let it never fear the unavoidable, let it constantly expect the unpredictable. **(4)** Do I need to speak of generals and the offspring of generals and men outstanding for their many consulships or many triumphs who encountered the inexorability of destiny? Entire kingdoms with their kings, and nations with their races, have endured their fate; everyone, or rather everything, faces its final day. The end is not the same in every case: life abandons one person in midcourse, deserts another right at the start, and reluctantly releases another in extreme old age, when he is wearied and longing to depart. Though the timetable differs, still we are all heading for the same place. I am not sure whether it is more foolish to be unaware of the law of mortality or more hubristic to object to it. **(5)** Come on, now, go and fetch the poems of either of your two authors,[21] poems that have become more widely known thanks to all the efforts of your literary genius, poems that you have turned into prose of such quality that, though their poetic texture has been lost, their appeal has remained (for in translating from one language to another you have ensured that all their finest characteristics followed you into the foreign tongue—something which was very difficult to achieve): in those works there is not a single book that will not supply you with numerous examples of human fragility, of unpredictable misfortunes, and of tears flowing for all sorts of different reasons. **(6)** Read and see how inspired was the thundering of your mighty words: you will be ashamed of suddenly going to pieces and abandoning the real greatness of your writing. Do not cause those who have unbounded admiration for your works to ask how such a frail mind could conceive something so powerful and enduring.

(12.1) Instead, turn from the things that torment you to the many great sources of comfort that you have. Look at your splendid brothers, look at your wife, look at your son: fortune has agreed with you that you should make this partial payment in return for the wellbeing of all of them.[22] You have many people in whom you can find comfort: make sure you avoid the disgrace of everyone thinking that a single source of grief counts for more with you than all these sources of consolation. **(2)** You can see that they have all been traumatized just as you have, and they cannot help you; indeed, you realize that they are actually looking to you for support. So, given that they are less highly educated and less talented than you, it is all the more essential for you to withstand the suffering that all of you face. Moreover, it is itself a form of comfort to share one's grief with many others: because it is being distributed among a number of people, only a tiny part of it should end up with you.

(3) I shall not stop bringing Caesar repeatedly to your attention: while he rules the world and demonstrates how much more effectively the empire is protected by generosity than by military power, while he is in charge of human affairs, there is no risk of your feeling that you have suffered any loss; in this one person you have sufficient security and comfort. So pick yourself up, and whenever tears well up in your eyes, turn them toward Caesar: they will be dried up at the sight of that most mighty and most glorious divinity; his radiance will dazzle them so that they can see nothing else, and it will keep them fixed on him. (4) You must think about him, the one you look at day and night, from whom you never divert your attention; you must invoke his aid against fortune. I have no doubt—so great is his kindness and his benevolence toward all who are close to him—that he has already dressed this wound of yours with many kinds of consolation, and has already amassed many medicines to counter your pain. Besides, even supposing he has done none of those things, is not the mere sight of Caesar, and the thought of him, a supreme comfort to you? (5) May the gods and goddesses extend their loan of him to the earth for a long time to come.[23] May he equal the achievements of the deified Augustus and exceed his years.[24] So long as he remains among mortals, may he not experience the mortality of anything in his own household. May he build up people's confidence in his son and win approval for him to be the ruler of the Roman Empire; and may he see him as his father's partner before he sees him as his successor.[25] May the day when his family claims him for heaven be long delayed, and be witnessed by our grandchildren.[26]

(13.1) Keep your hands off him, fortune, and do not demonstrate your power over him except in your beneficial aspect. Allow him to heal the human race, which has long been sick and ailing; allow him to reinstate and restore everything that the madness of the previous emperor destroyed.[27] May this star, which has dawned on a world that was plunged into the abyss and sunk in darkness, shine forever.[28] (2) May he pacify Germany,[29] open up Britain,[30] and conduct triumphs such as his father did,[31] and new ones. The virtue that occupies the highest place among his virtues, his clemency, holds out the promise that I too shall be a spectator of those triumphs.[32]

For he has not struck me down without being willing to raise me up, or rather he has not really struck me down; but when I was assailed by fortune and was falling, he held me up, and as I was hurtling to destruction, with a restraining touch from his divine hand he gently gave me a soft landing: he interceded for me with the senate, and did not just grant me my life but pleaded for it. (3) I leave it to him: let him think what he will of my case; either let his justice discern that it is a good one, or let his clemency make it a good one. Either favor will mean the same to me, whether he knows that I am innocent or wishes I were so. Meanwhile, it is a great comfort for my misery to see his mercy ranging across the whole world; from this very corner in which I have been buried it has already dug out several people who were overwhelmed by disaster many years previous, and has restored them to the light; so I am not afraid that I am the only one he will overlook. But he himself best knows the proper time to come to the rescue of each individual; I shall make every effort to ensure that he will not be ashamed when it is my turn. (4) O that blessed clemency of yours, Caesar, thanks to which exiles live a more tranquil life under you than the leading citizens did so recently under Gaius! They are not fearful, and do not await the sword every single hour, nor do they tremble every time they see a ship; thanks to you, they are enjoying not only an end to fortune's savagery but also hope of an improvement in fortune, and peace of mind while fortune remains as it is. One can tell that thunderbolts are entirely just when they are worshipped even by those they strike.[33]

(14.1) So this emperor, who is a universal source of comfort for everyone, has already, if I am not totally mistaken, restored your spirits, and to such a great wound he has applied even greater remedies. He has already used every means to give you strength; he has already, with his highly retentive memory, rehearsed all the precedents that could urge you toward equanimity; he has already expounded the precepts of all the philosophers with his customary eloquence. (2) So no one would better perform the role of comforter: when he is speaking, the words will have a special power, as if they were uttered by an oracle; his divine authority will crush all the force of your grief. So imagine him saying to you, "Fortune has not picked out you alone to subject to such grievous hurt: there neither is nor has been any household in the whole world exempted from mourning for someone. I shall pass over ordinary examples, which, even if they are less significant, are still numerous, and I shall take you to our public calendar and annals.[34] (3) You see all these portraits that have filled the atrium of the Caesars? Every single one of them is memorable for some family misfortune; every single one of those luminaries who brought distinction to past centuries was either racked with grief for lost relatives, or his relatives felt the most anguished grief for him.

(4) "Need I remind you of Scipio Africanus, who got the news of his brother's death while in exile?[35] This brother, who rescued his brother from prison, could not rescue him from fate; and it was evident to all how intolerant of equal rights was the brotherly love of Africanus, for on the same day as he had snatched his brother from the hands of a court official, he also vetoed a tribune of the plebs, although he was a private citizen.[36] But he mourned the loss of his brother with as much courage as he had defended him. (5) Need I remind you of Scipio Aemilianus, who at virtually one and the same time watched his father's triumph and the funerals of two brothers?[37] Although he was a mere youth, almost a boy, when his family was struck down hard on the heels of Paulus's triumph, he endured the sudden devastation with all the courage required of a man who was born to ensure that the city of Rome did not lack a Scipio and was not outlived by Carthage.[38]

(15.1) "Need I recall the closeness of the two Luculli, wrenched apart by death?[39] Or the Pompeii,[40] to whom savage fortune would not even concede that they should eventually die in the same catastrophe? Sextus Pompeius first of all outlived his sister, by whose death the bonds of the peace that had held together so well at Rome were undone;[41] he also outlived his excellent brother, whom fortune had raised up in order that it should topple him from a height no less than that from which it had toppled his father; and still after this misfortune Sextus Pompeius proved himself equal not just to the grief but also to the war. (2) From everywhere countless examples of brothers separated by death suggest themselves, or rather, to put it the other way around, scarcely any pairs of brothers have ever been seen growing old together. But I shall be content with examples from our own family; for no one will be so lacking in judgment and good sense as to complain that fortune has inflicted grief on someone else when he knows that it has even set its heart on the tears of the Caesars.

(3) "The deified Augustus lost Octavia, his beloved sister, and nature granted no dispensation from the inevitability of grief even to someone it had destined for heaven. Indeed, he was assailed by every kind of bereavement, losing his sister's son, who had been groomed to succeed him;[42] briefly, to save me listing his sorrows individually, he lost both his sons-in-law, his children, and his grandchildren, and of all mortals none was more conscious that he was a human being while he lived among human beings.[43] But his heart, which was well able to cope with everything, coped with all these numerous, severe losses, and the deified Augustus was victorious not just over foreign nations but also over his sorrows. **(4)** Gaius Caesar, <son> and grandson of the deified Augustus,[44] my maternal uncle,[45] in the earliest years of his manhood, while Leader of the Youth, lost Lucius, his beloved brother, also a Leader of the Youth, during the preparations for the Parthian War.[46] He suffered an emotional wound much more serious than his later physical one; but he bore both with outstanding love and outstanding courage.

(5) "<Tiberius> Caesar, my paternal uncle, lost Drusus Germanicus my father, a brother younger than he was, who at the time was opening up the interior of Germany and bringing the wildest tribes under Roman control; and he held him and kissed him as he died. Nevertheless he imposed a limit not only on his own grief but also on that of others: the whole army was not just sorrowful but traumatized, and claimed the body of its dear Drusus for itself; but Tiberius made it revert to the traditional Roman form of mourning, and judged that discipline had to be maintained not just in military matters but also in grief. He would not have been able to restrain the tears of other people if he had not first held his own in check. **(16.1)** Marcus Antonius, my grandfather, was second to none except the man who defeated him; just when he was reorganizing the state, when he was invested with triumviral power and acknowledged no superior authority, when, indeed, he saw everything, apart from his two colleagues, under his own control, he heard that his brother had been killed.[47] **(2)** Reckless fortune, how you amuse yourself with human suffering! At the very same time when Marcus Antonius was sitting in judgment on the life and death of his fellow citizens, the order was given for the brother of Marcus Antonius to be led away to execution. Marcus Antonius bore such a cruel wound with the same courageousness as he had endured all other adversities, and his mourning took the form of offering a sacrifice to his brother with the blood of twenty legions.[48]

(3) "But, to pass over every other example, and to ignore even the other deaths by which I have been affected, fortune has twice attacked me with grief for a brother, twice it has learned that I could be hurt but could not be defeated:[49] I lost my brother Germanicus, and anyone who considers how devoted to each other loyal brothers are can readily understand how I was devoted to him; but I kept my feelings under control so as not to neglect anything that was required of a good brother, and not to do anything that could be criticized in an emperor."

(4) So imagine the father of his people presenting you with these examples, and showing how nothing is sacred and inviolable for fortune, which has had the nerve to conduct funeral processions from the very household from which it was intending to seek gods. Let no one be surprised if it acts either cruelly or unjustly; can it know any sense of fairness or any restraint in its dealings with private houses when its implacable savagery has so often polluted the couches of the gods with death? (5) We may revile it not just with our own voices but also with the voices of the whole people, yet it will not change; it will stand its ground before all our prayers, all our complaints. This is how fortune has behaved toward humans, this is how it will behave: it has left nothing unventured, it will leave nothing unscathed; it will rampage violently everywhere, just as it always has done; in order to cause hurt it will even have the effrontery to enter those houses that are approached through temples, and it will drape black cloth over doorways festooned with laurel.[50] (6) Let us seek to obtain this one request from it with public vows and prayers, if it has not yet decided to reduce the human race to nothing, if it still looks favorably on the name of Rome: this emperor was a gift to a weary human world, so may it be willing to revere him as sacred, just as every mortal does; may it learn mercy from him, and be gentle with the gentlest of all emperors.

(17.1) So you should look at all those I have just mentioned who were either adopted into heaven or came very close to it: fortune does not even keep its hands off those by whose names we swear,[51] so you should react with equanimity when its hands reach out toward you as well. You should imitate the resoluteness with which these people have borne and overcome their grief, insofar as it is right for a human to walk in the footsteps of the divine. **(2)** Although in other spheres there are immense disparities of status and distinction, virtue is available to all: it thinks no one unworthy as long as he thinks himself worthy. You will certainly do well to imitate those who might have complained that they were not themselves exempted from this suffering, but who nevertheless judged that to be treated in the same way as everyone else in this one respect was not an injustice but the law of mortality, those who endured what had happened neither with excessive bitterness and resentment nor in a weak and womanish manner. For failure to acknowledge one's sufferings is inhuman; failure to shoulder them is unmanly.

(3) Since I have mentioned all the Caesars whom fortune robbed of brothers and sisters, I cannot omit one who deserves to be struck off every list of the Caesars, one whom nature created to bring ruin and shame to the human race, who burned and totally destroyed the empire which the clemency of our most kindly emperor is now restoring. **(4)** When he lost his sister Drusilla,[52] Gaius Caesar, that fellow who could no more grieve than rejoice as an emperor should, shunned the sight and company of his citizens, did not attend the funeral of his sister, and did not make the funerary offerings due to his sister, but in his residence at Alba he relieved the trauma of that agonizing bereavement with dice and gaming board and *** other such distractions.[53] What a disgrace to the empire! Gambling was the solace of a Roman emperor who was mourning his sister! **(5)** The same Gaius who, with insane inconsistency, sometimes let his beard and hair grow long, sometimes roamed aimlessly along the shores of Italy and Sicily, and was never quite sure whether he wanted his sister to be mourned or worshipped, all the while that he was setting up temples and couches for her,[54] was inflicting the cruelest punishment on those who had not been sufficiently mournful; for he endured the blows of adversity with the same lack of self-control with which, when buoyed up by favorable events, he swaggered far beyond the bounds of human decency. **(6)** Every Roman man should shun the example he set of distracting one's grief with ill-timed amusements, or inflaming it with unsightly mourning clothes and unkempt appearance, or entertaining it with other people's sufferings, an utterly inhuman form of comfort.

(18.1) You, however, need not change your usual behavior at all, since you have begun to devote yourself to those studies that best increase your happiness and most easily diminish your misfortune, that simultaneously bring both the greatest distinction and the greatest comfort to a human being. So now plunge yourself more deeply into your studies, now surround yourself with them, like fortifications for your mind, so that grief may not find a way in from any direction. **(2)** Also, prolong the memory of your brother in some literary monument of your own; in human life this is the only product that no storm can harm, no length of time consume. Other monuments, formed from stone structures and blocks of marble, or from mounds of earth raised up to a great height, do not guarantee a long survival, because they too perish: but a memorial built by literary genius is immortal. Lavish that on your brother, lay him to rest in that; it will be better for you to celebrate him with your literary genius, which is destined to last forever, than to mourn him with a grief that is pointless.

(3) As for fortune itself, although at the moment its case cannot be defended before you—for all that it has given us is made hateful by the fact that it has taken one thing away—nevertheless fortune will need to be defended as soon as time has enabled you to judge it more fairly; because then you will be able to achieve reconciliation with it. For it has made many provisions for remedying this hurt, and in future will give you many gifts to compensate for it; and finally, it itself had given you what it has taken away. **(4)** So do not employ your talent against yourself, do not be an advocate for your own grief. Your eloquence can make small things pass for great, and again it can belittle what is great and make it seem insignificant; but let it keep its powers for another occasion, now let it be wholly devoted to your own consolation. Yet watch out, in case this too is now superfluous; for nature demands some grief from us, but we bring more on ourselves through empty pride. **(5)** I shall never demand that you do not mourn at all, though I know that one can find men of a harsh rather than a courageous wisdom who say that the sage will not feel any grief.[55] They do not seem to me ever to have encountered this sort of adversity; otherwise fortune would have knocked their arrogant philosophy out of them, and forced them even against their will to confess the truth. **(6)** Reason will have achieved enough if it simply excises any grief that is superfluous and redundant; that reason should not allow grief to exist at all is something no one should either hope or wish for. Let reason rather maintain a midcourse that bears no similarity either to lack of love or to lack of sanity, and let it keep us in a frame of mind that is loving but not anguished: let tears flow, but let them also stop; let groans well up from the depths of the heart, but let them also come to an end; keep your mind under control in a manner that wins approval both from the wise and from brothers. **(7)** Make sure that you want to be reminded of your brother frequently, that you often mention him in your conversation, and also that through constant recollection you keep him in your mind's eye. You will be successful if you ensure that you find his memory pleasant rather than melancholy; for it is natural for the mind always to recoil from anything it returns to with sadness. **(8)** Think of his modesty, think of his resourcefulness when it came to action, his energy when it came to getting things done, his reliability when it came to promises. Pass on to others, and recall for your own benefit, all he said and did. Think of what he was like and of the hopes one could have had for him; for is there anything that one could not have confidently promised concerning such a brother?

(9) I have written this as best I was able, with a mind worn out and numbed by long disuse. If my words seem an inadequate match for your intellect or an inadequate cure for your grief, consider how one cannot be free to console someone else when one is preoccupied with one's own sufferings, and how Latin words do not come to one readily when the crude gabbling of barbarians, which even the ears of more civilized barbarians find harsh, is echoing all around.[56]

1. The Latin manuscripts begin in midsentence, but the general sense is clear.

2. That is, the Seven Wonders of the World; the list was fluid in Seneca's day.

3. Seneca is alluding to the Stoic doctrine of ecpyrosis.

4. Three cities destroyed by the Romans: Carthage and Corinth in 146 BCE, Numantia in 133 BCE.

5. There is nothing outside the universe, so it has nowhere to fall.

6. Seneca here alludes to his exile.

7. Reading *eum hominem <in sinu> continuisse.*

8. In Latin "lovable" (*amabilem*) picks up "friends" (*amicos*) in the previous sentence.

9. The liberal arts were the subjects covered in a general education; later the list was standardized to include grammar (chiefly the study of literature), dialectic, rhetoric, arithmetic, geometry, music, and astronomy.

10. That is, with his mind.

11. Literature was regarded as a safer pursuit than politics or other areas of public life.

12. Compare Lucretius 5.222–27.

13. In mythology, Atlas carried the world on his shoulders.

14. Polybius had translated Homer into Latin and Virgil into Greek.

15. Claudius had written on Roman, Etruscan, and Carthaginian history.

16. Seneca ignores, whether deliberately or through ignorance, the verse fables of Phaedrus, written during the reign of Tiberius.

17. "The divine" here includes the heavenly bodies, widely regarded as divine beings.

18. When Seneca wrote, Claudius had three children: Antonia, from his second marriage to Aelia Paetina, and Octavia and Britannicus, from his third marriage to Messallina.

19. Compare Lucretius 3.971.

20. Seneca is quoting a fragment of Roman tragedy of uncertain authorship (quoted also by Cicero *Tusculan Disputations* 3.28, 58, with slightly different wording). At birth, the Roman father lifted the baby off the ground, an act of formal recognition that the child was his own.

21. Homer or Virgil. From what follows it seems that Polybius's translations were in prose.

22. A financial image: fortune is a creditor who releases a struggling debtor from his debt upon payment of an agreed fraction of what is owed; in return for payment of his brother's life, Polybius can keep the lives of his other relatives.

23. It is a standard theme of Roman imperial panegyric that the emperor's true home is among the gods, but the writer appeals for him to stay on earth as long as possible.

24. Augustus died at the age of seventy-six; Claudius was in his fifties when Seneca wrote this.

25. The son in question is Britannicus; his mother was Claudius's third wife Messalina. Britannicus was born in 41 CE. Subsequently, after Claudius's marriage to Agrippina, her son Nero was promoted above Britannicus, who, according to the ancient sources, was murdered by Nero in 55 CE, the year after Nero became emperor. Claudius would see Britannicus as his successor after he had died and ascended to heaven.

26. Julius Caesar and Augustus, both ancestors of Claudius, had been deified, and they traced their ancestry to Venus, but "his family" may well refer to the gods in general.

27. The previous emperor was Gaius Caligula (r. 37–41 CE).

28. It was a commonplace of imperial panegyric to compare the ruler to a star.

29. Gabinius Secundus defeated the Chauci, a German tribe, during Claudius's reign. Gnaeus Domitius Corbulo also campaigned against the Chauci in 47 CE, but that was probably after the date of this work (see the next note).

30. Claudius led a successful invasion of Britain in 43 CE. This passage was clearly written before that, or at least before the news had reached Seneca in Corsica.

31. Claudius's father Drusus campaigned in Germany from 12 BCE till his death in 9 BCE, and won triumphal insignia. Claudius did celebrate a triumph after the conquest of Britain.

32. Suetonius (*The Life of Claudius* 34.3) reports that Claudius did allow some exiles back to Rome to watch his triumph. But Seneca was not among them.

33. Thunderbolts, wielded by Jupiter in mythology, are a regular metaphor for punishment inflicted by emperors. In Rome a traditional religious ritual was performed at any spot struck by lightning.

34. The public calendar, the Fasti, was the official record of magistrates who had held office each year. The public annals may refer to the *annales maximi*, the records kept by the pontifex maximus in the Early and Middle Republics, but more likely refer to Roman historical works more generally. Claudius himself was a historian; see 8.2 above.

35. This is Publius Cornelius Scipio Africanus the Elder, who defeated

Hannibal; the brother is Lucius Cornelius Scipio Asiagenes. But other writers, probably correctly, say that Publius died before Lucius. Publius probably went into voluntary exile in 184 BCE to avoid prosecution, and died the following year.

36. Publius rescued his brother a few years before his exile; the exact date is uncertain. Only a tribune in office could veto another tribune.

37. This is the younger Africanus, Publius Cornelius Scipio Aemilianus Africanus Numantinus, son of Lucius Aemilius Paullus, and subsequently adopted by the son of the elder Africanus. His natural father Paullus celebrated a triumph after his defeat of Perseus in 167 BCE. One son died five days before the triumph, the other three days after it.

38. This Scipio destroyed Carthage in 146 BCE.

39. Lucius Licinius Lucullus, who led the Roman army in the Third Mithradatic War and died in 57/56 BCE, and his brother Marcus Licinius Lucullus.

40. The sons of Pompeius Magnus (Pompey the Great): Gnaeus Pompeius Magnus Minor (who was executed after the battle of Munda in 45 BCE), and Sextus Pompeius Magnus (who was executed in 35 BCE, after being defeated at the battle of Naulochus the preceding year).

41. This sentence is problematic, for their sister was Pompeia, who married a Sulla, so that her death could not have had the effect here described. It is sometimes assumed that Seneca is confusedly thinking of the death of Julia, daughter of Julius Caesar. She married Pompey the Great in 59 BCE, cementing the alliance between Pompey and Caesar, and her death in 54 BCE was seen as a catalyst in the breakdown of the alliance. She was Pompey's second wife, and so stepmother, not sister, of the two Pompey brothers under discussion here. Another possibility is that Seneca refers to the baby daughter of Pompey and Julia, who was a half sister of the brothers: Julia died while giving birth to this baby daughter, who died a few days later.

42. Octavia died in 11 BCE; her son Marcellus had died in 23 BCE.

43. The sons-in-law were Marcellus and Agrippa, and the grandsons were Gaius and Lucius Caesar (see section 4 below). But he had only one child, his daughter Julia, and she died in banishment, having outlived Augustus; so Seneca may be thinking of Gaius and Lucius here too, for they were adopted as sons (see the next note).

44. He was grandson by birth (son of Agrippa and Julia, Augustus's daughter), son by adoption.

45. He was actually Claudius's maternal great-uncle (his mother Antonia was daughter of Octavia, Augustus's sister); possibly the Latin word has that meaning here.

46. In 2 CE. "Leader of the Youth," *princeps iuuentutis*, was a formal title they both received.

47. Marcus Antonius, the father of Claudius's mother Antonia, in 43 BCE formed the second triumvirate with Octavian, later Augustus, and Marcus Lepidus. He was defeated by Augustus in 31 BCE. His brother Gaius Antonius was killed in 42 BCE.

48. This refers to the defeat of the armies of Brutus and Cassius at Philippi in 42 BCE.

49. It is puzzling that fortune is described as attacking twice, but then Germanicus is the only brother mentioned. But Tacitus (*The Annals* 2.82) describes how in 19 CE two reports of Germanicus's death reached Rome: the first subsequently proved to be false, but the later one was true.

50. The entrance to the imperial palace resembled a temple, and a laurel tree grew in front of it.

51. In the imperial period people swore oaths by the current emperor, and by Augustus after his death.

52. Drusilla died in 38 CE.

53. Some corrupt words are omitted in the translation.

54. Images of the gods were regularly displayed on couches.

55. This was the Stoic view; but Seneca commonly distances himself from the strict Stoic view that the sage will have no emotions at all. Here he embraces the Aristotelian doctrine of the mean, i.e., the idea that one should shun excessive emotions (as he says in 18.6).

56. The conclusion recalls the end of Ovid's *Tristia* book 3 (3.14.47–52), where the poet complains about being surrounded by foreign voices in his place of exile, Tomi.

On the Shortness of Life

Introduction

The Paulinus addressed in this treatise is in all likelihood Pompeius Paulinus, a knight of Arelate (modern Arles) who, as *praefectus annonae* probably from 48 to 55 CE, was responsible for overseeing the Roman grain supply; it is now generally accepted that he was also the father of Pompeia Paulina, Seneca's wife (cf. Tacitus *Annals* 15.60.4). Given Seneca's direct injunction to Paulinus to retire from his important position (18.1–19.2), the work is apparently datable to between 48 and 55—a period in which Seneca was himself fully engaged in public life and court politics after his return from exile in 49. If this dating is accepted, two problems immediately present themselves: first, for all the attractive high-mindedness of Seneca's injunction to Paulinus to retire from his important business of state, just how practical an option can philosophical withdrawal be, not just for Paulinus (let alone for the state he serves) but also for Seneca's wider readership, ancient and modern, amid all life's responsibilities and challenges? Second, how can Seneca escape the charge of hypocrisy for urging Paulinus to retire in the very years when he himself was actively engaged at court?

The sheer provocation of both questions perhaps supplies the best answer to each: Seneca's exhortation to Paulinus hits home if it causes him (and *us*) to step back from the unrelenting march of life, to evaluate from a radical, alternative perspective the ordering of priorities in our existence, and so to reflect on how we daily use and allocate time. Real but immaterial, time was classified by the Stoics as one of the four "incorporeals" alongside the "sayable," void and place. At points in this treatise, however, Seneca portrays time as if it were a material commodity, or a form of property that can be given or taken away, conserved or spent, hoarded or wasted (cf. 3.1, 8.1)—a concretizing technique by which he casts time as a currency with transactional value and in need of careful budgeting. Time thus enters the moral sphere because our (Stoic) inner freedom depends on our mastery over time: hence the positive efficiency that Seneca inculcates by urging that time *can* be reclaimed from the depredations of others (cf. 2.4–5); by instilling a new discipline based on living "right now" (9.1); and by promoting an intolerance of time wasted through submission to vices (cf. 2.1–2), through procrastination (3.5, 9.1), or through pointless engagement in trivia (12.2–13.9). His brisk style, combining shafts of righteous indignation, diatribic broadside, aphoristic brevity, and cutting wit, itself underscores the urgency of his strictures about the value of time: his intolerant sureness of voice contributes to the essential optimism of a work which insists that there *is* another way.

The distinction drawn in *On Leisure* between the localized *res publica* and its counterpart in the cosmic megalopolis (4.1–2) is paralleled by the contrast drawn in *On the Shortness of Life* between Paulinus's onerous duties as *praefectus* (19.1; cf. 18.4: "Recall that energetic mind of yours . . . from an office that is certainly eminent but is hardly in keeping with the happy life") and the enlightened pursuits that await him in philosophical retirement (cf. 19.2: "You really ought to leave ground level and turn your mind's eye to these studies"). The change of perspective urged in 19.1–2 is anticipated by two important movements earlier in the treatise, the first in chapters 1–9. There, his condemnation of time-wasting through misguided preoccupation both comforts and cajoles: it comforts by distancing Paulinus (and, by extension, his readership) from the worst offenders whom he surveys; and yet it cajoles us to take stock of our own lives, and so (for example) to submit ourselves to the chastening audit of time squandered that he directs at an imaginary interlocutor in 3.2–3. The second movement extends from 10.2 to 17.6: despite the transition announced in 10.1 from straightforward denunciation to a more constructive approach ("the preoccupied . . . are to be taught a lesson, not simply given up for lost"), Seneca's condemnatory tone persists in his survey of time wasted on trivial pursuits in chapters 12–13; but those chapters are themselves offset by his change of direction to focus, in 14.1, on those philosophical devotees who "alone . . . are at leisure" and "alone really live." In contrast to the preoccupied, prominent among them the ordinary Roman client who breathlessly rushes from one obligation to the next in the daily circuit of obsequiousness (14.3–4), Seneca constructs a higher, figurative mode of clientship to accommodating philosopher-patrons such as Socrates or Carneades, Epicurus or Zeno (14.2, 5). Unlike ordinary clientship, this mode of *clientela* is paradoxically liberating, freeing the philosopher to live as his own master in full control of all times past, present, and future (cf. 15.5); the liberating effects of such *clientela* are akin to those of participation in the cosmic megalopolis of *On Leisure* 4.

From this higher perspective, Paulinus's status as *praefectus annonae*, however elevated in one way, resembles in another that of the burdened client of chapter 14; higher service awaits him if he can achieve the crucial "letting go" of everyday limitation and preoccupation. All speculation as to whether Paulinus was actually induced to retire by Seneca's persuasion is surely beside the point: what matters far more is the provocation that Seneca poses to settled attitudes by addressing a figure of Paulinus's prominence in so radical a fashion. Even if Seneca himself was *in officio* at the time of writing, the charge of hypocrisy is arguably a minor matter in comparison with the value of this appeal to vigilance and to the taking back of life. Alternatively, *On the Shortness of Life* may be viewed not so much as the work of a hypocrite but as an embodiment of its own message: even in the midst of the preoccupied life at court, Seneca exercises via his writing the very self-consciousness about the value of time that his treatise promotes in others.

Further Reading

Griffin, M. T. 1962. "*De Brevitate Vitae.*" *JRS* 52:104–13.

———. 1976. *Seneca: A Philosopher in Politics* (Oxford: Oxford University Press / Clarendon Press; repr. with postscript, 1992), esp. 317–21, 401–7.

Williams, G. D., ed. 2003. *Seneca: "De Otio," "De Brevitate Vitae"* (Cambridge: Cambridge University Press), esp. 18–25.

On the Shortness of Life

LUCIUS ANNAEUS SENECA

TRANSLATED BY GARETH D. WILLIAMS

(**1.1**) Most of mankind, Paulinus, complains about nature's meanness, because our allotted span of life is so short, and because this stretch of time that is given to us runs its course so quickly, so rapidly—so much so that, with very few exceptions, life leaves the rest of us in the lurch just when we're getting ready to live. And it's not just the masses and the unthinking crowd that complain at what they perceive as this universal evil; the same feeling draws complaints even from men of distinction. Hence that famous dictum of the greatest of physicians: "Life is short, art long."[1] (**2**) Hence also Aristotle's grievance,[2] most unbecoming a philosopher, when he called nature to account for bestowing so much time on animals that they can live for five or ten human life spans, while so much shorter a limit is set for humans, even though they are born to do so many great things.

(**3**) It's not that we have a short time to live, but that we waste much of it. Life is long enough, and it's been given to us in generous measure for accomplishing the greatest things, if the whole of it is well invested. But when life is squandered through soft and careless living, and when it's spent on no worthwhile pursuit, death finally presses and we realize that the life which we didn't notice passing has passed away. (**4**) So it is: the life we are given isn't short but we make it so; we're not ill provided but we are wasteful of life. Just as impressive and princely wealth is squandered in an instant when it passes into the hands of a poor manager, but wealth however modest grows through careful deployment if it is entrusted to a responsible guardian, just so our lifetime offers ample scope to the person who maps it out well.

(**2.1**) Why do we complain about nature? It has acted generously: life, if you know how to use it, is long. But one person's held in the grip of voracious avarice, another by the kind of diligence that busies itself with pointless enterprises. This one's sodden with wine, another slack with idleness. This one's tired out by his political ambition, which always hangs on the judgment of others, while another's passionate desire for trading drives him headlong over every land

and every sea in hope of profit. A passion for soldiering torments some men, who are always either bent on inflicting dangers on others or worried about danger to themselves. Some are worn down by the voluntary enslavement of thankless attendance on the great. (2) Many are kept busy either striving after other people's wealth or complaining about their own. Many who have no consistent goal in life are thrown from one new design to another by a fickleness that is shifting, never settled and ever dissatisfied with itself. Some have no goal at all toward which to steer their course, but death takes them by surprise as they gape and yawn. I cannot therefore doubt the truth of that seemingly oracular utterance of the greatest of poets: "Scant is the part of life in which we live."[3] All the rest of existence is not living but merely time.

(3) Vices assail and surround us on all sides, and they don't allow us to rise again and lift our eyes to the clear discernment of truth; but they press down on them, keeping them lowered and fixed on mere desire. It's never possible for their victims to return to their true selves. If by chance they ever find some respite, they still roll restlessly, just like the deep sea, which still swells even after the wind has settled; they never find full relaxation from their desires. (4) You think I'm talking only of those whose faults are admitted? Look at those whose prosperity draws crowds: they are choked by their own goods. How many have found their wealth a burden! How many are drained of their blood by their eloquence and their daily preoccupation with showing off their abilities! How many are sickly pale from their incessant pleasures! How many are left with no freedom from the multitude of their besieging clients! In short, look over all of them from lowest to highest: this person summons counsel to plead his case, another answers the call; this one stands trial, another acts for the defense, another presides as judge; no one acts as his own champion, but each is wasted for another's sake. Ask about those influential citizens whose names are studiously memorized, and you'll see that the following distinctions tell them apart: the first cultivates a second, the second a third; no one is his own man. (5) Again certain people give vent to the most irrational outbursts of anger: they complain about the haughtiness of their superiors, because the latter were too busy to receive them when they wanted an audience. Dare anyone complain about another's arrogance when he himself never has time

to spare for himself? Yet the great man has occasionally, albeit with a disdainful expression, condescended to look on you, whoever you are; he has deigned to listen to your words, he has allowed you to walk at his side. But you never thought fit to look on yourself or to listen to yourself. And so you've no reason to expect a return from anyone for those attentions of yours, since you offered them not because you wanted another's company but because you were incapable of communing with yourself.

(3.1) Though all the brilliant minds that have shone over the ages agree on this one point, they could never adequately express their astonishment at this dark fog in the human mind. No one lets anyone seize his estates, and if a trivial dispute arises about boundary lines, there's a rush to stones and arms; but people let others trespass on their existence—or rather, they go so far as to invite in those who'll take possession of their lives. You'll find no one willing to distribute his money; but to how many people each of us shares out his life! Men are thrifty in guarding their private property, but as soon as it comes to wasting time, they are most extravagant with the one commodity for which it's respectable to be greedy.

(2) And so I'd like to collar one of the older crowd: "I see that you've reached the limit of human life, you're pressing hard on your hundredth year or more; come now, submit your life to an audit. Calculate how much of your time has been taken up by a moneylender, how much by a mistress, how much by a patron, how much by a client, how much in arguing with your wife, in punishing your slaves, in running about the city on social duties. Add to your calculations the illnesses that we've inflicted on ourselves, and also the time that has lain idle: you'll see that you've fewer years than you count. (3) Look back and recall when you were ever sure of your purpose; how few days turned out as you'd intended; when you were ever at your own disposal; when your face showed its own expression; when your mind was free from disturbance; what accomplishment you can claim in such a long life; how many have plundered your existence without your being aware of what you were losing; how much time has been lost to groundless anguish, foolish pleasure, greedy desire, the charms of society; how little is left to you from your own store of time. You'll come to realize that you're dying before your time."

(4) What, then, is the reason for this? Your sort live as if you're

going to live forever, your own human frailty never enters your head, you don't keep an eye on how much time has passed already. You waste time as if it comes from a source full to overflowing, when all the while that very day which is given over to someone or something may be your last. You're like ordinary mortals in fearing everything, you're like immortals in coveting everything. (5) You'll hear many say: "After my fiftieth year I'll retire to a life of leisure; my sixtieth year will bring release from all my duties." And what guarantee, may I ask, do you have that your life will last longer? Who will allow those arrangements of yours to proceed according to plan? Are you not ashamed to keep for yourself only the remnants of your existence, and to allocate to philosophical thought only that portion of time which can't be applied to any business? How late it is to begin living just when life must come to an end! What foolish obliviousness to our mortality to put off wise plans to our fiftieth and sixtieth year, and to want to begin life from a point that few have reached!

(4.1) You'll find that the most powerful men of high position drop words in which they pray for leisure, praise it, and prefer it to all their blessings. They sometimes long to step down from that pinnacle of theirs, if they can safely do so; for even without any external disturbance or shock, fortune crashes down on itself under its own weight.

(2) The divine Augustus, to whom the gods gave more than to any man, never ceased to pray for rest for himself and to seek release from the affairs of state. Every conversation of his kept coming back to this theme, that he was hoping for leisure; he would relieve his toils with this sweet, even if illusory, consolation, the thought that one day he would live for himself. (3) In a letter that he sent to the senate, when he had given an assurance that his retirement would not be wanting in dignity and not be inconsistent with his former prestige, I find the following words: "But such things are more impressive in their fulfillment than in their promise. Yet my deep desire for that time, which I have long prayed for, has led me to anticipate something of its delight by the pleasure of words, since the joy of that reality is still slow in coming."[4] (4) Leisure seemed such a desirable thing that, because he couldn't enjoy it in reality, he enjoyed the thought of it in advance. He who saw that the world depended on him and him alone, who determined the fortunes of individuals and

nations, he was happiest in looking forward to that day on which he would lay aside his greatness. **(5)** He knew by experience how much sweat was wrung from him by those blessings that gleamed the world over; he knew the scale of the hidden anxieties they veiled.[5] Forced to contend in arms first with his fellow citizens, then with his colleagues, and finally with his relatives, he shed blood by land and sea. Driven by war through Macedonia, Sicily, Egypt, Syria, and Asia and almost every known land, he turned his armies to foreign wars when they were weary of slaughtering Romans. While he was pacifying the Alps and subjugating enemies embedded in the heart of the peaceful empire, and while he was extending its boundaries beyond the Rhine and Euphrates and Danube, in the city itself Murena, Caepio, Lepidus, Egnatius, and others were whetting their swords against him. **(6)** He had not yet escaped their intrigues when his daughter and so many noble paramours, bound by adultery as if by an oath of allegiance, kept causing him alarm in his now-failing years—as did Iullus and a woman once again posing a threat with her Antony.[6] He had cut away these sores, limbs and all, but others kept growing up in their place; as if overburdened with blood, the body politic was always hemorrhaging somewhere. That is why Augustus prayed for leisure, and why he found relief from his labors in hoping for it and thinking of it; this was the prayer of the man who could grant the prayers of other men.

(5.1) Marcus Cicero was storm-tossed among the likes of Catiline and Clodius, of Pompey and Crassus, declared enemies on the one side, doubtful friends on the other.[7] He was buffeted along with the ship of state, which he tried to keep steady as it was going down, but he was finally swept away. He was neither at ease in prosperity nor capable of withstanding adversity; how many times does he curse that very consulship of his,[8] which he had extolled not without reason but without ceasing! **(2)** How pitiful are the words that he wrings from himself in a letter written to Atticus, when the elder Pompey had been defeated and his son was still trying to revive his shattered forces in Spain![9] "You ask," he says, "what I'm doing here? I'm lingering in my Tusculan estate, half-free."[10] After that, he goes on to other statements in which he bemoans his former life, complains about the present, and despairs of the future. **(3)** "Half-free," Cicero said of himself. But needless to say, the sage will never resort to such an abject term. He will never be half-free but will always enjoy complete and unalloyed liberty. Not subject to any constraints, he will be his own master and tower above all others. For what can there be above the man who rises above fortune?

(**6.1**) Livius Drusus[11] was a vigorously energetic man who, thronged about by a huge crowd from the whole of Italy, had agitated for radical legislation and provoked the kind of troubles the Gracchi had. But he could see no clear way out for his policies, which he was unable to carry through and which, once started, it was no longer an option to abandon. He is said to have cursed the life of constant activity that he'd led from its very beginnings, saying that he was the only person who had never had a holiday even as a boy. While he was still a ward and had yet to assume the adult toga, he ventured to plead before juries on behalf of defendants and to exert his special influence in the courts—to such effect, in fact, that it's generally accepted that he captured several verdicts against the odds. (**2**) Where would such precocious ambition not find an outlet? You might have known that such premature presumptuousness would lead to disaster both for him and for the state. And so it was too late when he began complaining that he'd never had a holiday, since he'd been a troublemaker and a burden to the forum from his boyhood. It is unclear whether he died by his own hand. He fell suddenly from a wound to the groin; some doubted whether his death was self-inflicted, no one that it was timely.

(**3**) It would be superfluous to mention more figures who, although they seemed to others the happiest of mortals, themselves gave true testimony against themselves when they expressed intense hatred for every act of their lives. Yet by these complaints they changed neither themselves nor anyone else; for after the outburst, their feelings reverted to their normal state. (**4**) In reality, your life, even if you live a thousand years and more, will be compressed into the merest span of time; those vices of yours will swallow up any number of lifetimes. To be sure, this span of time, which good management prolongs even though it naturally hurries on, must in your case escape you quickly; for you fail to seize it and hold it back, and you do nothing to delay that speediest of all things, but you allow it to pass as if it were something overabundant that we can get back again.

(**7.1**) In fact, among the worst cases I count also those who give their time to nothing but drink and lust; for these are the most shameful preoccupations of all. Other people, even if the semblance of glory that grips them is false, nevertheless go astray in respectable fashion. You can cite for me people who are greedy, those quick to anger, or people who busy themselves with unjust hatreds or wars; but all of them sin in a more manly fashion. It is those abandoned to the belly and lust who bear the stain of dishonor. (2) Scrutinize every moment of such people's lives, and note how much time they spend on their ledger-keeping, how much on setting traps or fearing them, how much on cultivating others or being cultivated by others, how much on giving or receiving bail, how much on dinner parties which have themselves become business: you'll see that their affairs, whether good or bad, allow them no time to draw breath.

(3) To sum up, everyone agrees that no one area of activity can be successfully pursued by someone who is preoccupied—rhetoric cannot, nor can the liberal arts—since the distracted mind takes in nothing really deeply but rejects everything that is, so to speak, pounded into it. Nothing is less characteristic of a man preoccupied than living: there is no knowledge that is harder to acquire. Instructors of other disciplines are two a penny; indeed, mere boys have been seen to master some of these disciplines so thoroughly that they could even be masters in the classroom. But learning how to live takes a whole lifetime, and—you'll perhaps be more surprised at this—it takes a whole lifetime to learn how to die.[12] (4) So many men of the highest station have set aside all their encumbrances, renounced their wealth, their business, their pleasures, and right up to the very end of life they have made it their sole aim to know how to live. Nevertheless, the majority of them depart from life admitting that they did not yet have such knowledge—still less have those others attained it. (5) Believe me, it's the mark of a great man, and one rising above human weakness, to allow no part of his time to be skimmed off. Accordingly, such a person's life is extremely long because he's kept available for himself the whole of whatever amount of time he had. None of it lay fallow and uncultivated, and none of it was under another's control; for being a most careful guardian of his time, he found nothing worth exchanging for it. And so that man had enough time; but those deprived of much of their life by the public have necessarily had too little.

(6) Nor should you imagine that those people aren't sometimes conscious of their loss. Certainly you'll hear many of those burdened by their great prosperity occasionally cry out amid their hordes of clients or their pleadings of cases or their other respectable forms of wretchedness: "I've no chance to live." (7) Of course you don't! All those who engage you in their business disengage you from yourself. How many days did that defendant of yours take from you? How many that candidate? Or that old lady, wearied as she is by burying her heirs? Or that character who feigns illness to excite the greed of legacy hunters? Or that powerful friend who holds on to you not for true friendship but for show? Check off, I say, and review the days of your life: you'll see that very few of them, and those the worthless ones, have stayed in your possession. (8) The man who's achieved the high office he'd prayed for longs to lay it aside and repeatedly says: "When will this year end?" The man who puts on the games thought it a great privilege that responsibility for giving them fell to him. Now he says: "When will I be free of them?" That advocate has people competing for his attention throughout the forum; with the crowd he draws, he fills the whole place further than he can be heard: "When," he says, "will there be a vacation?" Everyone sends his life racing headlong and suffers from a longing for the future, a loathing of the present. (9) But the person who devotes every second of his time to his own needs and who organizes each day as if it were a complete life neither longs for nor is afraid of the next day. For what new kind of pleasure is there that any hour can now bring? Everything has been experienced, everything enjoyed to the full. For the rest, fortune may make arrangements as it wishes; his life has already reached safety. Addition can be made to this life, but nothing taken away from it—and addition made in the way that a man who is already satisfied and full takes a portion of food which he doesn't crave and yet has room for. (10) So there's no reason to believe that someone has lived long because he has gray hair and wrinkles: he's not lived long but long existed. For suppose you thought that a person had sailed far who'd been caught in a savage storm as soon as he left harbor, and after being carried in this direction and that, was driven in circles over the same course by alternations of the winds raging from different quarters: he didn't have a long voyage, but he was long tossed about.

7777777777777

(8.1) I am always astonished when I see people requesting the time of others and receiving a most accommodating response from those they approach. Both sides focus on the object of the request, and neither side on time itself; it is requested as if it were nothing, granted as if it were nothing. People trifle with the most precious commodity of all; and it escapes their notice because it's an immaterial thing that doesn't appear to the eyes, and for that reason it's valued very cheaply—or rather, it has practically no value at all. (2) People set very great store by annuities and gratuities, and for these they hire out their services or their efforts or their attentions. But no one values time: all use it more than lavishly, as if it cost nothing. But if mortal danger threatens them, you'll see the same people clasping their doctors' knees; if they fear a capital charge, you'll see them ready to spend all they have to stay alive. So great is the conflict in their feelings. (3) But if each of us could see the number of years before us as precisely as the years that have passed, how alarmed would be those who saw only a few years left, and how carefully would they use them! And yet it's easy to manage an amount, however small, which is clearly defined; we have to be more careful in conserving an amount that may give out at any time.

(4) Yet there's no reason to believe that those people are unaware of how precious a commodity time is. They habitually say to those they love most intensely that they are ready to give them some of their own years. And they do give them without knowing it; but they give in such a way that, without adding to the years of their loved ones, they subtract from themselves. But this very point, namely, whether they are depriving themselves, eludes them, and so they can bear the loss of what goes unnoticed in the losing. (5) No one will bring back the years, no one will restore you to your former self. Life will follow the path on which it began, and it will neither reverse nor halt its course. It will cause no commotion at all, it will call no attention to its own swiftness. It will glide on in silence. It will prolong itself at neither a king's command nor his people's clamor; it will run on just as it started out on the first day, with no diversions and no delays. And the outcome? You've been preoccupied while life hurries on; death looms all the while, and like it or not, you have to accommodate it.

(9.1) Can there be anything sillier than the view of those people who boast of their foresight? They are too busily preoccupied with efforts to live better; they plan out their lives at the expense of life itself. They form their purposes with the distant future in mind. Yet the greatest waste of life lies in postponement: it robs us of each day in turn, and snatches away the present by promising the future. The greatest impediment to living is expectancy, which relies on tomorrow and wastes today. You map out what is in fortune's hand but let slip what's in your own hand. What are you aiming at? What's your goal? All that's to come lies in uncertainty: live right now. (2) Hear the cry of the greatest of poets, who sings his salutary song as if inspired with divine utterance:

> Each finest day of life for wretched mortals
> is ever the first to flee.[13]

"Why are you holding back?" he says. "Why are you slow to action? If you don't seize the day, it slips away." Even when you've seized it, it will still slip away; and so you must compete with time's quickness in the speed with which you use it, and you must drink swiftly as if from a fast-moving torrent that will not always flow. (3) This too the poet very aptly says in chastising interminable procrastination: not each best "age" but each best "day." Carefree and unconcerned even though time flies so quickly, why do you project for yourself months and years in long sequence, to whatever extent your greed sees fit? The poet is speaking to you about the day—about this very day which is slipping away. (4) So can there be any doubt that each finest day is ever the first to flee for wretched mortals—that is, the preoccupied? Old age takes their still childish minds unawares, and they meet it unprepared and unarmed; for they've made no provision for it. Suddenly, unsuspecting, they've stumbled upon it, without noticing that it was drawing nearer every day. (5) Just as conversation or reading or some deep reflection beguiles travelers and they find that they've reached their destination before being aware of approaching it, so with this ceaseless and extremely rapid journey of life, which we make at the same pace whether awake or sleeping: the preoccupied become aware of it only at its end.

(10.1) If I wanted to divide my subject into categories, each with its proofs, I could come up with many arguments to demonstrate that the life of the preoccupied is very short. But Fabianus,[14] who was not one of today's chair-holding professionals but a true philosopher of the old-fashioned sort, was in the habit of saying that we must battle against the passions with a vigorous attack, not with nicety of argument; the enemy line is to be turned by a full-frontal assault, not by tiny pinpricks. He has no regard for mere quibbling, for vices are to be crushed, not merely nipped at. Nevertheless, for the preoccupied to be censured for their distinctive failing, they are to be taught a lesson, not simply given up for lost.

(2) Life is divided into three parts: past, present, and future. Of these, the present is brief, the future doubtful, the past certain. For this last is the category over which fortune no longer has control, and which cannot be brought back under anyone's power. Preoccupied people lose this part; for they have no leisure to look back at the past, and even if they had it, there's no pleasure in recalling something regrettable. (3) And so they're unwilling to turn their minds back to times badly spent, and they dare not revisit the past because their vices become obvious in retrospect—even those that insinuated themselves by the allurement of momentary pleasure. No one gladly casts his thoughts back to the past except for the person whose every action has been subjected to his own self-assessment, which is infallible. (4) A man who's been ambitious in the scale of his desires, arrogant in his disdainfulness, unrestrained in prevailing over others, treacherous in his deceptions, greedy in his plunderings, and lavish in his prodigality—such a man must inevitably be afraid of his own memory. Yet this is the part of our existence that is consecrated and set apart, elevated above all human vicissitudes and removed beyond fortune's sway, and harried by no poverty, no fear, no attacks of disease. This part can be neither disrupted nor stolen away; our possession of it is everlasting and untroubled. Days are present only one at a time, and these only minute by minute; but all the days of time past will attend you at your bidding, and they will allow you to examine them and hold on to them at your will—something which preoccupied people have no time to do. (5) It takes a tranquil and untroubled mind to roam freely over all the parts of life; but preoccupied minds, as if under the yoke, cannot turn around and look backward. Their life therefore disappears into an abyss; and just as it does no good to pour any amount of liquid into a vessel if there's nothing at the bottom to receive and keep it,[15] so it makes no difference how much time

we are given if there's nowhere for it to settle, and it's allowed to pass through the cracks and holes in the mind. **(6)** The present time is very brief—indeed, so very brief that to some people[16] it seems to be nonexistent. For it's always in motion, slipping by and hurrying on; it ceases to be before it arrives, and it no more suffers delay than do the firmament or the heavenly bodies, whose ever-tireless movement never lets them remain in the same position. So the preoccupied are concerned with the present alone, and it is so fleeting that it can't be grasped, and even that little amount is stolen away from them because they're pulled in many different directions.

(11.1) In a word, do you want to know how briefly they really live? See how keen they are to live a long life. Enfeebled old men beg in their prayers for an additional few years; they pretend they are younger than they really are; they flatter themselves by this falsehood, and deceive themselves as gladly as if they deceived fate at the same time. But when some real illness has at last reminded them that they are mortal, how terrified they are when they die, as if they're not leaving life but are being dragged from it! They cry out repeatedly that they've been fools because they've not really lived, and that they'll live in leisure if only they escape their illness. Then they reflect on how uselessly they made provision for things they wouldn't live to enjoy, and how fruitless was all their toil. **(2)** But why should life not be ample for people who spend it far removed from all business? None of it is made over to another, none scattered in this direction or that; none of it is entrusted to fortune, none wasted through neglect; none is lost through being given away freely, none is superfluous; the whole of life yields a return, so to speak. And so, however short, it is amply sufficient; and for that reason, whenever his last day comes, the sage will not hesitate to go to his death with a sure step.

(12.1) You perhaps want to know whom I'd term the preoccupied? Don't imagine that I mean only those lawyers who are driven out of the law court only when the watchdogs are finally let in for the night; or those patrons you see crushed either with impressive display in their own crowd of admirers or more contemptuously in someone else's crowd; or those clients whose duties summon them from their own houses in order to dash them against the doors of others; or those the praetor's spear keeps busy for disreputable gain which is someday bound to fester.[17] **(2)** Even the leisure of some people is preoccupied: in their country retreat or on their couch, in the midst of their solitude, and even though they've withdrawn from everyone, they are troubling company for themselves; their existence is to be termed not leisurely but one of idle preoccupation. Do you call a man at leisure who arranges with meticulous attention to detail his Corinthian bronzes, which are made so expensive by the collecting mania of a few, and who spends most of the day on rusty strips of copper? Or a man who sits at a wrestling ring (for—shame on us!—we suffer from vices that are not even Roman), enthusiastically watching boys brawling? Who separates the troops of his own well-oiled wrestlers into pairs of the same age and skin color? Who maintains a stable of the freshest athletes? (3) Tell me, do you call those people leisured who spend many hours at the barber's while any overnight growth is trimmed away, solemn consultation is taken over each separate hair, and disheveled locks are rearranged or thinning hair is combed forward from both sides to cover the forehead? How angry they get if the barber has been a little too careless, as if he were cutting a real man's hair! How they flare up if anything is wrongly cut off their precious mane, if a hair lies out of place, or if everything doesn't fall back into its proper ringlets! Which of those people wouldn't rather have their country thrown into disarray than their hair? Who isn't more concerned about keeping his head neat rather than safe? Who wouldn't rather be well groomed than well respected? You call leisured these people who are kept busy between the comb and the mirror? (4) What about those who are absorbed in composing, listening to, and learning songs? The voice, whose best and simplest flow is naturally straightforward, they twist into sinuous turns of the most feeble crooning. Their fingers are always snapping in time to some song that they carry in their head, and when they've been asked to attend to serious and often even sorrowful matters, you can overhear them quietly humming a tune. Theirs isn't leisure but idle occupation. (5) And heaven knows! I'd not class their banquets among leisurely pastimes, because I see how anxiously they arrange their silver plate, how carefully they gather up the tunics of their pretty boys-at-table, how they are on tenterhooks to see how the boar turns out from the cook, how quickly the smooth-skinned slaves hurry to discharge their duties at the given signal, how skillfully birds are carved into carefully shaped portions, and how attentively wretched little slave boys wipe away the spittle of drunks. By these means they seek a reputation for refinement and sumptuous living, and their evils follow them into every corner of their lives to such an extent that they cannot eat or drink without ostentation. **(6)** Nor would I count among the leisured those who have themselves carried around in a sedan chair and litter, and who arrive precisely on time for their rides, as if they were forbidden to skip them; and who have to be reminded of their scheduled time for bathing, for swimming, or for dining: they are so enervated by the excessive sloth of a pampered mind that they can't tell by themselves if they are hungry. **(7)** I hear that one of these pampered creatures—if *pampered* is the right word for unlearning life and normal human practice—was manually lifted out of the bath and set down in his sedan chair, and asked: "Am I now seated?" Do you think that someone like this, who doesn't know if he is sitting, knows whether he's alive, whether he can see, whether he's at leisure? It's hard for me to say whether I pity him more if he really didn't know as much or if he pretended not to know. **(8)** They are oblivious to many things, but they also affect forgetfulness of much. They find certain vices pleasing as evidence of their prosperity: to know what you're doing seems to be the mark of a man who's lowly and contemptible. What folly to think that mime actors[18] feign many details in order to attack luxury! Truth be told, they pass over more than they fabricate, and such a wealth of unbelievable vices has arisen in an age that has applied its fertile talents in this one direction that by now we can charge the mime actors with ignoring them. To imagine that there's anyone so ruined by pampering that he takes another's word as to whether he's seated! **(9)** So here is not a person of leisure; you should apply a different term to him. He is sick or rather as good as dead; the truly leisured person is one who is also conscious of his own leisure. But a person who needs a guide to make him aware of his own bodily positions is only half-alive; how can he be in control of any of his time?

(13.1) It would be a long business to run through the individual cases of people who've spent their whole lives playing checkers or playing ball, or baking their bodies in the sun. People whose pleasures put them to considerable work are not at leisure. For instance, nobody will doubt that those who devote their time to useless literary questions—Rome too now has a significant number of such people—are busily engaged in doing nothing.[19] (2) It was once the well-known failing of the Greeks to ask how many rowers Ulysses had, whether the *Iliad* or the *Odyssey* was written first, and also whether they belong to the same author, and other questions of the same stamp which, if you keep them to yourself, do nothing to improve your private knowledge; and if you divulge them, you're made to appear not more learned but more annoying. (3) And now this vacuous enthusiasm for acquiring useless knowledge has infected the Romans as well. Only a few days ago I heard someone[20] mentioning which Roman general had been the first to do what: Duilius was the first to win a battle at sea,[21] Curius Dentatus the first to parade elephants in a triumph.[22] So far, even if such items as these hardly steer us toward true glory, they still involve models of service to the state; such knowledge isn't going to profit us, but it's nevertheless of the sort to hold our interest because its subject matter, though empty, is appealing. (4) We may also excuse investigators who ask who first persuaded the Romans to deploy a naval force (it was Claudius,[23] who was called Caudex for this reason, because the ancients termed the composite structure of several planks a *caudex*; hence the public records are called *codices*, and the barges which carry provisions up the Tiber are still called *codicariae* in accordance with ancient practice). (5) Doubtless also this may have some relevance—the fact that Valerius Corvinus was the first to conquer Messana,[24] and was the first of the family of the Valerii to be called Messana after appropriating the name of the captured city; common usage gradually changed the lettering, so he became Messalla. (6) But will you also allow interest in the fact that L. Sulla was the first to display lions off the leash in the circus,[25] though as a general rule they were shown in chains, and that javelin throwers were supplied by king Bocchus[26] to dispatch them? All right, let's allow that as well; but is any useful purpose really served by knowing that Pompey was the first to put on a fight in the circus involving eighteen elephants,[27] with noncriminals arrayed against them in mock battle? A leader of the state and a man of outstanding kindliness, as his reputation has it; among leaders of old, he thought it a memorable form of spectacle to destroy human beings in unheard-of fashion. "They fight to the death? That's not enough. They're torn to pieces? Not enough: let them be utterly crushed by animals of massive bulk!" (7) It would certainly be preferable for such stuff to be forgotten, for fear that some future strongman might learn of it and be envious of an utterly inhuman episode. O what darkness great prosperity casts on our minds! He thought he was above the laws of nature when he was throwing so many hordes of human wretches to beasts born under a different sky, when he was arranging war between such disparate creatures, when he was shedding so much blood before the eyes of the Roman people—people he'd later force to shed still more blood themselves. But this same man was later taken in by Alexandrian treachery and offered himself to be run through by the meanest of his chattels;[28] then at last he recognized the empty boast that was his own surname.[29]

(8) But to return to the point from which I digressed, and to demonstrate the futility of the pains that some people take in these same matters: the same source[30] reported that Metellus, in his triumph after conquering the Carthaginians in Sicily, was alone of all Romans in having 120 captured elephants led in procession before his chariot;[31] and that Sulla was the last Roman to extend the *pomerium*, which it was the custom of old to extend after the acquisition of Italian, but never provincial, territory.[32] Is there any more benefit in knowing this than to know that the Aventine Hill is outside the *pomerium*, according to him, for one of two reasons: either because that was the rallying point for the plebeians in secession from Rome,[33] or because the birds had not been propitious when Remus took the auspices there;[34] and to know countless other items besides that are either crammed with lies or improbable? (9) For even if you grant that people say all these things in good faith, and even if they guarantee the truthfulness of their writing, whose mistakes will such items of information make fewer? Whose passions will they hold in check? Whom will they make braver, or more just, or more generous of spirit? My friend Fabianus used to say that he sometimes wondered whether it was better to apply oneself to no researches at all than to be embroiled in these.

(14.1) Of all people, they alone who give their time to philosophy are at leisure, they alone really live. For it's not just their own lifetime that they watch over carefully, but they annex every age to their own; all the years that have gone before are added to their own. Unless we prove most ungrateful, those most distinguished founders of hallowed thoughts came into being for us, and for us they prepared a way of living. We are led by the work of others into the presence of the most beautiful treasures, which have been pulled from darkness and brought to light. From no age are we debarred, we have access to all; and if we want to transcend the narrow limitations of human weakness by our expansiveness of mind, there is a great span of time for us to range over. (2) We can debate with Socrates, entertain doubt with Carneades,[35] be at peace with Epicurus, overcome human nature with the Stoics, and go beyond it with the Cynics.[36] Since nature allows us shared possession of any age, why not turn from this short and fleeting passage of time and give ourselves over completely to the past, which is measureless and eternal and shared with our betters? (3) As for those who run about performing their social duties, agitating themselves and others: when they've duly acted like madmen, when they've crossed every threshold on their daily rounds and passed no open door, and when they've delivered their moneygrubbing greeting to houses very distant from one another, how few patrons will they be able to catch sight of in a city so vast and so fragmented by varied passions! (4) How many patrons will there be whose sleep or self-indulgence or churlishness denies their callers access! How many who, after they've tortured them with the long wait, pretend to be in a hurry as they pass them by! How many will avoid going out through a reception hall packed with clients and make their escape through a door that's hidden from view, as if it were not even crueler to deceive them than to refuse them admittance! How many, half-asleep and weighed down by the effects of yesterday's drinking, will yawn with utter disdain and address those wretched clients, who cut short their own sleep in order to wait on another's, by the right name only after it's been whispered to them a thousand times over by lips that hardly move![37] (5) Do we suppose these clients spend time on morally commendable duties? But we can say as much of those who'll want to have Zeno, Pythagoras, Democritus, and the other high priests of philosophical study, and Aristotle and Theophrastus, as their closest companions every day. None of these will ever be unavailable to you, none of these will fail to send his visitor off in a happier condition and more at ease with himself. None will let anyone leave empty handed; they can be approached by all mortals by night and by day.

(15.1) None of these philosophers will force you to die, but all will

way of living. We are led by the work of others into the presence of teach you how.[38] None of them will diminish your years, but each will share his own years with you. With none of them will conversation be dangerous, friendship life threatening, or cultivation of them expensive. From them you'll take whatever you wish; it will be no fault of theirs if you fail to take in the very fullest amount you have room for. **(2)** What happiness, what a fine old age lies in store for the person who's put himself under the patronage of these people! He'll have friends whose advice he can seek on the greatest or least important matters, whom he can consult daily about himself, from whom he can hear the truth without insult and receive praise without fawning, and who will provide a model after which to fashion himself.

(3) There is a common saying that it was not in our power to choose the parents we were allotted, and that they were given to us by chance; yet we can be born to whomever we wish. There are households of the most distinguished intellects: choose the one into which you'd like to be adopted, and you'll inherit not just the name but also the actual property, which is not to be hoarded in a miserly or mean spirit: the more people you share it with, the greater it will become. **(4)** These will open for you the path to immortality, and raise you to an elevation from which no one is cast down. This is the sole means of prolonging mortality, or rather of transforming it into immortality. Honors, monuments, all that ostentatious ambition has ordered by decree or erected in stone, are soon destroyed: there's nothing that the long lapse of time doesn't demolish and transform. But it cannot harm the works consecrated by wisdom: no age will efface them, no age reduce them at all. The next age and each one after that will only enhance the respect in which they are held, since envy focuses on what is close at hand, but we more freely admire things from a distance. **(5)** So the sage's life is ample in scope, and he's not constricted by the same limit that confines others. He alone is released from the limitations of the human race, and he is master of all ages as though a god. Some time has passed? He holds it in recollection. Time is upon us? He uses it. Time is to come? This he anticipates. The combining of all times into one makes his life long.

(16.1) But for those who forget the past, disregard the present, and fear for the future, life is very brief and very troubled. When they reach the end of it, they realize too late, poor wretches, that they've been busied for so long in doing nothing. **(2)** And the fact that they sometimes pray for death need hardly be taken as evidence that their life is long. In their folly they are afflicted by fickle feelings that rush them into the very things they fear; they often pray for death precisely because they fear it. (3) And there's no reason to find evidence that they live long in the fact that the day often seems long to them, or that they complain that the hours pass slowly until the appointed hour for dinner arrives; for when their usual preoccupations fail them and they are left with nothing to do, they fret without knowing how to apply their free time or how to drag it out. And so they move on to some other preoccupation and find all the intervening time burdensome, precisely as they do when a gladiatorial show has been announced for a given day, or when the date of some other show or amusement is keenly awaited, and they want to skip over the days in between. Any postponement of something they look forward to is long to them. (4) But the time of actual enjoyment is short and fleeting, and made far shorter by their own fault; for they desert one pleasure for another and cannot persist steadily in any one desire. Their days aren't long but hateful; yet, on the other hand, how short seem the nights that they spend cavorting with prostitutes or drinking! (5) Hence the mad inspiration of poets too who feed human frailty by their stories and imagine that Jupiter actually doubled the length of the night[39] when seduced by sexual pleasure. All this inflaming of our worst passions amounts to nothing but enlisting the gods as setting a precedent for our vices, and giving a license for corruption that is justified by divine example. How can the nights that they pay for so dearly not seem so very short to these people? They lose the day in looking forward to the night, the night in fear of the dawn.

(17.1) The very pleasures of such people are anxious and disturbed by various kinds of alarm, and at the very moment when they are rejoicing the agitated thought steals in on them: "How long will this last?" It is this feeling that has caused kings to weep over their own power; the extent of their prosperity gave them no pleasure, but the prospect of its eventual end terrified them. (2) When that exceedingly arrogant king of the Persians ranged his army over the vast plains and could only measure its size, not count it, he wept at the thought that within a century not one soldier from that huge force would still be alive.[40] Yet the very man who wept was destined to bring their fate on them, to lose some troops at sea, others on land, some in battle,[41] others in flight, and so to destroy in a very short time all those for whose hundredth year he feared. **(3)** And what of the fact that even the joys of such people are anxiety ridden? This is because they don't rest on stable causes but are disrupted as frivolously as they are produced. But what do you think their times are like when they are wretched even by their own admission, since even the joys which lift and transport them above their fellow men are by no means unmixed? **(4)** All the greatest blessings cause anxiety, and fortune is never less wisely trusted than when at its most advantageous. To maintain prosperity we need fresh prosperity, and other prayers are to be offered instead of those that have already turned out well. Everything that comes our way by chance is unsteady, and the higher our fortunes rise, the more susceptible they are to falling. But what must inevitably collapse gives no one pleasure; and so the life of those who acquire through hard work what they must work harder to possess is necessarily very wretched, and not just very brief. **(5)** They obtain with great effort what they desire, and they anxiously hold on to what they've obtained; and meanwhile they give no consideration to time's irretrievability. New preoccupations take the place of old, hope arouses new hope, ambition new ambition. They don't look for an end to their wretchedness, but change the cause of it. We've been tormented by our own public office? We spend more time on somebody else's. We've stopped toiling as candidates? We start canvassing for others. We've given up the vexation of being a prosecutor? We take on that of being a judge. A man stops being a judge? He starts presiding over a special commission. A man's spent all his working life managing other people's property for a salary? He's diverted by looking after his own wealth. **(6)** Marius was done with army service, and the consulship kept him busy.[42] Quintius hurries to get through his dictatorship, but he'll be called back to it from his plow.[43] Scipio will go up against the Carthaginians before being fully ready for such an undertaking.[44] Victorious over Hannibal, victorious over Antiochus, he will win distinction in his own consulship and act as surety for his brother's consulship;[45] and but for his own objections, his statue would be placed in Jupiter's company in the Capitoline temple. But discord among the citizens will bring trouble to their savior, and after he has scorned as a young man public honors rivaling those of the gods, in old age he'll eventually take pleasure in an ostentatiously defiant exile. Reasons for anxiety will never be wanting, whether because of prosperity or wretchedness. Life will be driven on through one preoccupation after another; we shall always pray for leisure but never attain it.

(18.1) And so, my dearest Paulinus, remove yourself from the crowd and, storm-tossed more than your years deserve, withdraw at last to a more peaceful haven. Consider how many waves you've endured and, on the one side, how many storms you've weathered in private and, on the other, how many you've brought on yourself in your public career. Long enough has your virtue been demonstrated through toilsome and unceasing proofs; put to the test what it can achieve in leisure. The greater part of your life, and certainly the better part, has been given to the state: take some of your time for yourself as well. (2) It's not to a sluggish and idle state of inaction that I summon you, or to drown all your lively energy in sleep and in the pleasures that are dear to the crowd. That's not to find peace of mind: you'll find tasks to busy yourself about in serene seclusion that are more important than any you've dealt with so energetically thus far. (3) You manage the revenues of the world, it is true, as scrupulously as you would a stranger's, as diligently as you would your own, as conscientiously as you would the state's. You win affection in a post in which it is hard to avoid being hated. Yet it is nevertheless better—believe me—to know the balance sheet of one's own life than that of the public grain supply. (4) Recall that energetic mind of yours, which is supremely qualified to deal with the greatest challenges, from an office that is certainly eminent but is hardly in keeping with the happy life. And consider that you didn't make it your aim, with all your training in the liberal arts from the earliest age, for many thousands of grain measures to be safely entrusted to you; you'd shown promise of something greater and higher. There'll be no shortage of men of both scrupulous good character and diligent service. But slow-moving pack animals are far better suited to carrying heavy loads than thoroughbred horses; who ever hampered the fleetness of these well-bred creatures with a weighty burden? (5) Consider, moreover, how stressful it is to subject yourself to such a heavy responsibility; you have to deal with the human stomach, and a hungry people neither submits to reason nor is soothed by fair treatment or influenced by any entreaty. Only recently, within those few days after Gaius Caesar died, he was still pained to the utmost (if the dead have any consciousness) because he saw that the Roman people survived him and still had enough rations for seven or at all events eight days; because he made his bridges of boats and played with the empire's resources,[46] we faced the worst kind of disaster even for people under siege: a shortage of food. His imitation of a crazed foreign king of ill-fated arrogance almost came at the cost of mass destruction by starvation, and of the general catastrophe that follows famine. **(6)** What was the frame of mind of the officials in charge of the grain supply when they were destined to face stones, weapons, fires, and Gaius? With the greatest concealment they covered over such a great sickness lurking amid the state's innermost organs, and with good reason, to be sure. For certain complaints are to be treated without the patient's being aware of them; knowing about their disease has caused many to die.

(19.1) Retire to those pursuits that are calmer, safer, and more important. Do you think it amounts to the same thing whether you're in charge of seeing that imported grain is transferred to the granaries undamaged by either the dishonesty or the carelessness of the transporters, that it doesn't absorb moisture and then get spoiled through heat, and that it corresponds to the declared weight and measure; or whether you occupy yourself with these hallowed and lofty studies, so as to learn the substance of god, his will, his general character, and his shape; what outcome awaits your soul; where nature lays us to rest upon release from our bodies; what it is that bears the weight of all the heaviest matter of this world in the center, suspends the light components above, carries fire to the highest part, and rouses the stars to their given changes of movement; and to learn other such matters in turn that are full of great wonders? **(2)** You really ought to leave ground level and turn your mind's eye to these studies. Now, while enthusiasm is still fresh, those with an active interest should progress to better things. In this mode of life much that is worth studying awaits you: the love and practice of the virtues, forgetfulness of the passions, knowledge of how to live and to die, and deep repose.

(3) The plight of all preoccupied people is wretched, but most wretched is the plight of those who labor under preoccupations that are not even their own, whose sleep schedule is regulated by some-body else's, who walk at somebody else's pace, and who are under instructions in that freest of all activities—loving and hating.[47] If these people want to know how short their life is, let them reflect on how small a part of it is their very own.

(**20.1**) So, when you see a man repeatedly taking up the robe of office, or a name well known in public, don't envy him: those trappings are bought at the cost of life. For one year to be dated by their name, they'll waste all their own years.[48] Life deserts some of them amid their first struggles, before the arduous climb up to the peak of their ambition. Some, after they've clambered up through a thousand indignities to arrive at the crowning dignity, are assailed by the wretched thought that all their toil has been for an inscription on an epitaph. Some map out new aspirations for their extreme old age as if in their youth, and they succumb to weakness amid their great and immoderate endeavors. (**2**) It's a shameful end when an old man acting in court for litigants who are perfectly unknown to him breathes his last even at the moment when he's winning the applause of impressionable bystanders. It's a disgraceful end when the man who's sooner worn out by living than by working drops dead in the middle of his duties; and a disgraceful end when a man dies in the act of going over his accounts and draws a smile from the heir who's long been kept waiting. (**3**) I can't pass over one example that occurs to me. Gaius Turannius was an old man of proven diligence who was past ninety when, on the emperor's initiative, he was granted retirement from his administrative post by Gaius Caesar;[49] he gave instructions for himself to be laid out on his bed and to be mourned by his as-sembled household as if he were dead. The house lamented its elderly master's unemployment and didn't cease their mourning until his job was restored to him. Is it really such a pleasure to die preoccupied? (**4**) Yet many have that same attitude, and their desire for work lasts longer than their capacity for it. They struggle against their bodily infirmity, and old age itself they adjudge a hardship for no other rea-son than because it removes them from office. The law doesn't draft a soldier after fifty, it doesn't require a senator's attendance after sixty: it's harder for people to obtain retirement from themselves than from the law. (**5**) All the time while they plunder and are plundered and break in on each other's rest and make each other miserable, life is without profit, without pleasure, without any progress of mind. No one holds death in view, no one refrains from distant hopes. Indeed, some people even make arrangements for things beyond life—huge tomb structures, dedications of public buildings, gladiatorial shows for the funeral, and ostentatious funeral processions. Yet in truth, the funerals of such people should be conducted by the light of torches and wax tapers,[50] as if they'd lived for the briefest span.

1. From the first *Aphorism* of Hippocrates of Cos, probably Socrates' contemporary in the later fifth century BCE.

2. Attributed by Cicero (*Tusculan Disputations* 3.69) to Theophrastus, Aristotle's associate and successor; possibly a simple misattribution, unless Seneca deliberately invokes Aristotle as a weightier presence here alongside Hippocrates.

3. A nonmetrical rendering of a poet whose identity is much disputed. Cf. 9.2 for Virgil hailed as "the greatest of poets," and *Letters* 63.2 for Homer as "the greatest of Greek poets"; but no clear trace of the dictum here is to be found in either.

4. The letter is lost; Seneca is our sole witness to its existence. Its date is unclear, as is its possible relation or relevance to historical reports of Augustus contemplating retirement in the first decade of his rule.

5. Seneca proceeds to give a summary of Augustus's consolidation of power, from the death of Caesar in 44 BCE to Antony's defeat at Actium in 31; his pacification of the near empire (the Alpine tribes, 7–6 BCE); and his expansion of the imperial margins. This emphasis on external gains is dramatically contrasted with the threat brought increasingly closer to home in 4.5–6, first by domestic troubles at Rome (through the conspiracies of M. Aemilius Lepidus in 29 BCE, Varro Murena and Fannius Caepio in 23/22, and M. Egnatius Rufus in 19), then by sedition in the imperial household itself through the dangerous liaisons of Julia, Augustus's daughter, who was banished in 2 BCE.

6. Iullus, Antony's second son, was punished by death in 2 BCE for adultery with Julia, who is cast here as a second Cleopatra.

7. Catiline's notorious conspiracy to transform the Roman order by overthrowing aristocratic senatorial power was thwarted by Cicero as consul in 63 BCE. In 61 Cicero testified against P. Clodius Pulcher, on trial for violating the mysteries of the cult of Bona Dea; acquitted by bribery, Clodius took revenge by securing Cicero's exile in 58. Pompey and Crassus were allies, with Julius Caesar, in the First Triumvirate of 60; Cicero found Pompey in particular "a doubtful friend" when he was faced with exile in 58.

8. Apparently a Senecan distortion: Cicero's extant writings yield no evidence of any such detestation.

9. After Pompey's defeat by Caesar at Pharsalus in 48 BCE, Gnaeus, his elder son, was defeated at Munda (Spain) in 45. But the allusion could extend to Sextus, Gnaeus's brother, who prolonged Pompeian activities in Spain until after Caesar's death in 44.

10. The words are nowhere found in Cicero's extensive extant correspondence with T. Pomponius Atticus, his friend from boyhood and relation by marriage.

11. As tribune in 91 BCE Drusus introduced radical social legislation, including land distributions for the poor and the enfranchisement of all Italians, which provoked vigorous opposition. Drusus was assassinated, but in suggesting that he committed suicide, Seneca here develops his most dramatic illustration yet of the need for escape from the pressures of high but dangerous responsibility, and of personal fortunes collapsing on themselves (cf. 4.1).

12. The Stoic notion of "meditation on death" is Platonic in origin (e.g., *Phaedo* 67e: "true philosophers diligently practice dying"). Seneca repeatedly urges such meditation (e.g., *Letters* 70.18, 114.27) because of the liberation it brings from fear of death (e.g., *Letters* 30.18, 36.8) by anticipating the soul's release from bodily captivity (e.g., *Consolation to Marcia* 23.2).

13. Virgil *Georgics* 3.66–7; also quoted at *Letters* 108.24, 26.

14. Papirius Fabianus, ca. 35 BCE–before 35 CE, was a talented rhetorician who, by ca. 10 BCE, became a follower of Q. Sextius, founder of Rome's only indigenous philosophical school. Fabianus's teachings made a deep impression on the young Seneca (cf. *Letters* 40.12, 58.6, 100 *passim*) as well as his father (cf. *Controuersiae* 2 pref. 1–2).

15. A likely allusion to the fate of the Danaids, punished in the underworld for killing their new husbands by having always to draw water with leaking vessels or sieves.

16. Including those Stoics for whom the "now" point is itself ever fleeting and never fully "real" or "here," being a part of the temporal continuum which consistently moves along with the Stoic universe.

17. A spear was fixed in the ground at public auctions, apparently after the ancient practice of selling war spoils under the victor's symbol of ownership. The auctioneers overseeing the sale of state property (*praecones publici*) belonged to the staff of magistrates, including praetors; hence "the praetor's spear."

18. Mime was a theatrical medium for risqué and often vulgar realism, which Seneca elsewhere presents as having a popular moralizing component (cf. *Letters* 8.8–9).

19. For Seneca the pedantry of the *grammatici*, whose numbers grew at Rome in the first century CE, ignores the real relevance of literature and philology in nurturing mature judgment.

20. Unknown; the elder Pliny has been suggested, but with no strong supporting evidence. Seneca may simply be using a rhetorical device to introduce the point in colloquial fashion.

21. Gaius Duilius; after leading the Roman fleet to victory over the Carthaginians off Mylae (Sicily) in 260 BCE, he celebrated the first naval triumph in 259.

22. In 275 BCE, after Dentatus defeated Pyrrhus, the Molossian king of Epirus; as a hero of the Samnite and other wars, and as an exemplar of humble living, see *Consolation to Helvia* 10.8.

23. Appius Claudius Caudex, consul in 264 BCE; he crossed to Sicily in the First Punic War to counter the alliance between the Carthaginians and Hieron II of Syracuse.

24. M.'Valerius Maximus Messalla, consul in 263 BCE, forced Hieron II of Syracuse to come to terms with Rome in that year, and celebrated a triumph for his capture of Sicilian Messana.

25. As *praetor urbanus* in 93 BCE; leashed lions were apparently first exhibited in games at Rome in 104 BCE.

26. King of Mauretania, who was persuaded by Sulla to betray Jugurtha, his son-in-law, to the Romans; he remained on cordial terms with Sulla after the end of the Jugurthine War.

27. In 55 BCE, when Pompey celebrated the opening of his new stone theater in the Campus Martius. Seneca's ensuing protest against public slaughter (13.6–7; cf. *Letters* 7.3–5, 95.33) is already anticipated by Cicero's report (*Letters to His Friends* 7.1.3; cf. Pliny *Natural History* 8.21) that the crowd was moved to compassion for the persecuted elephants.

28. After defeat at Pharsalus in 48 BCE, Pompey sought protection from Ptolemy XIII of Egypt, his *cliens* and possible ward; but while going ashore at Alexandria he was murdered by Ptolemy's agent.

29. *Magnus* = "Great."

30. As in 13.3 above.

31. L. Caecilius Metellus, consul in 251 BCE, triumphed after defeating Hasdrubal at Panormus (Palermo) in 250; the exact number of elephants is disputed.

32. At Rome the *pomerium* was the sacral boundary, plowed and then marked by stone pillars, beyond which the city auspices (*auspicia urbana*) could not be taken. Post-Sullan extensions are in fact attributed to Julius Caesar, Augustus, and Claudius; but Seneca (or his informant) arguably presses the point that Sulla was the last to extend the *pomerium* for *legitimate* reasons (*Italian* territory acquired).

33. Twice according to Livy, in 494 BCE and then in 449.

34. In their legendary contest to become Rome's founder, Remus was defeated when, taking auspices on the Aventine, he counted six birds, Romulus on the Palatine twelve.

35. If Socrates effectively founded the skeptical Academy (cf. Cicero *Tusculan Disputations* 5.11), Arcesilaus (316/15–242/1 BCE) was founder of the second or Middle Academy, and Carneades of Cyrene (214–129 BCE) the third or New Academy.

36. While the Stoic strives to be free of the passions (*apathês*), Stoic *apatheia* did not connote complete impassivity (cf. *On Anger* 1.16.7). But the more extreme Cynic position casts the sage as completely detached, even *un*emotional.

37. The *nomenclator*, or guest-announcer, discreetly attends his master.

38. Cf. 7.3 and n. 12 above.

39. During his visit to Alcmena, wife of Amphitryon and mother of Hercules.

40. Xerxes, on his campaign against Greece in 480 BCE; cf. Herodotus 7.45–46.

41. Most obviously, at sea at Salamis in 480 BCE, on land at Thermopylae in 480 and Plataea in 479.

42. Gaius Marius won election to the consulship in 107 BCE. After Jugurtha's defeat, he was elected again in 104, and four more times down to 100, and then again in 86. The full impact of the allusion here lies not just in Marius's rapid transition from soldier to statesman but implicitly also in the sheer number of his consulships, offering their own illustration of how "new preoccupations take the place of old" (17.5).

43. According to tradition L. Quintius Cincinnatus was appointed dictator in 458 BCE (after defeating the Aequi in fifteen days, he laid down his office), and again in 439. The legend that he was called from the plow is usually associated with his first dictatorship, but by linking it with the second and overlooking the distance between 458 and 439 Seneca stresses Cincinnatus's restlessness *ex officio*.

44. P. Cornelius Scipio Africanus (235–183 BCE), appointed at age twenty-six to the command against Carthage in the Second Punic War. Resentment at his successes may have fueled the accusations of financial dishonesty leveled in the so-called trials of the Scipios of the 180s; embittered, he withdrew to Liternum on the Campanian coast, where he died in 184/83.

45. As legate serving under his brother, Scipio negotiated peace terms after the defeat in 189 BCE of Antiochus III, king of Syria, at Magnesia.

46. Gaius was assassinated on January 22 or 24 in 41 CE. Seneca conflates events by connecting a food crisis in 41 with Gaius's notorious construction of a bridge of boats from Baiae to Puteoli in 39. Gaius allegedly sought to emulate Xerxes' bridging of the Hellespont in 480 BCE.

47. I.e., clients rise early to pay their patron the formal morning call (*salutatio*; cf. 14.4), then escort him in public; the client-patron relationship also dictated political and social allegiances.

48. The *consules ordinarii* ("normally appointed" consuls, as opposed to *suffecti*, or "replacement" consuls), after whom the year of their office was dated.

49. According to Tacitus (*Annals* 1.7.2, 11.35.1), Gaius Turannius was *praefectus annonae* in 14 CE (hence naturally an example of special relevance to Paulinus) and, still in office, close to Claudius in 48. If, as Seneca has it, he was past ninety before the end of Gaius's reign in 41, it hardly seems likely that he would still be in office some seven years later. Hence the case for reading *S[extus]* with the Senecan MS tradition, and for positing another elderly Turannius apart from the impossibly old Gaius—unless Seneca simply exaggerates his age before 41 CE.

50. To avoid attention, the funerals of children were conducted at night by torchlight and taper.

On the Constancy of the Wise Person

Title, Topic, and Structure

Somewhat surprisingly, *On the Constancy of the Wise Person* (*De Constantia Sapientis*) does not contain a single instance of the Latin word *constantia*. The fact is, at some point in the tradition this short title became a more convenient way to refer to the work than the longer, original title, which asserts a famous Stoic paradox: *That the wise person receives neither injury nor insult.* As Seneca tells Serenus, his friend to whom the work is addressed, the Stoics stand out from the other schools of philosophy in alone pursuing "a man's path" (1.1–2). This challenges Serenus (the path is steep and direct), but it also encourages him (the slope will become easier), and it adumbrates the work's central topic: the path "rises ... beyond the reach of any missile" (1.1).

We soon learn that Serenus has recently expressed outrage that Cato the Younger was verbally abused and spat on (1.3–3.2). Seneca's response at the time, he recalls, was to reassure Serenus that "the wise person is safe and sound" (2.3). The present dialogue is launched from that dispute: Seneca now presents a skeptical and impassioned speech of Serenus (3.1–2) and responds to it with an initial clarification of what is meant by "not receiving" an injury or insult (3.3–4.3).

The exordium and narration are followed by a division of topics (5.1–2) in which Seneca bifurcates his theme into "injury" (*iniuria*) and "insult" (*contumelia*), and explains that he will deal with each separately. As it happens, his separate treatment goes somewhat against the grain of the Roman law of delicts, in which the *actio iniuriarum* since the second century BCE had encompassed not only physical injury (the primary sense of *iniuria* in early Roman law such as the Twelve Tables) but also defamatory actions and words.[1] Seneca's goal, however, is not to scrutinize Roman law but to demonstrate how, for each of the distinct ways in which the reader might understand a person's being intentionally harmed, the wise person remains untouchable. Distinguishing injury and insult at 5.1 allows him to explore the full spectrum more gradually: he uses the category of injury to focus primarily on instances comparable to physical assault, that are objective and in clear violation of laws, whereas he uses the category of insult to focus on instances in which harm is inflicted by words, involves interpretation, and may lie beyond the laws (i.e., even if we know that clear instances of defamation lay firmly within the *actio iniuriarum*). This is also Seneca's way of homing in on the recipient's interpretation as the real determinant of whether harm has been inflicted at all.

In the discussion of "injury"[2] that fills out the work's first half (5.3–9.5), Seneca directly addresses the question of how someone can do an injury, yet the wise person not receive it—something which, as Serenus's skeptical reaction already suggests, sounds just as counterintuitive in Latin as it does in English. One broader supposition helps us to make sense of this: injury relates to the body and other external things that are irrelevant to the security of the mind. This idea is reinforced by clusters of syllogistic argument (5.3–5, 7.2, 8.1–2), all of which seek to separate the agent's intention from the action's outcome.[3] Intentionality, it turns out, can be actively ignored by the wise person, who brushes off wrongdoers' deeds as if they were chance events of no importance (8.2–9.1). The discussion is brought to life with the historical example of Stilpo of Megara (ca. 360–280 BCE; 5.6–6.7), who shows what it means to distinguish between a "well-founded mind" (6.4) and the destroyed foundations of his city belonging to fortune.

The second topic, insult, is dealt with more extensively than the first (10.1–18.6). Insult is classified in one sense as a lesser, or less real, form of injury (10.2, 16.3). Yet insult also receives sensitive treatment in its own right, with Seneca focusing on the more ambiguous matter of interpreting people's words.[4] The psychological profile of what makes a person likely to perceive insult (10.3) is the opposite of the wise person's magnificence of mind (11.1), and the analysis of "insult" (*contumelia*) as deriving from "scorn" (*contemptus*) introduces considerations of the two parties' relative status. This allows Seneca to dismiss the different causes of supposed insults typically received by elite Roman men from their social inferiors (e.g., 10.2), except that real superiority is not social but moral: someone's status as, say, king of the Medes (13.3) is irrelevant in the eyes of the wise person.

The extended example with which the discussion of insult concludes centers on the assassination of Gaius Caesar (Caligula), both an avid user of insults and a hostile interpreter of them (18.1–5).

In his peroration (19.1–4) Seneca recasts the topic: what he has really been talking about is mental freedom (*libertas*), and he suggests a replacement of political freedom with an interiorized, personal autonomy grounded in reason. Indeed, Seneca now hints to his contemporary readers, living in the conditions of the principate, that "those who are not perfect . . . should be put on alert that they themselves must live among injuries and insults" (19.3). In the work's closing sentence also, he hints at a replacement of one *res publica* with another: of traditional political freedom with the cosmopolitan ideal of a community of reason shared in by human beings and gods alike.

Constancy and Wise Men

Despite what was said above, the later-added title, *On the Constancy of the Wise Person*, helps us to perceive a major thread of the work. Seneca elsewhere uses *constantia* to characterize consistency of behavior from one day to the next or perseverance in what one has proposed or judged, without giving ground (e.g., *Letters* 55.5, 92.3, 120.19–22).[5] In the present work he places particular emphasis on two characteristics of the wise person that are elsewhere closely linked with *constantia* and with its corresponding Greek term, *karteria*. One is *patientia*, "endurance" (2.2), which in the case of the wise person is closely connected to another characteristic: *magnitudo animi* or *magnanimitas* (Greek *megalopsuchia*), "magnificence of mind" (11.1).[6] These notions are elaborated by the work's two main patterns of imagery. One is hardness (the Latin terms include *duritia* and *robur*), which captures both the wise person's immunity and the dynamic weakening effect the wise person has on those who attack him. The second is vertical elevation, which brings together such distinct spatial metaphors as ascending to virtue, rising above fortune, being out of the reach of missiles, contemplating others from a tranquil vantage point, and proximity to god; the theme also tends to trigger a shift to a "sublime" style in Seneca's prose (e.g., at 9.4).

This portrait of inviolability is aided further by Seneca's focus on the wise person as such: the work is not about constancy in the abstract but is "a complex meditation on the nature of the Stoic *sapiens*,"[7] both as instantiated in Cato and Stilpo and as seen against the background of popular paradigms (Hercules, Ulysses, 2.1) and abstract philosophical definitions. Although Seneca makes concessions to his reader, focusing at one point not on the *sapiens uir* ("wise man," 16.3) but on the *consipiens* ("man in his right mind"), the work's last sentence serves as a reminder of the didactic possibilities that come from knowing of a wise person's having existed at some point in time.[8]

Seneca's picture of the Stoic "wise person" (*sapiens*) in this work is decidedly masculine. This is signaled in the first sentence, with its gendered distinction between Stoics (for whom *uirtus*, originally "manliness," is the highest good) and other philosophers (1.1). It is worth pointing out, however, that the emphasis on *uir* is also about being an adult. In a possible allusion to Lucretius (*On the Nature of Things* 2.55–58) or to Plato's cave, Seneca describes children frightened by shadows and other illusory objects as a comparison for how people are led by the mere "thought of pain" to perceive insults as injuries (5.2). This enhances our understanding of the "man's path" of Stoic philosophy as a progression to the adulthood defined by perfection of our rational nature.

Serenus and the Paradoxes of Roman Public Life

In seeking to offer its addressee, Serenus, a path toward enduring the injuries and insults of everyday high society, this work already has a lot in common with *On Anger*, addressed to Novatus. Both works argue against revenge and place particular emphasis on magnificence of mind, and both also draw on the reign of Caligula to illustrate the extremes of supposed injury and equally the advantages of restraint.

Annaeus Serenus was a friend of Seneca (or, as his family name may suggest, a relative) whose position during the reign of Nero, if not also in prior emperors' reigns, clearly shadowed Seneca's own. Most scholars have wanted to date *On the Constancy of the Wise Person* to the mid- to late 50s, and prior to *On Tranquility of Mind*, which is also addressed to Serenus; prior also to *On Leisure*, if that is addressed to him too.[9] Their reasoning is that in *On Tranquility of Mind* and *On Leisure*, Serenus speaks for the most part from the position of a Stoic, whereas in the present work he is referred to as suspicious of Stoic claims (3.2), even if he should probably not be seen as one of the Epicureans to whom Seneca refers quite critically later in the work (15.4–16.1). The different portrayals of Serenus certainly invite us to speculate that he converted to Stoicism—the very thing he jokes about here (3.2).

Serenus's indignation is prompted in large measure by the Stoics' use of paradoxes, which he catalogs, with counterexamples, at 3.1. In fact, most of the paradoxes mentioned by Serenus here are attested elsewhere in the Stoic tradition,[10] including the one that is central to the present work. Plutarch, for example, alludes to Chrysippus's claim "that the wise person is not wronged (*adikeisthai*)."[11]

What annoys Serenus is that the Stoic paradoxes are often falsified by reality: Cato *was* abused and spat on, despite being wise. Seneca's response is not to pretend that the climate of the Late Republic was anything other than poisonous, and indeed, the Caligula example at the end of the work, in which the ambiance of the popular assembly (*contio*) has migrated from the forum into the imperial dining room (18.2), shows new dishes of indignity being served up. His response, rather, is to clarify: his analytical arguments, as well as his forays into satire, are intended to throw into relief the misguided values and attachments of Roman social life. In the process of revealing the central paradox to be no paradox at all, Seneca seeks in turn to reveal the far worse and more genuine contradictions (if not technically paradoxes) in how people value what has no value.

The Stilpo and Caligula examples help in particular to counter Serenus's resorting to history to prove that the paradoxes are wrong. Though Stilpo himself belonged to his own, Megarian school, and his actions might be taken more generally as an illustration of "self-sufficiency" (*autarkeia*), his example here (5.6–6.7) embodies Stoic paradox by having the conquered come out on top as the conqueror.

The Caligula example (18.1–5) offers its own kind of vindication that is grounded in the syntax of Julio-Claudian history.[12] Seneca's argument throughout the work would lead us to expect that when Caligula insulted Valerius Asiaticus, simply Valerius's magnificence of mind would allow him to rise above the insult and live in tranquility (18.2). Yet surprisingly Seneca does not dwell much on Valerius's response, except for giving the impression that Valerius let the insult go. He proceeds instead with retelling history and juxtaposing the insult to Valerius to the assassination of Caligula led by Chaerea (18.3) in such a way that it appears that one is the punishment for the other.[13] This turns the story into an illustration of the claim that the perpetrator of an injury "sooner or later will meet his match: someone will emerge to avenge you also" (17.4; cf. 18.5). But Seneca is not explicitly endorsing revenge: as he soon emphasizes, Caligula's assassination was self-inflicted, stemming from his own pathological tendency to see insults where there were none, and to react to these with cruelty (18.4–5). So although the Caligula example begins as an illustration of how the restrained man (Valerius) will be vindicated, it serves equally as an illustration of how the unrestrained man (Caligula) who allows himself to be offended by what people say will meet with a self-inflicted punishment—thereby reinforcing a central lesson of the work. It is always easy to suspect that Seneca himself savored Caligula's assassination as vindication for himself and others who were mistreated by Caligula but showed restraint; he does this here, however, in a way that allows him to remain opposed to the act of revenge while finding some satisfaction in its outcome.[14]

On the Constancy of the Wise Person

LUCIUS ANNAEUS SENECA

TRANSLATED BY JAMES KER

(**1.1**) It would not be unfair for me to say, Serenus, that there is as much of a difference between the Stoics and the rest of those who make a claim to wisdom as there is between females and males. Both contribute to communal life in equal measure, but the one was born to comply, the other to command. The other wise persons give soft and soothing treatment, just like doctors when they are friends of the sick people whose bodies they are treating, or when they belong to the same household: they do not treat them in the way that is best and most direct, but as they are permitted. The Stoics, having embarked on a man's path, are not concerned with making it seem pleasant to those who enter on it, but are concerned rather that the path should remove us as soon as possible and lead us out to that elevated peak which rises so far beyond the reach of any missile that it towers over fortune.

(**2**) "But the way we are being called to is steep and rough." Well? Can the heights be reached by a flat path? Yet the way is not even as steep as some people think. Only the first part has rocks and cliffs and looks impassable. It is just as when things we spy from afar often seem broken or intertwined because our eyesight is deceived by the distance; but then, when we get closer, those same things that the error of our eyes had lumped together are gradually spread out. Beyond that point, the things that from far off seemed precipitous are reduced to a gentle slope.

(**3**) Recently, when mention happened to be made of Marcus Cato,[15] you expressed outrage (as you can never tolerate injustice) that Cato's own age did not fully appreciate him: although he surpassed the Pompeys and the Caesars, his own age ranked him below the likes of Vatinius.[16] It seemed outrageous to you also that when Cato was preparing to oppose a law, his toga was torn off him in the forum, he was shoved by the hands of a seditious faction all the way from the rostra to the Fabian arch, and he endured verbal abuse, and spitting, and all the other insults of a frenzied crowd.

(**2.1**) At that time I responded that you had reason to be upset on behalf of the republic, which was being put up for sale by Publius Clodius[17] on the one side, and on the other by Vatinius and all the most shameful persons. These men were so swept away by their blind desire that they did not understand that while they were selling the republic they were also putting themselves up for sale. As for Cato himself, I told you not to be concerned. For I said that the wise person can receive neither injury nor insult, and that the immortal gods had given Cato to us as a more reliable exemplar of the wise man than they had given Ulysses and Hercules to previous ages. Our fellow Stoics, you see, declared that these men were wise, being unbeaten by labors and being scorners of pleasure and victors over every kind of fear.[18]

(2) Cato did not go into hand-to-hand combat with beasts, which are typically pursued by hunters and country dwellers, nor did he chase monsters with fire and steel, nor did he happen to live in times when it could be believed that the heavens rested on the shoulders of a single man. Now that the gullibility of the ancients had been fully shaken off and the age had reached new heights of cunning, Cato fought against ambition, a bad thing that comes in many shapes, and unbounded lust for power, which the entire world divided into three was not able to satisfy.[19] He stood alone against the vices of a decadent city sinking under its own weight, and he kept a hold on the falling republic as much as it could be dragged back by just one hand. Ultimately, he lost his grip and gave himself as a companion to the ruin he had long postponed, and the two of them were snuffed out together (it would have been an unthinkable offense for them to be separated). For Cato did not outlive freedom, nor freedom Cato.

(3) Do you think an injury could have been done to this man by the people because they took away either the praetorship or his toga, or because they spattered that sacred head with the scum from their mouths? The wise person is safe and sound, and he cannot be affected either by any injury or by any insult.

(3.1) It seems to me that I can see your mind burning up and boiling over. You are on the verge of crying out: "These are the things that take authority away from your school's teachings. You people promise things greater than can even be wished for, let alone believed.[20] Then, making your huge pronouncements, after saying that the wise person is not poor, you do not deny that he usually lacks a slave, shelter, and food. After saying that the wise person is not insane, you do not deny that he departs from himself and utters words of little sanity, that he dares to do whatever the force of his sickness compels him to do.[21] After saying that the wise person is not a slave, you (the same people who said this!) do not contest that he will be put up for sale and will do what has been commanded and will perform servile duties for his master. So it is that, while haughtily holding your nose in the air, you descend to the same level as the rest, simply changing the names of things. (2) I suspect, then, there is something similar in this, that at first glance seems beautiful and grand: that the wise person will receive neither injury nor insult. It makes a great difference, however, whether you place the wise person beyond indignation or beyond injury. For if you say that he will bear it with a calm mind, he has no special status: he possesses a thing that is common and that can be learned through nothing more than being repeatedly subjected to injury, namely, endurance. If you say that he will not *receive* an injury, that is, that no one will try to *do* him an injury, I am abandoning all my occupations and becoming a Stoic!"

(3) Indeed, it was my intention not to adorn the wise person with an illusory honor composed of words, but to situate him in that place where no injury is permitted. "What? There will be no one who challenges him, who makes trial of him?" Nothing in the nature of the world is so sacred that it does not encounter sacrilege. But divine things are no less sublime because there exist those who, though they will never touch the greatness that is located far beyond them, nevertheless attack it. An invulnerable thing is not what is not struck but what is not harmed. This will be what distinguishes the wise person I present to you. (4) Surely there is no dispute that firmness is more certain if it is undefeated than if it is not challenged, since strength that has not been tested is open to doubt, whereas durability is rightly judged more certain if it has repelled all attacks? In the same way, you should know that the wise person is of a better nature if no injury harms him than if no injury is perpetrated. And I will say that that man is brave whom wars do not defeat, and who feels no fear at the approach of an enemy force—not the man who lives off the fat of peacetime among inactive peoples.

(5) This I say, therefore: that the wise person is vulnerable to no injury. So it does not matter how many missiles are thrown at

him, because none can penetrate him. Just as the hardness of certain stones cannot be penetrated by iron, and adamant cannot be cut or crushed or worn away but actually blunts the things that hit it; just as certain things cannot be consumed by fire but, even when surrounded by flames, still preserve their sturdiness and their form; and just as certain rocks projecting upward break the sea and yet show no traces of its ferocity despite being assaulted through the ages—just so solid is the wise person's mind, and it has gained such robustness that it is as safe from injury as those things I have recounted.

(4.1) "What? Will there not be someone who tries to do an injury to the wise person?" He will try, but the injury will not reach him. For he is too far removed from contact with lower things for any harmful force to carry its strength all the way to him. Even when the powerful seek to do him harm, being held aloft by their power and kept strong by the compliance of their subjects, their attacks will all fall as far short of wisdom as objects that are shot high into the air from bows and catapults, even if they fly further than the eye can see, nonetheless fall back before reaching the sky. (2) What? Do you think, on the occasion when that foolish king darkened the day with so many missiles, that any arrow hit the sun, or that Neptune could have been touched by the chains that he threw into the deep sea?[22] As celestial things elude human hands, and as no harm is done to divinity by those who demolish temples and melt down statues, so too, no matter what shameful, reckless, arrogant thing is done against the wise person, the attempt is made in vain. (3) "Yet it would have been better if there had been no one who wanted to do this." You are hoping for a difficult thing for the human race: innocence. Further, for this not to be done is in the interest of those who would do it, not of him who can endure even if it should be done. Indeed, I suspect that tranquility amid provocations provides a better display of wisdom's strength, just as the greatest proof that a general is powerful in arms and men is for him to be safe and free of anxiety within the land of the enemy.

(5.1) Let us distinguish, if you will, Serenus, between injury and insult. The first of these is more serious by nature, the second slighter and only serious to those who are coddled: people are not harmed by it but simply offended. Yet such is the weakness and vanity of people's minds that some think nothing is more harsh. Thus you will find a slave who prefers to be whipped than to be boxed on the ears, and who believes death and beatings (*uerbera*) to be more bearable than insulting words (*uerba*). (2) We have reached such a height of absurdity that we are vexed not only by pain but by the thought of pain, like children who are frightened by a shadow, by grotesque masks, or by a disfigured appearance; and who are brought to tears by names unpleasant to their ears, by gesticulations of the fingers, and by other things which in their ignorance they try to flee, driven by erroneous thinking.

(3) Injury's intention is the following: to affect someone with bad. But wisdom does not leave a place for bad, since for wisdom the only bad is shamefulness, which cannot enter where virtue and the morally good already are. If, then, there is no injury without bad and there is nothing bad except what is shameful, and what is shameful cannot reach one who is engaged in morally good things, injury does not reach the wise person. For if an injury is the suffering of something bad, but the wise person suffers nothing bad, no injury pertains to the wise person. (4) Every injury is a diminishing of that which it attacks, and no one can receive an injury without some detriment to his status, to his body, or to the things that are placed outside us. But the wise person is not able to lose anything: he has placed everything in himself, he places no trust in fortune, and he has his goods on solid ground, being content with virtue, which does not have need of fortuitous things and therefore cannot be increased or diminished. For it is the case both that things that have reached the highest point have no place for increase, and that fortune snatches away nothing except what it has given. But fortune does not give virtue, and therefore does not take it away. Virtue is free, inviolable, unmoved, unshaken, so hardened against chance events that it cannot be made to bend, let alone be defeated. It stares down the devices of terror: whether it is presented with hardships or with blessings, its expression remains unchanged. (5) He will not, then, be losing a thing whose passing he will feel. For he is in possession of virtue alone, from which he can never be dislodged. Other things he uses as if on loan. And who is upset by the loss of what is not his? But if injury cannot harm any of the things that are a wise person's own, because his things are safe so long as virtue is safe, then injury cannot be done to the wise person.

(6) Megara had been captured by Demetrius, who was called Poliorcetes (Stormer of Cities). The philosopher Stilpo, being asked by Demetrius whether he had lost anything, said, "Nothing: all my things are with me."[23] Yet his estate had become plunder, the enemy had seized his daughters, his fatherland had fallen under foreign domination, and he himself was being interrogated by a king backed up by the weapons of his victorious army and standing on higher ground. **(7)** Even so, Stilpo wrested that man's victory from him by testifying that although his city had been captured, he was not only unconquered but actually unscathed. For he had with him his real goods, which none can lay claim to, whereas those things that had been snatched away and scattered around and were being passed from hand to hand he judged to be not his but rather things that come and go at fortune's beck and call. Therefore he had enjoyed them, but not as his own, because the possession of things that flow in from outside is slippery and uncertain.

(6.1) Now consider whether a thief, a defamer, an insolent neighbor, or some wealthy man lording it like a king over Stilpo's destitute old age could do an injury to this man. War, an enemy, and that expert in the fine art of storming cities could wrest nothing away from him! **(2)** Amid swords flashing everywhere and the tumult of soldiers pillaging, amid the flames and blood and carnage of an overthrown city, amid the crash of temples falling down on their gods, one man was at peace.

There is no reason, then, for you to think my promise is reckless. If, though, you do not fully trust me, I have a guarantor I can give you. For you are skeptical that such great endurance, or such greatness of mind, can be present in a human being. But one comes forth in our midst to say:[24] **(3)** "You have no reason to doubt that someone born a human being can raise himself above human affairs; that he can look without anxiety on griefs and losses, sores and wounds, and great catastrophes crashing down around him; that he can bear hardships calmly and favorable conditions moderately, neither yielding to the former nor depending on the latter, but rather can remain the same amid diverse events; and that he can think nothing to be his except himself—and even himself only in that part in which he is better. **(4)** Look, I am present to prove to you that under the command of that destroyer of so many cities the fortifications are being shaken with a battering ram; the high towers, undermined by tunnels and secret trenches, are suddenly toppling; and a mound is rising up that will rival the height of the tallest citadels—and yet no machinery can be found that will unsettle a well-founded mind. **(5)** Just now I crawled out from the ruins of my house, and with fires blazing all around me I fled the flames through a trail of blood. As for the fate my daughters met, whether it was worse than our public fate, I do not know. Old and alone, and seeing only enemies around me, I nevertheless declare that my assets are intact and unharmed. Whatever I had that was mine, I have and I hold. **(6)** You should not think that I am conquered and that you are the conqueror. Your fortune conquered my fortune. As for the whereabouts of those fleeting things whose masters are changing, I do not know. As far as my things are concerned, they are with me. They *will* be with me. **(7)** The wealthy folks have lost their estates; the lustful have lost their lovers and their favorite whores, purchased at great expenditure of shame; the ambitious have lost the Senate house, the forum, and places designated for exercising vices in public. The moneylenders have lost their account books, in which avarice gleefully hallucinates its wealth. As for me, I have everything intact and uncompromised. Go, then, and question those people who weep and lament, who cast their naked bodies before drawn swords in defense of their money, who flee from the enemy with their pockets weighed down."

(8) This is the way, then, Serenus, you should understand how that perfected man, full of human and divine virtues, suffers no loss. His goods are encircled by solid and insurmountable fortifications. With these walls you cannot compare the walls of Babylon, which Alexander entered, not the walls of Carthage or Numantia captured by a single hand, not [Rome's] Capitol or citadel. Those bear the traces of the enemy. These walls that protect the wise person are safe both from flame and from infiltration. And they offer no way in, being lofty, unstormable, equal to the gods.

(7.1) You cannot say, as you often do, that this wise person of ours is found nowhere. We are not making up an empty paragon of human nature or inventing a huge image of something false. Rather, we have produced, and we *will* produce, such a one as we fashion— perhaps rarely, and just one, even after great intervals of time. For great things that surpass the normal and common measure are not generated often. And yet I feel awe to think that Marcus Cato himself, from whose mention this disputation proceeded, may surpass our model.

(2) Ultimately, that which harms needs to be stronger than that by which it is harmed. But wickedness is not stronger than virtue. Therefore the wise person cannot be harmed. Injury is not attempted against the good except by the bad. Good people are at peace among themselves, whereas bad people are as malicious to good people as they are to one another. But if only a weaker person can be harmed, and a bad person is weaker than a good person, and the good need not fear injury except from one who is not his equal, then injury cannot befall a wise man. You no longer need to be reminded, of course, that no one is good except the wise man.

(3) "If Socrates," he says, "was condemned unjustly (*iniuste*), then he received an injury (*iniuriam*)." At this point we need to understand that it can be the case that someone does an injury to me and I do not receive it. It is just as when someone puts a thing in my city house that he has surreptitiously taken from my country villa: he has committed a theft, but I have lost nothing. **(4)** Someone can be harmful, even though he has not harmed. If a man should sleep with his own wife thinking she is another man's wife, he will be an adulterer, even though she is not an adulteress. Someone gave me poison, but the poison lost its power when mixed with food: he, by giving poison, made himself guilty of a crime, even if he did not harm. A bandit is no less a bandit if his weapon was thwarted by a barrier of clothing. As far as guilt is concerned, all crimes are complete even before the outcome of the action. **(5)** Certain things by their very nature are joined together in such a way that A can be without B, but B cannot be without A. I will try to make clear what I mean. I can move my feet without running; I cannot run without moving my feet. I can, despite being in water, not be swimming; if I swim, I cannot not be in water. **(6)** The thing we are dealing with is also in this category: if I have received an injury, necessarily it was done; if it was done, I did not necessarily receive it. For many things can come about that can avert injury. Just as some chance event can knock away an outstretched hand or divert missiles that have been shot, so too something can repel injuries, no matter what sort, and can intercept them halfway, so the injuries have been done but not received.

(8.1) In addition to this, justice (*iustitia*) cannot suffer anything unjust (*iniustum*), because opposites do not combine; and injury (*iniuria*) cannot be done except unjustly (*iniuste*); therefore injury cannot be done to the wise person. Nor can you be surprised if no one can do an injury to him, when no one can even benefit him![25] The fact is that nothing is lacking to the wise person that he could receive in the place of a gift, and equally, that the bad person can confer nothing that is worthy of the wise person. For he needs to have before he can give, but he has nothing which the wise person will rejoice over when it is passed on to him.

(2) No one is able, then, either to harm the wise person or to benefit him, since divine things need no help and are incapable of being harmed; and the wise person exists as the closest neighbor to the gods, being godlike except for his mortality. Struggling and striving toward those things that are lofty, orderly, fearless, flowing in an even and harmonious course, free from anxiety, kind, existing for the public good, and healthy both for him and for others, he will not desire anything that is lowly, and he will not shed tears for anything. **(3)** One who rests on his reason for support and proceeds through human events with a divine mind does not have anywhere he can receive injury.

Do you think I mean injury from human beings alone? Not even from fortune: whenever fortune has come into combat with virtue, it never walks away virtue's equal. If we receive with calm and placid mind the biggest thing of all, beyond which angry laws and the cruelest masters have nothing further with which to threaten us, and in which fortune uses up its power; if we know that death is not a bad thing, and thus that it is not even an injury—then we will tolerate other things more easily: losses and griefs, dishonors, changes of location, deaths of kin, and separations. These things do not submerge the wise person, even if they encircle him all at once. Still less does he grieve over their individual assaults. And if he bears the injuries of fortune moderately, how much more will he bear those of powerful human beings, whom he knows are the hands of fortune!

(9.1) So he endures all things just as he endures a numbing winter and bad weather in the skies, just as he endures fevers and illnesses and other things that happen by chance. Nor does he form such a high opinion of anyone that he thinks the other has done anything deliberately. That belongs to the wise person alone. All other people engage not in deliberations but in deceptions and treachery and un-considered motions of the mind. He counts these as accidents. But chance events all rage around us, seeking worthless targets.

(2) Consider also the following: that the material for injuries is most widely available in those things by which someone has sought to endanger us, such as a hidden accuser, false charges, or powerful men provoked into hating us, and whatever other banditry there is among togate citizens. That other kind of injury is frequent too: if someone's profits or a prize long hunted are forced from their hands, or if an inheritance earned by hard work is diverted, or the goodwill of a well-to-do household is withdrawn. The wise person escapes these things: he does not know how to live in either hope or fear.

(3) Now add the fact that no one who receives an injury does so with thoughts unmoved, but is disturbed at the perception of injury, whereas someone removed from errors, who controls himself, a man of deep and placid peacefulness, is without disturbance. For if injury touches him, it also moves and pushes him, whereas the wise person is without anger, which is aroused by the appearance of injury. Nor could he have been without anger if he were not also without injury, which he knows cannot be done to him. This is how he is so up-standing and joyful, how he is buoyed up by unceasing joy. But so far is he from being caught up in the offenses caused by things and by people, that injury itself is useful to him, allowing him to put himself to the test and to make trial of his virtue.

(4) Let us show our favor for this plan, I beg you all, and let us be present with calm minds and ears while the wise person is withdrawn from injury. Nothing is thereby subtracted from your petulance, your rapacious desires, or your blind recklessness and your arrogance: your vices are safe while this freedom is acquired by the wise person. We are acting not to prevent you from being permitted to do an injury, but rather so that he can cast all injuries down to the depths and can defend himself through endurance and magnificence of mind.

(5) Just so, in the sacred games, most men defeat their opponents' hands by wearing them out with stubborn endurance. Consider the wise person to be of this kind—to be one of those who through long and committed training have acquired the firmness to withstand ev-ery hostile force, and to wear it out.

(**10.1**) Since we have run to the end of the first part, let us pass on to the second, in which we will argue against insult—in part through certain specific arguments, but indeed mostly through ones that are common.[26] Insult is something less than injury: we can complain about it more than we can pursue it, and the laws too have not thought it worthy of any punishment. (**2**) This emotion is stirred up by the lowliness of a mind that recoils because of some dishonoring word or deed: "That man did not admit me today, though he was admitting others," "When I was speaking, he insolently turned away from me, or he mocked me openly," "He seated me not in the middle of the couch but at the foot," and other things of this kind.[27] What shall I call these except the quibbles of a seasick mind? Usually it is the luxurious and the fortunate who are found uttering them, because no one has the time to notice such things if he has worse things to contend with. (**3**) Minds with too much leisure, that are weak by nature, feminine, and idling around in the absence of genuine injury— they are the ones disturbed by these things. And the majority of these things are due to the fault of the interpreter.

Someone, then, who is affected by insult does not show that he has any good sense in himself or any confidence. For he judges, without a hint of doubt, that he has been disrespected, and this sting does not occur without a certain lowliness in the mind, which depresses itself and slumps down. The wise person, by contrast, is not disrespected by anyone: he knows his own greatness, and he informs himself that no one has that much power over him. And as for all these things that I would call not miseries of the mind but rather annoyances, he does not defeat them: rather, he does not even feel them.

(**4**) There are other things that strike the wise person even if they do not overthrow him, such as physical pain, loss of a limb, loss of friends and children, and during wartime the calamity of his fatherland in flames. I do not deny that the wise person feels these,[28] for we do not endow him with the hardness of stone or of iron. To endure without feeling what you endure is not virtue at all. What, then, is my point? He receives some cuts, but those that he receives he overcomes, he heals, he stanches. Yet these lesser blows he does not even feel, and he does not use against them that customary virtue we have been talking about, by which he tolerates hardships, but either he does not register them or he thinks they are laughable.

(11.1) Besides, the fact that the majority of insults are made by arrogant and insolent men who bear their good fortune poorly means the wise person has something by which he can reject that inflated emotional reaction: magnanimity, the most beautiful of all the virtues. Virtue passes by anything of that sort, like empty images from dreams and nocturnal visions without a trace of substance or truth. (2) At the same time, he considers that all are too low to be bold enough to look down on things that are elevated so much higher. Insult (*contumelia*) is so called from scorn (*contemptus*), because no one marks someone with an injury unless he has scorned him. But no one scorns someone greater and better, even if he does something that scorners typically do. For children strike their parents' faces, and a toddler has been known to mess up its mother's hair and tear it, and to spit on her, or to expose her naked skin in full view of her family, and to utter obscenities—and we do not call any of these insults. Why? Because the one who does them is incapable of scorning. (3) It is the same reason why we are entertained by our slaves' insult-filled humor against their masters. Their boldness even gives itself license against dinner guests, if it has been initiated by the master. And the more worthy of scorn each one is, the more unrestrained is his tongue. For this very purpose some people buy up cheeky boys and sharpen up their rudeness and put them under an instructor so that they can pour out abuse like experts. And we call these not insults but witticisms. What madness it is, though, to be entertained one moment and offended the next by the same things, and to call something that a friend has said a slander, but something that a mere slave has said a humorous reproach!

(12.1) The attitude we have in our minds toward children is what the wise person has toward all those whose childishness persists even after the arrival of adulthood and gray hair. Or has any progress been made by those whose minds have problems and errors that have grown greater—who differ from children only in the size and shape of their bodies, but otherwise are no less misguided and astray, seeking after pleasures indiscriminately, anxiously, and peaceful only from terror and not from good character? (2) No one can say that there is a difference between these men and children just because children are possessive toward knucklebones or nuts and little copper coins, whereas the men are possessive toward gold, silver, and cities! Because children play magistrates among themselves and make believe at having a purple-fringed toga, fasces, and judge's throne, whereas the men play at the same things seriously in the Campus Martius, the forum, and the Senate house. Because children make imaginary houses by piling up sand on the seashore, whereas the men, as if they are doing something great, busy themselves with piling up stones and walls and roofs, and take what was invented for sheltering bodies and convert it into something dangerous. The situation is similar, then, for children and for these men who have proceeded further— except that the latter's error concerns other, greater things. (3) So the wise person is justified in receiving these people's insults as jokes. On occasion too, he admonishes them, like children, with harm and punishment, not because he has received an injury but because they did an injury, and so that they might stop doing it. For stock animals too are tamed just so, with a lash of the whip, and we are not angry at them whenever they refuse a rider, but we curb them so that pain can break their insolence. You will see, then, how this neutralizes the objection that is made against us: "Why does the wise person, if he has not received an injury or an insult, punish those who did them?" If you want to know: he is not avenging himself but rather is correcting them.

(13.1) But how can you not believe that this mental durability is able be present in a wise man, when you can observe the same thing in others due to a different cause? For what doctor gets angry at someone who is out of his mind? Who takes umbrage when someone utters curses because he is in a fever and has been forbidden cold water? (2) The wise man has the same feeling toward all people that the doctor has toward his patients: the doctor is willing to handle their private parts if they need a remedy, to examine their excrement or urine, or to take abuse from the raving mad. The wise man knows that all those who walk around in togas or in purple, though fit and of healthy complexion,[29] are in poor health. He regards them as no different from sick people lacking in self-control. So he does not even get annoyed at them if in their illness they try something reckless against their healer. He regards their honors as having no value, and brings the same attitude to their actions which are performed without virtue. (3) Just as he will not feel smug when a beggar fawns on him, and will not judge it an insult just because a person of the lowest station does not return his greeting, so too he will not admire himself when many wealthy people admire him. For he knows that wealthy people are no different from beggars—and indeed are more deserving of pity, because the latter lack a little, whereas the former lack a lot.

Likewise, he will not be affected if the king of the Medes or king Attalus of Asia should pass over his greeting in silence, with a haughty expression.[30] He knows that there is nothing more to be envied in that man's position than in the position of a slave in a large household whose responsibility it is to restrain the sick and the insane. (4) Surely I need not be annoyed if my name is not returned by one of those who do business at the temple of Castor buying and selling wretched human chattels, whose stalls are crammed with a crowd of the lowliest slaves? I think not. What good, anyway, does someone have who has only the bad beneath him? And thus, just as he overlooks this one's courtesy or discourtesy, so too he overlooks the king's: "You have beneath you Parthians, Medes, and Bactrians. But you contain them by fear, and they do not allow you to slacken your bow. They are your bitterest enemies, they allow themselves to be bought, and they are on the lookout for a new master."

(5) He will not be moved, then, by anyone's insult. The fact is that although all men are different from one another, the wise person regards them all as equal, on account of their equal stupidity. For if he lets himself just once descend to being disturbed by either injury or insult, he will never be able to be free from anxiety. And freedom from anxiety is the wise person's hallmark. Nor will he be caught out judging that an insult has been done to him and thereby allowing the one who did it to have honor. For one who succeeds in making someone annoyed by scorning him, by implication can rejoice at being admired.

(14.1) Some are so crazy that they think that an insult can be done them by a woman. What does it matter how privileged she is whom they are dealing with, how many litter bearers she has, how heavy her earrings are, how spacious her sedan chair? She remains an equally thoughtless animal and, unless knowledge and much learning are added, wild, and lacking control over her desires. Some get annoyed if they are bumped by a hairdresser, and they call it an insult when a doorman gives them trouble, when a name announcer is arrogant, or a bedroom slave gets uppity. O how ridiculous these things are! And how much pleasure one can fill one's mind with from the hurly-burly of other men's errors while contemplating one's own peace and quiet!

(2) "What? Will the wise person not approach doors where a harsh gatekeeper presides?" Indeed he will try this, if necessity demands it, and he will soothe that man, whoever he is, as he would by throwing food to a fierce dog. And he will not think it unworthy to spend something to cross the threshold, considering how certain bridges too require a gift for crossing. And so he will give to that man also, whoever he is, who manages this revenue at the morning receptions. He knows that things that are for sale are bought with money. It is a small-minded person who is smug over having replied freely to a doorman, over having broken his staff, over having gone through to the master and asked for him to be flogged. He who puts up a fight makes himself into an opponent, and even though he may win, he is at his level.

(3) "But what will the wise person do when he is punched?" What Cato did, when his face was struck: he did not get angry, he did not avenge the injury, and he did not even forgive it, but rather he denied that an injury had been done. His ignoring it required a greater mind than would have been required for him to forgive it. (4) We will not linger on this point for long. After all, who is unaware that none of the things that are thought bad or good seem to the wise person as they seem to everyone else? He does not respect people's judgments about what is shameful or pitiful. He does not go on the popular path, but as the planets pursue a course contrary to the movement of the heavens, so does the wise person advance against popular opinion.

(15.1) Stop saying, therefore: "Will the wise person not receive an injury, then, if he is cut, if his eye is gouged out? Will he not receive an insult if he is jostled through the forum with abusive taunts by foul-mouthed men; if, at a king's banquet, he is ordered to recline beneath the table and to eat with the slaves who are responsible for the most humiliating chores;[31] if he is compelled to endure any other contrivance that is offensive to the sensibilities of a freeborn person?" (2) However great those things become in number or in scale, they will be of the same nature. If the little ones do not touch him, not even the greater ones will. If a few do not touch him, not even a great many will. You, though, take your own weakness as a guide in making a guess about his huge mind, and when you consider how much you think you are able to endure, you place the limit of the wise person's endurance just a little further. But his virtue locates him in another part of the universe: he has nothing in common with you. **(3)** Go and find some things that are harsh and heavy to bear, from which you retreat when you hear them or see them: a plurality of these will not overwhelm him, and he will withstand them all just as he withstands them singly. If someone says that one thing is tolerable to the wise person, another intolerable, and he keeps the mind's greatness within fixed limits, he has it wrong. Fortune defeats us unless our defeat of it is total.

(4) But so that you do not think this hardness is exclusive to the Stoics, Epicurus—whom you people adopt as the patron of your inactivity, thinking that he teaches soft and lazy things and pathways to the pleasures—says: "Fortune rarely gets in the wise man's way." How close he came to uttering a *man's* words![32] Do you want to speak still more bravely and to separate fortune from the rest? **(5)** The wise man's meager house, where there is no adornment, no clamor, no finery—this house is not watched over by gatekeepers who divide the crowd but can be bribed to give their approval. Rather, over this empty threshold, which has no doorman, fortune does not pass. It knows that, where there is nothing that belongs to it, there is no place for it.

(16.1) But if even Epicurus, who indulges the body a great deal, rises up against injuries, what part of what we are saying seems hard to believe or beyond the measure of human nature? He says that the wise person can tolerate injuries, whereas we say that there are no injuries.[33] **(2)** And you cannot say, indeed, that this goes against nature. We do not deny that being beaten, being struck, or losing a limb is an unfortunate thing, but we deny that all these things are injuries. We remove from these not the sensation of pain but only the name injury, which cannot be sustained with virtue intact. We will see which of us speaks more truly. Certainly we both agree on scorning injury. Do you seek to know what the difference is between the two of us? The same difference as there is between two courageous gladiators, of whom one clamps his wound and stands his ground, while the other looks to the people applauding and indicates that it is nothing, and does not allow them to intercede. (3) You should not think that our divergence is great. As to the thing that is at issue, and the one thing that need concern you, both examples urge it: to scorn injuries (and insults, which I would call the shadows and suspicions of injuries). Despising these requires not a wise man (*sapiente . . . uiro*) but simply one in his right mind (*consipiente*), who can say to himself: "Are these things happening to me deservingly or undeservingly? If deservingly, it is not insult, but judgment. If undeservingly, we should be embarrassed for him who does what is unjust." (4) And what is that thing that is called an insult? He made a joke about my smooth head, my poor eyes, my bandy legs, and my height. What insult is it to be told what is evident? When a thing is said before an audience of one, we laugh, but when in front of many, we get mad. And we do not give others the freedom to say the same things that we ourselves are accustomed to saying. By mild jests we are entertained; at excessive ones we get angry.

(17.1) Chrysippus reports how a certain man got mad when someone had called him a "muttonhead of the deep."[34] In the Senate we saw Fidus Cornelius, Ovidius Naso's son-in-law, weeping when Corbulo had called him a "shaved ostrich."[35] Against all the other abuses intended to wound his character and his life, his brow retained its firmness, but at this absurdity the tears welled forth. So great is the weakness of our minds when reason has departed. (2) What about our being offended if someone imitates our way of speaking, our walk, some flaw in our body or in our voice? As if those things would be more obvious when another imitates them than when we ourselves do them! Some are reluctant to hear about their old age, their gray hairs, and other things which we pray we will attain. Others are inflamed by an accusation of poverty, when in fact anyone who seeks to conceal his poverty is accusing himself. And thus do we deprive of material those petulant persons who make humor through insult: you need to take the initiative and get in before they do. No one prompts laughter if he has already gotten a laugh at his own expense. (3) Tradition relates how Vatinius, a man born for both laughter and hatred, was a charming and witty joker. He said a great many things at the expense of his own feet and his scarred neck. This is how he avoided being made fun of by his enemies, who were as numerous as his deformities, and especially by Cicero.[36] If Vatinius was able to accomplish this by the hardness of his words—he whom constant invectives had long since taught to feel no shame—then why can it not be accomplished by one who, through his liberal studies and his cultivation of wisdom, has actually made some progress? **(4)** Add the fact that it is a kind of revenge to snatch away the pleasure of having made an insult from the one who made it. People often say, "Oh dear. I do not think he understood." So contingent is the outcome of an insult on the victim's feeling it and becoming incensed. Moreover, sooner or later the perpetrator will meet his match: someone will emerge to avenge you also.

(18.1) Gaius Caesar,[37] a practitioner of insults along with his other copious vices, was driven by a strange urge to brand every person with some mark, though he himself offered rich material for laughter—so hideous was the pallor that betrayed his insanity, so savage were the eyes concealed beneath his old woman's brow, so misshapen was his desolate head strewn with fiercely defended hairs;[38] not to mention his neck covered in bristles, the thinness of his legs, and the enormity of his feet. If you wish to recall the individual instances in which he was insulting to his parents and grandparents, and to persons of every rank, there is an endless supply. I will recall those that sealed his fate.

(2) Valerius Asiaticus was among the emperor's foremost friends, a fierce man who could scarcely be expected to bear with a calm mind insults made against *others*.[39] During a banquet—really, during a public assembly—and so that all could hear, the emperor reproached Valerius for how his wife was in bed. Good gods! For a man to listen to this, for the emperor to know this, and for free speech to have reached such an extreme that, not just to an ex-consul, not just to a friend, but to a husband, the emperor should narrate his adultery and his dissatisfaction! **(3)** By contrast, Chaerea, the military tribune, had a way of talking that did not match his prowess.[40] It was weak in volume and, if you were not aware of his deeds, would have made him seem suspect. When Chaerea asked for the watchword, Gaius once gave him the sign of Venus, another time the sign of Priapus, in one way after another reproaching the soldier for his softness. All of these things he did while himself dressed in diaphanous robes, slippers, and earrings! And so he compelled Chaerea to use his sword so that he would not have to ask for the watchword anymore. That man was the first among the conspirators to raise his hand, and it was he who severed his neck in a single stroke.[41] A great many swords were then thrust in from all sides, avenging public and private injuries. Yet the first man was the one who least seemed to *be* a man.

(4) But the same Gaius saw insults wherever he looked, as those with the greatest appetite for making insults are incapable of enduring them. He was angry with Herennius Macer, because he had greeted him as "Gaius." And he did not let a top-ranking centurion go unpunished for having called him "Caligula" (Little Boot). For this is what he used to be called, having been born in camp and being a child of the legions, and he was never known to the soldiers more closely by any other name. But now, wearing the high boots of tragedy, he regarded "Caligula" as a taunt, an abuse. (5) And so this itself will serve as a consolation: that even if, in our leniency, we will pass over revenge, there will be someone who exacts punishment from the person who is wanton, arrogant, and revels in doing injury—vices that are never used up in a single person or a single insult.

(6) Let us look to the examples of those we praise for their endurance, such as Socrates. He received in good spirits the witticisms that were published and staged against him, and he laughed at them no less than when he had filthy water poured over him by his wife Xanthippe.[42] Antisthenes was abused for having a foreign, Thracian mother. He replied that even the mother of the gods was from Mount Ida.[43]

(19.1) There is no need to resort to a quarrel or a physical struggle. We must use our feet to get far away. We must ignore whichever of these things is done by senseless people (they can be done only by senseless people). And we must make no distinction between the honors and the injuries given by the common people, (2) neither grieving over the latter nor rejoicing over the former. Otherwise, from fear of insults or from weariness at them, we will neglect many necessary things, and we will fail to attend to public and private duties (which are sometimes also beneficial)—all because we are vexed by a womanly concern about hearing something contrary to our thinking. Sometimes we will even get angry at the powerful, and will reveal this feeling in an uncontrolled exercise of freedom. But to put up with nothing is not freedom: there we are deceived. Freedom is putting one's mind above injuries, making oneself into the sole source of one's joys, and separating external things from oneself so that one does not have to live an unsettled life, afraid of everyone's laughter and everyone's tongue. For if *anyone* can make an insult, who then is not capable of making one?

(3) Different remedies, however, will be used by the wise person and by one who is aspiring to wisdom. You see, those who are not perfect and are still holding themselves to the standard of public judgment should be put on alert that they themselves must live among injuries and insults: everything that happens will be lighter, if they know to expect it. The more respectable each person is in his birth, his reputation, his inheritance, the more bravely should he conduct himself, knowing that the tall ranks stand at the front of the battle line. Let him bear insults, abusive words, dishonors, and other humiliations as if they were the clamor of the enemy, weapons thrown from a distance, and rocks clattering around his helmet but not making any wound. As for injuries, like wounds, some piercing the armor and some the breast, let him withstand them without being knocked down or even giving ground. Even if you are pushed and shoved by a hostile force, giving way is still shameful: keep the position assigned to you by nature. Do you ask what this position is? Being a man.

(4) The wise person has a different thing to help him that is the opposite of this. For you are all still fighting, whereas for him the victory has been won. Do not struggle against your good. And while you are still on your way to the truth, foster this hope in your minds, and willingly take up better things, and help them along with your attitude and your will: the existence of something unconquered, the existence of someone against whom fortune has no power at all, is in the interest of the commonwealth of the human race.

Abbreviations

OCD   *Oxford Classical Dictionary*, 3rd ed., ed. Simon Hornblower and An-
thony Spawforth. Oxford: Oxford University Press, 1996.

SVF   *Stoicorum Veterum Fragmenta*, ed. Hans F. A. von Arnim. Leipzig,
1903–24.

Use.   Usener, Hermann. *Epicurea*. Leipzig, 1887.

Introduction

1. Insult (*contumelia*) was a frequent grievance in the *actio iniuriarum*; see
in general the discussion by Riggsby 2010, 191–94; also, *OCD* s.v. "*iniuria* and
defamation." Seneca's discussion shows some traces of legal categorization and
juristic argumentation (e.g., 5.3, 7.3–6).

2. Though it would have been possible to translate *iniuria* with "wrong,"
as Robert Kaster has appropriately done in his translation of *On Anger*, in the
present context I have used *injury* to sustain the contrast with insult—the first
primarily physical, the second primarily verbal—that is central to the division of the work; and to register the fact that Seneca often draws analogies
with physical assault (e.g., 1.1, 3.5, 16.2). But caution is needed: Latin *iniuria*,
like Greek *adikia*, places more emphasis on the perpetrator's agency ("unlaw-
ful conduct," "unjust treatment," "an injustice") than does the English term
injury.

3. The syllogistic arguments here differ from the logical game-playing Seneca criticizes elsewhere (e.g., *Letter* 49.5–6), as noted by Barnes 1997, 18 n. 19.
See also Cooper 2006.

4. Seneca's discussion is placed in a broader sociological context by Roller
2001, 146–54, esp. 151 n. 32.

5. On *constantia* in Seneca's prose and tragedies, see Star 2006.

6. On *constantia* in Seneca and its association with *patientia* and *magnitudo
animi*, see Viansino 1988, 66. Serenus's lack of special respect for *patientia* is
a reminder of that term's associations with not only endurance but also, depending on the context, problematic submission, mapped in detail by Kaster
2002.

7. Wright 1974, 59. The convenient but misleading abbreviated title *On
Constancy* may owe something to the fact that Justus Lipsius adapted Seneca's

title for his neo-Stoic work *De Constantia* (1584). Lipsius's work draws on a variety of Seneca's works, not this one alone.

8. For subtle analysis of the sage's function in Seneca, see Inwood 2005, 295–96.

9. The only certain dating criterion is the posthumous mention of Valerius Asiaticus at 18.2, which puts the work later than 47 CE, the year of Valerius's suicide under Claudius (Tacitus *Annals* 11.3.2). On Serenus, and the chronology of the works associated with him, see Seneca's recollection of his death in *Letter* 63.14–15. For discussion see Griffin 1992, 316–17, 354, 396, 399, 447–48; Williams 2003, 12–15; also Grimal 1953, 13–17, 19.

10. On the tradition see Lee 1953; the relevance of paradoxes in Seneca's *Consolation to Helvia* is demonstrated by Williams 2006.

11. Plutarch *On Stoic Contradictions* 1044a. For this and other fragments preserving this paradox (including Seneca *On Benefits* 2.35.2), see *SVF* 3:567–81. The various Greek terms include *adikia* ("injustice"), *blabē* ("harm"), *diabolē* ("slander"), *hubris* ("rough treatment").

12. On the Caligula example, see Wilcox 2008, 466–72; Wright 1974, 63.

13. As Matthew Roller has noted (2001, 161–62).

14. Griffin 1992 observes: "Perhaps [the Caligula example here] is a reference to Seneca's own insulting treatment and his passive role in 41, but Seneca does not go out of his way to enlighten us biographically" (215).

On the Constancy of the Wise Person

15. Cato the Younger (95–46 BCE); on Cato in Seneca, see the note at *On Providence* 2.9.

16. P. Vatinius had defeated Cato in the election for praetor in 55, and this is the scenario that Serenus has in mind, as is made clear at 2.3 below (cf. *On Providence* 3.14; *Letters* 118.4).

17. P. Clodius Pulcher (d. 52), one of Cicero's main adversaries, became a symbol of political corruption and mob violence in the 50s BCE.

18. Seneca presents Hercules as a moral exemplar alongside Regulus and Cato at *On Tranquility of Mind* 16.4, and he is ubiquitous in the tragedies; Ulysses (Odysseus) arises as an occasional example, especially in *Letters* (e.g., 88.7).

19. I.e., the first triumvirate, in the 50s, with power shared between Caesar, Pompey, and Crassus.

20. On the Stoic paradoxes, see my introduction to this essay.

21. This perhaps refers to situations when the wise person undergoes a temporary loss of sobriety or sanity, as in drunkenness (Cato's, at *On Tranquility of Mind* 17.4); on drunkenness, however, see *Letters* 83.9–27.

22. Actions of King Xerxes during the Persian Wars.

23. Demetrius (336–283 BCE) was the son of Antigonus and king of Macedonia. Stilpo (ca. 370–290 BCE) belonged to the Megarian school of philosophy begun by Euclides of Megara, a student of Socrates; their ethics emphasized, among other things, self-sufficiency.

24. Still Stilpo.

25. Another Stoic paradox: "The wise person is never moved by gratitude" (cf. Cicero *On Behalf of Murena* 61).

26. I.e., common to insult and injury alike.

27. I.e., insults at the morning greeting (*salutatio*) and the evening dinner party (*conuiuium*).

28. Apparently a reference to pre-emotions (*propatheiai*), which the Stoic wise person feels without assenting to them. On Seneca's account of these, see Graver 2007, 93–101.

29. The text here (MSS *ualentes coloratos*, emended to *ualentes colorati*) remains uncertain.

30. King of the Medes: probably a loose reference to Xerxes, the Persian king. Attalus: i.e., one of the three kings of Pergamon named Attalus, in the third and second centuries BCE.

31. The servile chores included wiping up spit and vomit; see *Letters* 47.5.

32. Epicurus *Sententiae* 16 Use.

33. Usener excerpts this as frag. 585.

34. *Veruex marinus*: literally, "a marine castrated sheep"; source unknown (= *SVF* 2:11).

35. Seneca's "eyewitness account" is "hard to place," but probably in the reign of Caligula or later (Griffin 1992, 44 n. 4).

36. For Vatinius's deformities and Cicero's attacks, see Plutarch *Cicero* 9 and 26; Cicero's speech *Against P. Vatinius* was published ca. 56–54 BCE, after the trial of P. Sestius. On Vatinius see also 1.3 above with note.

37. On Caligula (12–41 CE; emperor 37–41), many of the details below arise also in Suetonius's *Caligula*: physiognomy (50), adultery (36), clothing (52), Chaerea and the assassination (56–58), the name Caligula (9).

38. I follow Gertz's emendation *emendicaticiis capillis aspersi* ("hairs obtained by begging") for †*emendacitatis*† *capillis adspersi*.

39. I.e., let alone against himself. Basore translates with "by others"; I prefer to follow Viansino and Lanzarone.

40. Cassius Chaerea.

41. As Wilcox 2008, 467 observes, this ironically echoes Caligula's saying (recorded by others, and by Seneca in *On Anger* 3.19.2) that he wished the Roman people had one neck, so he could punish them all in a single stroke.

42. On Xanthippe's ill-tempered provocations of Socrates, see Seneca's

On Marriage frag. 31 Vottero and *Letters* 104.27. On Socrates as the butt of comedians' jokes, see *On the Happy Life* 27.2.

43. Antisthenes (444–365 BCE) and a few other students of Socrates encountered abuse for not being Athenian citizens. The "mother of the gods" is Cybele.

Editions and Translations

Basore, John, trans. 1928. *Seneca, Moral Essays.* Vol. 1. Loeb Classical Library. Cambridge, MA: Harvard University Press.

Grimal, Pierre, comm. 1953. *De constantia sapientis.* Paris: Belles Lettres.

References

Barnes, Jonathan. 1997. *Logic and the Imperial Stoa.* Leiden: Brill.

Cooper, John M. 2006. "Seneca on Moral Theory and Moral Improvement." In *Seeing Seneca Whole: Perspectives on Philosophy, Poetry and Politics*, ed. K. Volk and G. Williams, 43–56. Columbia Studies in the Classical Tradition. Leiden: Brill.

Griffin, Miriam T. 1992. *Seneca: A Philosopher in Politics.* 2nd ed. Oxford: Oxford University Press.

Inwood, Brad. 2005. *Reading Seneca: Stoic Philosophy at Rome.* Oxford: Clarendon Press.

Kaster, Robert A. 2002. "The Taxonomy of Patience, or When Is "Patientia" Not a Virtue?" *Classical Philology* 97:133–44.

Lanzarone, Nicola, trans. and notes. 2001. *La fermezza del saggio: La vita ritirata.* Milan: Rizzoli.

Lee, A. D., intro. and notes. 1953. *M. Tulli Ciceronis Paradoxa Stoicorum.* London: Macmillan.

Riggsby, Andrew M. 2010. *Roman Law and the Legal World of the Romans.* Cambridge: Cambridge University Press.

Roller, Matthew B. 2001. *Constructing Autocracy: Autocrates and Emperors in Julio-Claudian Rome.* Princeton: Princeton University Press.

Star, Chistopher. 2006. "Commanding *Constantia* in Senecan Tragedy." *Transactions of the American Philological Association* 126:207–44.

Viansino, Giovanni, trans. and comm. 1988, 1990. *I Dialoghi.* 2 vols. Milan: Mondadori.

Volk, Katharina, and Gareth D. Williams. 2006. *Seeing Seneca Whole: Perspectives on Philosophy, Poetry, and Politics.* Columbia Studies in the Classical Tradition. Leiden: Brill.

Vottero, Dionigi, ed. 1998. *Lucio Anneo Seneca: I frammenti.* Bologna: Pàtron.

Wilcox, Amanda. 2008. "Nature's Monster: Caligula as *Exemplum* in Seneca's *Dialogues*." In *KAKOS: Badness and Anti-Value in Classical Antiquity*, ed. R. Rosen and I. Sluiter, 451–75. Leiden: Brill.

Williams, Gareth D. 2003. *Seneca: "De Otio," "De Brevitate Vitae."* Cambridge: Cambridge University Press.

———. "States of Exile, States of Mind: Paradox and Reversal in Seneca's *Consolatio ad Helviam Matrem*." In Volk and Williams 2006, 178–95.

Wright, J. R. G. 1974. "Form and Content in the *Moral Essays*." In *Seneca*, ed. C. D. N. Costa, 39–69. London: Routledge and Kegan Paul.

On Tranquility of Mind

Addressee and Circumstances

Seneca's *On Tranquility of Mind* is unique among his *Dialogues*, because it presents a genuine exchange between its addressee, Annaeus Serenus, and Seneca. Serenus, most probably a Spanish kinsman, seems to have come to Rome under Seneca's patronage; he is also the addressee of *On the Constancy of the Wise Person* and probably of the truncated dialogue *On Leisure*, but only this dialogue gives him a voice, which characterizes a young man's crisis of identity.

The opening chapter raises the question whether the dialogue is supposed to be a letter or a dramatized interview. As an interview it could be modeled on, for example, the master-pupil interviews of Cicero's *Tusculan Disputations*; as a letter, it could act as a forerunner to Seneca's one-sided correspondence with Lucilius from the years 63–64 BCE. While the confessional opening chapter can be read as based on genuine requests for help from Serenus, Seneca has most likely adjusted the statements he puts in Serenus's mouth to include issues he himself wants to discuss in his "reply." There are features in this first chapter, such as the preoccupation with senatorial magistracies and with the artistry of writing and speaking, that are more relevant to Seneca's own life than to his young consultant.[1] In fact, 1.13–14, with its positive emphasis on the need for grandeur so that the mind can soar, although neatly matched at the close by 17.11, invokes a standard far from, even opposed to, the goal of tranquility.

I read the dialogue as an oral consultation with Serenus as Seneca's patient: his appeal is couched in terms of sickness, but that of the mind;[2] and the situation closely resembles therapy. Serenus has endorsed Stoic principles for a virtuous life, and observed them in his own simple life-style: but he is susceptible to the material values and display of his associates, and is struggling to deny assent to their values. His problem, then, is an inner conflict between instinctive and learned values.

The first sentence focuses on self-examination; the expressions of self-discontent and corresponding attempts at self-adjustment will articulate both Serenus's speech and the movement of Seneca's reply from 2.7 and 9 to 14.2, and in the last section, 17.1. This concern with interiority is particularly strong in the systematic therapy of Seneca's *Letters to Lucilius*. But although *On Tranquility* is a therapeutic response to Serenus's explicit recognition of his own mental dis-ease (even using the medical terms of actual disease) and uses cognitive interrogation as part of its proposed cure, neither it nor Stoic approaches to moral issues conform to modern methods of psychotherapy.[3]

Where do we place this dialogue within Serenus's known career? He held a responsible administrative position as prefect of the corps of *Vigiles* (combined watch and police), probably from 54, when the post was vacated, until Tigellinus took over in 62; but nothing in *On Tranquility* implies that Serenus was already holding this position. His appointment would reflect Seneca's influence—still strong at that time—with Agrippina and Nero. Allusions to the difficulty of participating in political life, especially in 3.2–3, are relatively low-key, but suggest the dialogue was composed quite early in Nero's principate.[4] We know only that in *Letters to Lucilius* 63 (probably written in 63) Seneca looks back to his own grief and distress at the sudden death of Serenus (from accidental poisoning at an official banquet): since Seneca had no children, he may have given Serenus the love appropriate to the son he never had.

Structure

Several attempts have been made to determine the structure of the dialogue as a whole, based either on the subject matter of successive chapters or on fitting it, like Procrustes, to a rhetorical pattern. But the rhetorical model was designed for courtroom oratory; it does not fit philosophical protreptic.

CHAPTER I

Serenus's opening speech is a key to the concepts that control the sixteen chapters of Seneca's reply: this address, almost a confession, has been designed to introduce nearly all the leitmotifs that we can trace in the analysis that follows. Two metaphors are introduced as analogies that will recur throughout the dialogue; first, that of mental sickness (1.2 and 1.4), and second, the analogy of life to a voyage, together with the image of mental peace as calm at sea (1.17; cf. 1.11). Seneca's reply opens by recalling both these analogies in his references to convalescing patients and to the sea's residual disturbance after a storm. Throughout the dialogue conventional allusions to sea and storm are meant to remind the reader of the original maritime context of *tranquillitas* ("a sea-calm after storm").

Serenus begins with self-scrutiny: after describing his discontent in 1.9, he anticipates Seneca's prescription, moving in 1.11 to develop the idea of focusing within himself, which is often called Senecan interiority: "Let my mind keep to itself, tend to itself, and do nothing foreign to its needs." This leitmotif will be taken up pointedly by Seneca's diagnosis in 2.7: "There are countless characteristics of this vice but only one outcome, to be dissatisfied with oneself," recalled in 2.11. The many reflexive idioms in this dialogue will concentrate, toward the end of Seneca's survey of obstacles to calmness, in this admonition concerning the mind (14.2): "Let it have faith in itself, rejoice in itself, respect its own qualities, and as far as possible withdraw from what is alien to it."

Serenus is represented as a Stoic student, or *proficiens*, halfway toward control of his own spirit: he has learned Stoic standards of indifference to exterior goods sufficiently to apply them in his domestic frugality, but not sufficiently to escape depression at other men's luxury. He calls his trouble the weakness of purpose of a good mind (1.15). He has learned enough to regret but not to resist his own wavering (1.9); but it will be left to Seneca to diagnose this regret as "self-disgust" (*fastidium*: 2.5; cf. 2.10, 2.15, 3.1).[5] Serenus describes but cannot name the condition that Seneca identifies in his response. Almost cured of his worldly desires and hopes (hopes are even more harmful than fears), the student still suffers from inner conflict. His ranking of "goods" inverts that of the worldly man; but while based on Stoic values, it is still insecure and tends to aversion to the outside world.

CHAPTER 2

Seneca's reply offers a new, deeper sense of *tranquillitas* (2.3), identified as the equivalent of *euthumia* in Greek. Serenus first uses the word (1.11) without scrutiny as freedom from exterior disturbance, but Seneca interiorizes it, defining it as "stable balance of the soul," and refers to Democritus's treatise *Euthumia* (2.3).[6] Three citations (*Dialogues* 1.6.2, 4.10.5, and 7.27.5) mention Democritus's indifference to money; Seneca comes closest to *On Tranquility* 2.3 at *On Anger* 5.6.3: "We will benefit from the salutary rule of Democritus showing how to achieve tranquility if we do not do many things or things beyond our powers, either privately or publicly."

CHAPTERS 3–5

The best choice for life would be active involvement in public affairs and service as a citizen to fellow citizens, collectively and individually. For the elite these would have been among Stoic *kathekonta*, personal duties, or obligations determined by their status, translated by Cicero as *officia*. One metaphor, that of the soldier on military duty, becomes prominent in chapter 3, developing from a complex analogy between different levels of civil and military service (3.5). This is Roman: no Hellenistic Greek living in the age of mercenaries would have implied the superiority of military to civic duty.

CHAPTER 6

Chapter 6 offers a statement of themes: "We ought to examine ourselves first of all, then the business we are going to tackle, then the people for whom and with whom we will take it on" (6.1). This is true to Democritus, but marks a program that Seneca only partially follows.

CHAPTERS 8–11

Chapters 8 through 11 treat the external assets of wealth and property, which can distract the man striving for tranquility and virtue. But here Seneca brings into play two concepts that govern human circumstance: nature, identified in Stoic thinking with god and providence, and fortune, held responsible for all bad experiences, the attacks of which on the good man dominate these chapters.

CHAPTERS 12–16

Chapters 12 through 16 move from precepts to examples of reversals of fortune, then to models of virtue in face of death (Julius Canus under the tyrannical Caligula at 14.4–9, and Cato of Utica, glorified beyond even Hercules and Regulus, at 16.4).

The final chapter 17 is more upbeat. After new warnings against pretense and self-scrutiny distorted by undue concern with outsiders' values, 17.3 advises protection of one's integrity by withdrawal, relaxation, and the discreet use of drinking (17.9–11) to stimulate the mind before closing with the short coda of good wishes to Serenus.

Acknowledgments

I am most grateful to Professor Doug Hutchinson and six students from his course on Seneca for compiling a bibliographical survey for me to use in the fuller discussion of *On Tranquility* that I hope to publish elsewhere. I would also like to thank James Ker for advice and access to his own introductions in this series.

On Tranquility of Mind

LUCIUS ANNAEUS SENECA

TRANSLATED BY ELAINE FANTHAM

[Serenus] (1.1) When I was taking stock of myself,[7] Seneca, I found some faults openly displayed for me to take in hand, and others less obvious and hidden, and yet others that were not constant but recurred at intervals. I would call the latter the most distressing. They jump out like enemies on the move and attacking according to circumstances, and prevent me from being either prepared for action as if in wartime, or free of anxiety as if there were peace. (2) However, I find myself most commonly in this condition (why shouldn't I admit the truth, as I would to a doctor?),[8] neither genuinely released from the things I feared and hated, nor vulnerable. Even though I could be in a worse state, it is still extremely plaintive and moody: I am neither sick nor well.

(3) You don't have to tell me that the beginnings of all virtues are delicate, but they gain hardiness and strength with time. I know quite well that even the effort we put into appearances—prestige and renown for eloquence and whatever depends on another man's vote—gains strength in the lapse of time. In fact, both the talents that produce true strength and those adornments acquired to impress others wait for years to pass until duration gradually puts on a healthy color. But I am afraid habit which produces constancy may drive this fault more deeply into me; long association brings as much love for bad behavior as for good.

(4) I cannot show you once and for all the nature of this weakness of a mind[9] torn between tendencies, not veering strongly to either what is right or what is perverse; but I can explain it by taking parts of it. I will tell you what happens to me, and you will find a name for my affliction. (5) I admit I have a deep love of thrift; I don't like a couch arranged for display, or clothing fetched out from a chest, forced to shine by a thousand weights of the clothes press. Rather, I like homely and inexpensive clothing that does not have to be preserved or put on with anxious care. (6) I like food that is neither prepared nor watched by troops of servants, not something ordered many days ahead and proffered by many hands, but available and eas-

ily so, with no exotic or precious ingredients. This will not run out on any occasion, or be a burden to my budget or my body, or be brought up in vomiting.[10] **(7)** I like an ungroomed attendant and a simple homebred slave, the heavy silver plate of my country father without the signature of any craftsman: I like a table that does not seize the eye with its many colored markings, and has not become famous in the community through successive ownership by many masters, but is put there for use, not to beguile the gaze of any guest with pleasure or inflame them with envy. **(8)** Yet although all this pleases me well, the show of someone's corps of pages grazes my mind, fellows bought and more fussily clothed than usual and decked with gold, a whole squadron of gleaming slaves. Even the floor of the house which they tread is costly and the rooms glitter with riches spread in every corner, and the common people pay homage as escorts and attendants to the inheritance that is being squandered. Need I mention the channels flowing around the dinner guests, transparent to the very bottom, and the banquets matching their staging? **(9)** As I emerge from the prolonged inattention induced by thrift, this extravagance with its immense splendor has engulfed me and reverberated all around me. My gaze trembles and I raise my mind toward it more easily than my eyes. So I depart not worse but saddened, and I walk less tall among my possessions, and an unspoken sting comes over me, and uncertainty whether those luxuries are not better after all. None of this changes me, but it does not fail to disturb me.

(10) I decide to follow the commands of our teachings, and enter political life; I decide to win office and the fasces, not because I am seduced by purple and rods, but to be more useful and ready to assist my friends and relations and all our citizens, in fact all humankind. I readily follow Zeno, Cleanthes, and Chrysippus, although none of them entered public life, and none of them failed to send others. **(11)** When something has shaken my heart, unaccustomed to being buffeted around, when something occurs either undeserved—as many things are in all human life—or too slow in progress, or when insignificant matters demand a great deal of time, I turn away to leisure, just as for wearied cattle too the homeward steps are faster. I decide to confine my life within my own walls: "Let no one take any day from me that yields no return for so much expense; let my mind keep to itself, tend to itself, and do nothing foreign to its needs, nothing that requires the approval of an arbiter; let it love tranquility, free of public and private preoccupation." (12) But when some sterner reading matter has stimulated my mind and noble examples have goaded me on, I want to leap into the public life of the forum, lend my voice to one man and my services to another,[11] trying to do some good even if it will not benefit him, and check the arrogant behavior of some fellow wrongly puffed up by good fortune.

(13) Certainly I think it better where writing is concerned to contemplate the real themes and speak on account of them, but otherwise to let the words follow the ideas, so that unpretentious speech follows where they lead: "What is the use of composing material destined to last for ages. Won't you stop trying to ensure that you are not passed over in silence by posterity? You were born for death: a funeral kept silent is less troublesome. So to keep the time occupied, write something in a simple style for your own use, not for self-advertisement. (14) Men need less effort if they study for each day's needs." On the other hand, when the mind is uplifted by the grandeur of its contemplation, it becomes aspiring in its language and is eager to speak more loftily to match the inspiration, and speech is produced matching the dignity of its matter; then, forgetting the rule and a more disciplined judgment, I am borne aloft with an expression that is not my own.

(15) Not to pursue details for too long, this weakness of a good mind follows me in every affair. I am afraid that I shall shortly run empty, or what is more disturbing, that I shall be suspended on the edge of falling, that the affair may be more serious than I myself can discern. For we look at our personal affairs with easy affection, and favor always hinders good judgment. (16) I think many people could have achieved wisdom if they did not believe they had done so already, if they had not concealed some aspects of themselves, and passed over others with covered eyes. There is no reason for you to judge that we are ruined more by other men's flattery than our own. Who has dared to tell himself the truth? Who though set among flocks of praising and wheedling fellows has not flattered himself most of all? (17) So I am asking you, if you have any cure to put an end to my wavering, to believe that I deserve to owe my tranquility to you. I know that these disturbances of the mind are not life threatening, and bring no real disruption, but to express my complaint to you

by a true analogy, I am distressed not by the storm[12] but by seasickness; so take from me whatever evil this is and come to my aid as I flounder in sight of land.

[Seneca] (2.1) Indeed, I have been asking myself silently for some time now, Serenus, what to compare with this emotional state of mind, and I could not come to any closer parallel than the case of those who, recovering from a long and serious illness, are intermittently bruised by slight fevers and trivial jolts. When they have escaped the aftermath they are still disturbed by insecurity and stretch their hands out to doctors when they are already healthy, and think ill of every hint of fever in their body. The body of these men, Serenus, is not unhealthy but too unaccustomed to health, like the quivering of even a calm sea just when it has recovered from the storm. (2) So there is no need of those harsher remedies which we have already run through—to resist yourself at one time, at another be angry with yourself, and at another press on severely—but you need what comes last, to have faith in yourself and believe you are following the right path, not letting yourself be diverted by the cross tracks of many people running hither and yon, and of some who even wander around the path itself. (3) For what you are longing for is a great thing and the highest achievement, near to god: never to be shaken. The Greeks call this stable balance of the mind *euthymia* (there is a splendid treatise by Democritus about it). I call this tranquility, since we do not have to imitate and transpose their words in the form they use; but the actual thing must be marked by some name that ought to have the meaning, not the form, of the Greek designation. (4) So we are investigating how the mind may always move at an even and favorable pace and be well disposed to itself and glad to see its own qualities and not interrupt this joy, but always remain in a calm condition, neither rearing itself up nor thrusting itself down; this will be tranquility. Let us investigate in general how this can be reached. (5) You will take as much as you want from this generic cure. Meanwhile, the vice must be dragged into the open in its entirety so that everyone may recognize his own share; this is when you will understand how much less trouble you have with your self-disgust[13] than those who, bound to a showy proclamation and burdened by an immense claim, are kept in their pretense by shame rather than their own will.

(6) Everyone experiences the same problem, both persons harassed by instability and boredom and constant change of purpose, who always prefer what they have left behind, and others who wilt and yawn. Add another group who toss and turn like insomniacs and change position this way and that until they find rest from sheer exhaustion. By remaking the condition of their life, they finally settle in the mood in which they are overtaken not by distaste for change but by old age, too sluggish to innovate. Add others who are too unstable, not by fault of consistency but from lack of energy, persons who live not as they want but as they began. (7) There are countless characteristics of this vice but only one outcome, to be dissatisfied with oneself. This comes from a badly tuned mind and desires that are timid or unrealized, when they either don't dare as much as they desire, or don't achieve it and are utterly straining with hope; they are always unstable and fickle, as inevitably happens to men in suspense. They strain toward their goals by every method, and train and force themselves to dishonorable and difficult endeavors; and when their effort goes unrewarded they are tormented by the futile disgrace, and grieve, not that they wanted base things but that they wanted them in vain. (8) Then regret at their undertaking possesses them and fear of attempting it, and there steals into them the tossing of a mind that finds no way out, because they can neither command their desires nor gratify them, and the hesitation of a life that is not working itself out, and the neglect of a sluggish soul among its abandoned goals. (9) All these things are more burdensome when out of distaste for their laborious failure they take refuge in leisure, in solitary study, which a mind roused up for civil duties and eager for action cannot endure, nor can a restless nature containing too little inner consolation. So when the pleasures are withdrawn which sheer busyness offers to people running around, their mind cannot bear the house and solitude and its walls, and one hates to contemplate being left to oneself. (10) Hence that boredom and discontent with oneself and tossing around of a mind that never settles and that grim and sickly endurance of its leisure. This happens most of all when one feels shame to admit the reasons and one's shamefulness drives torments within, and desires confined in a small space choke themselves without any escape: hence comes the grief and wilting and thousand waves tossing an uncertain mind, kept in suspense by hopes unfulfilled and sad-

dened by hopes given up for lost. Hence comes the emotional state of persons abominating their leisure and complaining that they have nothing to do, and envy that is most hostile to others' progress. For unsuccessful inaction feeds their spleen and they want everyone to be destroyed, because they have not been able to advance. **(11)** Then this loathing of others' successes and despair of achieving one's own produces a mind enraged with fortune, lamenting the modern age and withdrawing into corners to brood over one's punishment, until a person is weary and ashamed of himself—since by nature the human mind is active and disposed to movement. Any source of arousing and distracting oneself is welcome, more so to the worst kind of intellects which are glad to be worn away by keeping busy. Just as some sores seek for hands that will hurt them and enjoy the contact, and whatever irritates delights the ugly disfigurement of their body, I would say that minds in which desires have broken out like nasty ulcers take pleasure in toil and harassment. **(12)** Some things delight our body too with a kind of pain, like tossing and shifting to the side that is not yet tired and seeking refreshment from one position after another. This sort of person is just like Achilles in Homer, now lying on his face and now his back, rearranging himself in different positions like a sick man, enduring nothing for long, and treating changes as a kind of cure.

(13) This is why men go touring on their travels and wander around the beach resorts; and their restlessness, ever hostile to present circumstances, tests itself now by sea, now on land. "Let's make for Campania now." Soon they are sated with fancy resorts. "Let's go and see wild country, making for the moorland of Bruttium and Lucania." But even in uninhabited places they miss some charm to give their pampered eyes relief from the stretches of neglect of rough terrain. "Let's make for Tarentum, with its much-praised harbor and milder winter weather, and a hinterland wealthy enough even for a crowd of long ago." "Now let's turn about toward the city": their ears have been deprived for too long of the din of applause, and now they are eager to enjoy human bloodshed.[14] **(14)** They embark on one journey after another and exchange one show for another. As Lucretius says:

This is how each man constantly is fleeing himself,

but what is the point of fleeing if he doesn't escape himself? He is his own escort and drives himself on, the most burdensome of companions. **(15)** So we ought to realize that we are suffering, not the fault of our surroundings, but our own fault; we are too weak to bear anything, enduring neither toil nor pleasure nor ourselves nor any thing for long. This condition has driven some people to death, because when they constantly changed their purpose, they returned to the same setup and had left no room for any novelty; they began to be sated with life and the world itself, and that old lament of spoiled indulgence came over them: "How long will we experience the same things?"

(3.1) You ask me what aid you should use against this boredom. It would be best, as Athenodorus[15] says, to keep oneself occupied with business and handling public affairs and the services of a citizen. For just as some men spend the day in the open sun doing exercises and tending their physical health, and it is most beneficial by far for athletes to nourish their arms and strength—the only task to which they have devoted themselves—for the greater part of their time, so when you prepare your mind for the contest of civil affairs, it is by far the finest thing to be actively occupied; for when a man resolves to make himself useful to his fellow citizens and mankind, he both exercises and advances, by setting himself in the midst of public services and administering both shared and private business according to his capacity. **(2)** "But," he says, "because simplicity is unsafe in this crazed life of ambition with so many slanderers twisting right action to make it seem worse, and because there will always be more hindrance than support, we ought to withdraw from the forum and public life. Yet a great mind has a way to unfold itself even in private; nor, in the way that the impulses of lions and wild creatures are confined by cages, is it true of humans, given that their greatest deeds are conducted in retirement. **(3)** So let him go into retreat on condition that wherever he has secluded his leisure, he will want to benefit individuals and the whole community by his intellect, his speech, and his advice. Indeed, it is not only the person who presents candidates for office and defends the accused, and gives his judgment on war and peace, who benefits the state; instead, whoever encourages the young; whoever, given the great scarcity of good instruction, instills virtue in minds; whoever seizes and holds back those rushing to make money and enjoy luxury and, if nothing more, at least slows them down, this person is doing public business in a private role. (4) Or does the magistrate who arbitrates between foreigners and citizens, or as urban praetor declares the views of his assessor to those who consult him, do more than whoever explains what is justice, or piety, or endurance, or courage, or contempt for death and knowledge of the gods, and how freely given a blessing is a good conscience?[16] (5) So if you devote the time to studies that you have subtracted from public duties, you will not have been a deserter or shirked your offering. Indeed, it is not only the fighter who stands in the battle line and defends the right or left wing who serves as a soldier, but the man who guards the gates or performs a function less dangerous but far from idle, and keeps the watch and is in charge of the equipment. Though these services are free of bloodshed, they count among military offices. (6) If you call yourself back to your studies you will escape any distaste for life, and not long for night from weariness of daylight; you will be neither a burden to yourself nor a superfluous nuisance to others; you will win many to your friendship, and all the best persons will come flowing toward you. For virtue, however hidden, never goes unnoticed but sends out signals of itself; whoever deserves it will find it from its tracks. (7) For if we eliminate all social intercourse and abjure the human race and live turned in on ourselves alone, the consequence of this isolation deprived of every study will be a dearth of things to do: we will start to raise some buildings and demolish others, and thrust back the sea, then channel streams to combat the difficulty of the site and make bad use of the time that nature has given us to spend. (8) Some of us use it sparingly, others squander it; some of us spend it in such a way that we can give an account of it, others so that we have nothing left over, the most shameful of situations. Often, an old man of advanced years has no evidence to prove he has lived long except his actual age."

(4.1) My dear Serenus, Athenodorus seems to me to have surrendered himself to our times, and retreated too soon. Not that I would deny that we should give way at some time, but we should do so stepping back gradually with our standards and military dignity still preserved: men are more respected and safer with their enemies when they surrender fully armed. This is what I think virtue and the lover of virtue should do. (2) If fortune[17] overcomes him and forestalls his ability to act, he should not instantly turn and flee unarmed seeking a hiding place, as if there were anywhere that fortune could not catch up with him, but he should approach his duties more sparingly and selectively find some activity in which he can be useful to the state. (3) He is not allowed to serve as a soldier; then let him seek office. He must live as a private citizen; let him be an advocate. He is enjoined to silence; then let him benefit his citizens with his silent encouragement. Is it dangerous even to enter the forum? Let him play the good companion and loyal friend and moderate guest in private homes, at the games, and at parties. Has he lost the duties of a citizen? Then let him perform those of a human being. (4) In this way and with exalted mind we have not confined ourselves within the walls of a single city, but released ourselves to do business with the whole world and declared the universe our native land, so as to give a wider battleground to our virtue. If the magistrate's tribunal is closed to you and you are banned from the speaker's platform or the assembly,[18] look behind you to see how great a space of vast regions and peoples lies open beyond; no place barred to you will be so great that there is not a greater area left. (5) But think whether all those scruples of yours are not a vice, since you are only willing to take part in state affairs as a consul, or a presiding magistrate or a herald in Greece, or head of state at Carthage. Supposing you were not willing to campaign except as a commanding officer or a captain? Even if others will occupy the front line and fate has set you back in the third line, fight from there with your voice, encouragement, example, and spirit; even with his hands cut off, the person who stands firm and supports it with his shouting finds something to contribute to his side.[19] (6) So do something of this sort. If fortune has displaced you from the first level in government, stand and give support with your shouting; and if someone chokes you by the throat, stand and give support with your silence. The effort of a good citizen is never without use; heard and seen, by his expression and nod and silent persistence and even by his gait, he is of help. (7) Just as some medications benefit by their mere smell, without taste or contact, so virtue, even hidden and at a distance, spreads advantage. Whether it strides and exercises its right over itself, or finds sorties risky and is forced to furl its sails; whether it is idle and silent and confined to a narrow place, or it is in the open field, in every kind of condition virtue is beneficial. Why do you think a man who keeps quiet is not useful as an example? **(8)** So it is by far the best to mix leisure with your affairs whenever a life of action will be barred by chance hindrances or the condition of the state. For never are all options so utterly fenced off that no room is left for honorable action.

(5.1) Can you find any city more wretched in any way than the Athenians' city[20] when the thirty tyrants tore it apart? They had killed thirteen hundred citizens, all the best men, but did not make an end of it; but their sheer savagery stimulated itself. In a city which held the Areopagus, that most scrupulous of courts, in which there was a senate and a people similar to the senate, the grim college of executioners met each day, and the unhappy senate house was crammed with tyrants: could that state repose in which there were as many tyrants as there were henchmen? Their minds could not even entertain any hope of recovering their freedom, and no scope for a cure appeared against such a powerful force of evils; for how could the poor city find so many Harmodii? **(2)** Yet Socrates was openly out in public life and comforted the mourning fathers and exhorted men despairing of the state, and reproached wealthy men fearing the consequences of their riches because they came too late to regret the dangers brought on by their greed; he bore himself as a mighty example for those willing to imitate him, walking as a free man among the thirty masters. **(3)** But Athens herself killed him in jail, and liberty did not tolerate the liberty of the man who had safely provoked the horde of tyrants; you learn from this that even in an oppressed state there is a chance for the wise man to put himself forward, and that in a flourishing and happy state envy and a thousand other evils dominate. **(4)** So, however the government presents itself, however fortune allows, we shall either expand ourselves or shrink ourselves in such a way that we shall, at any rate, be taking action, not paralyzed or strangled with fear. In fact, that man will be a hero who, when dangers threaten on all sides and weapons and chains clash all around, will not crush or conceal his virtue. For burying oneself is not a form of salvation. **(5)** Curius Dentatus[21] spoke the truth, as I think, when he said he preferred to be dead than go on living, for it is the worst of misfortunes to leave the ranks of the living before you die. But if you happen upon a less flexible period of politics, you will have to see to it that you claim more time for leisure and study;

just as you would make quickly for the harbour on a dangerous voyage, you should not wait for affairs to send you away but extricate yourself from them.

(6.1) Now we ought to examine ourselves first of all, then the business we are going to tackle, then the people for whom or with whom we will take it on.[22]

(2) We must perform a self-assessment[23] before all else, because we generally think ourselves able to do more than we actually can: one man is tripped up by confidence in his eloquence, another has demanded more from his inherited property than it could sustain, another has weighed down a weak constitution with a strenuous duty. The modesty of some is not suited to public life, which needs a confident gaze, and the arrogance of others does not suit the court; others do not keep their anger under control, and any cause for indignation carries them away into rash words; others again cannot control their wit and do not refrain from dangerous jokes; for all such men retirement is more advantageous than business. A fierce and impatient nature should avoid the provocations of frankness that will bring it harm.

(3) Then we must assess the enterprises we are tackling, and match our strength against the affairs we are going to attempt, since the performer must always have more strength than the work requires; burdens that are too great for the bearer necessarily overwhelm him. Besides, some enterprises are not so great as they are productive, bringing a load of other business with them. Others too should be shunned which will give birth to new and many-sided preoccupations; nor should you approach anything from which there is no freedom to withdraw; you should put your hand to such affairs as you can or at least hope to bring to an end, and abandon whatever spreads further in the process and does not come to an end where you intended.

(7.1) We should in any case be careful in choosing people, checking whether they are worthy to trust with a part of our life or whether the loss of our time will extend to them, since some people debit to us our services at their own initiative. (2) Athenodorus says he will not even attend a dinner at the house of a man who will not feel indebted to him on this account. You realize, I think, that he will go much less willingly to those who use the table to make themselves quits with the duties of friends, who count the courses as if they were acts of generosity, and as if they were being unrestrained in honor of an outsider; take away their witnesses and onlookers, and a private eating house[24] will give no pleasure. You must consider whether your nature is more suited to active business or leisured study and meditation, and lean in the direction your power of intellect will carry you. Isocrates laid hands on Ephorus and took him away from public life, believing him to be better suited to composing records of history.[25] In fact, coerced intellects respond badly; when nature resists, effort is wasted. (3) However, nothing will delight the mind as much as a true and sweet friendship. What a great blessing it is when there are breasts ready to receive your every secret and keep it safe, whose awareness you fear less than your own, whose talk soothes your anxiety, whose opinion eases your decision, whose cheerfulness routs your sadness, so that the mere sight of them delights you! We will choose those who are free of desires, as far as this is possible; for vices spread and leap to whoever is close at hand, doing harm by their contagion. (4) Just as in a plague we should take care not to keep vigil by people whose bodies have already been possessed and inflamed with disease because we will contract dangers and suffer from being merely breathed on, so when we select the character of friends we will take pains to take on the least infected; it is the beginning of disease to mix healthy elements with sickness. Yet I would not advise you to follow or draw to yourself no one except a wise man. For where will you find that person whom we have been seeking for so many ages? Let the least bad serve as the best. (5) You would hardly have the opportunity of a better choice if you sought out good men among the Platos and Xenophons and that crop of Socrates' brood, or if you had access to the generation of Cato, which produced numerous men worthy to be born in Cato's age[26] (as it did many men worse than at any other time, and contrivers of the greatest crimes; indeed, both groups were needed for Cato to be appreciated: he had to have both good men to commend himself and wicked men to test his power). As it is now, when there is such a shortage of good men, the choice would be less discriminating. (6) One should especially avoid grim fellows who deplore everything, men whom any excuse pleases to make complaints. Even if his loyalty and goodwill are certain, a troubled companion who groans at everything is the enemy of tranquility.

(8.1) Let us move on to inherited property, the worst fuel of human woes. If you were to match all the other causes of our distress against it, death, sicknesses, fears, longings, and the endurance of pains and toils, with those anxieties which our wretched money supplies, this side of the scale will weigh down heavily. (2) So we should think how much less pain comes from not having wealth than from losing it, and we will realize that poverty has less scope for torment because it has less to lose. You are wrong if you think wealthy people bear their losses with more spirit; the pain of a wound is the same for the biggest and smallest bodies. (3) Bion[27] said neatly that it was no less discomfort for bald men to be depilated than men with a good head of hair. You can be sure of the same in the case of rich and poor: their discomfort is the same, for each person's money has stuck to him and cannot be pulled away without his feeling it. So, as I said, it is more bearable and easier not to accumulate money than to lose it: that is why you will see people whom fortune has never smiled upon more happy than those it has deserted.[28] (4) Diogenes, a man of mighty intellect, saw this and made sure that he had nothing to be snatched from him.[29] Call that poverty, want, neediness, put any shameful name you want on this freedom from care; I will think he lacks happiness if you find me any other man who has nothing to lose. Either I deceive myself, or it is a king's life to be the one person among misers, frauds, robbers, and thieves who cannot be harmed. (5) If anybody doubts Diogenes' happiness, he can also have the same doubt about the condition of the immortal gods, wondering whether they live with too little happiness because they have neither estates nor parks nor lands made valuable by another farmer, nor a vast amount of interest in the market. Aren't you ashamed, whoever you are, to gape at riches? Come, then, look at the world: you will see that the gods are bare, conferring everything but possessing nothing. Do you think a man who has shed all his gifts of fortune is a pauper, or like the immortal gods? (6) You call Demetrius, Pompey's freedman,[30] happier, because he felt no shame at being wealthier than Pompey himself? He had the number of his slaves reported to him every day just like armies reported to a commander, although his riches should long before have consisted of two deputies and a larger cell. **(7)** But Diogenes' only slave ran away, and he did not think it worthwhile to fetch him back when he was pointed out. He said, "It's a disgrace if Manes can live without Diogenes, but Diogenes cannot live without Manes." I think he meant: "Fortune, mind your own business, you have nothing of yours with Diogenes; my slave has run away, or rather I have gone free." **(8)** A slave household wants clothing and diet, and you have to watch over so many bellies of ravenous creatures, to buy their clothes and guard their thieving hands and rely on the services of men weeping and cursing. How much more happy the man who owes nothing to anyone except himself, whom he can so easily refuse! **(9)** But since we don't have that much strength, we should shrink our inheritance to be less vulnerable to the wrongs of fortune. Bodies are more nimble in warfare which can be contracted into their armor than those which spill over, so that their own size exposes them to wounds; the best measure of money is one that neither sinks into poverty nor departs far from it.

(9.1) This measure will suit us, moreover, if we have already determined on thrift, without which no wealth is enough or sufficiently available, especially since the cure is nearby; and poverty itself with the aid of economy can turn itself into wealth. **(2)** Let us get used to rejecting display and calculating the usefulness of things, not their decorative value. Food should slake our hunger, drink our thirst, let lust flow where it has to; let us learn to rely on our own limbs and devise our grooming and diet not to match new models but as our ancestors suggested; let us learn to increase our restraint and restrain our extravagance, to moderate our vainglory, soothe our irritability, look on poverty with steady eyes, and practice thrift, even if it will cause more shame.[31] We should apply cheaply made remedies to our natural longings, keep in chains, as it were, our unbridled hopes and our mind hovering over the future, and focus on seeking wealth from ourselves rather than fortune. **(3)** Such a variety and unevenness of chances cannot ever be driven off without a great deal of storms assailing ships that spread out wide riggings; we must compress our affairs in a small space so that missiles fall wide, and this is why sentences of exile and disasters have turned into a cure and more grievous losses are cured by lighter ones. When the mind pays little heed to advice and cannot be healed more gently, why is it not in its interest if poverty and disgrace and overthrow are applied, and we set one evil against another? So let us get used to dining without an assembly of guests and being servants to fewer slaves and providing garments for the purpose for which they were invented and living more modestly. Not only in races and chariot contests but in these laps of life we must turn on the inside.

(4) The most liberal form of expense, that on studies, has justification as long as it has a limit. What is the point of countless books and libraries when their owner can scarcely read their labels in a lifetime? This overload burdens the student, and does not educate him; it is much better to entrust yourself to a few authors than be misled by an abundance of them. (5) Forty thousand books burned at Alexandria;[32] some other person may have praised this most noble monument to royal wealth, as did Livy, who called it the distinguished work of the refinement and dedication of kings. Yet this was not refinement and dedication but a studious extravagance, and not even studious, since they had procured the books not for study but for display. In the same way, most men ignorant of elementary education see books not as the tools of study but as the adornment of dinner parties. So let us obtain just as many books as is enough, but nothing for show. (6) You will say, "These expenses have been poured out more honorably like this than on Corinthian bronze and painted pictures." But whatever is excessive anywhere is a vice. What reason have you to pardon a man chasing bookcases of citrus and ivory, hunting the oeuvre of authors either unknown or disapproved, and yawning surrounded by so many thousand books, when the exterior and labels of his volumes are what please him the most? (7) So you will see in the houses of the laziest fellows all the histories and speeches, with pigeonholes rearing up to the roof; now even a library is fitted out between the cold baths and hot pools as an essential adornment of the house. Obviously I would forgive this if the blunder arose from an excessive desire for study; but in fact, those volumes searched out and copied with their images,[33] and the works of holy intellects, are obtained for show and to decorate the walls.

(10.1) But suppose you have fallen into some difficult kind of life, and either public or private fortune has set a noose for you unwittingly which you can neither untie nor break through. Think that men shackled together can at first scarcely endure the burden and hindrance on their legs; then, when they have resolved not to resent them but to endure, necessity teaches to wear them bravely, and habit makes it easy. You will find enjoyment and relaxation and pleasure in any kind of life if you want to make light of misfortunes rather than make them odious. (2) Nature has served us better on no other count: knowing the sorrows to which we were born, it invented habit as a softener of disasters, quickly making the most burdensome experiences grow familiar. No one would endure if the persistence of misfortunes had the same force as the first blow. (3) We are all shackled to fortune; some have a golden chain and a loose one, others narrow and dingy chains, but what difference does it make? The same watch has been set around all, and even those who have bound others are themselves bound, unless you think a chain is lighter on the left.[34] Some are bound by high offices, others by wealth; nobility weighs down on certain men and lowly birth on others; some men have the dominion of others hanging over their head, others their own dominion; sentences of exile keep some men in one place, priesthoods keep them in another. All life is a servitude. (4) So we must become used to our condition and complain about it as little as we can, seizing on whatever advantage it brings with it: there is nothing so bitter that a steady mind cannot find comfort in it. Often, small spaces have been opened up for many purposes by the skill of the architect, and organization has made even the narrowest place habitable. Apply reason to your difficulties; harsh circumstances can be softened and narrow spaces expanded and heavy burdens made less oppressive to people who bear them skillfully. (5) Besides, we should not send our desires into a far distance but permit them to emerge near at hand, since they will not bear being utterly confined. Once you have left aside what is impossible or difficult, we may follow goals set near and teasing our hope, but we must know that everything is equally trivial, with a different exterior but all equally hollow inside. And we should not envy those who stand above us; what seemed lofty is merely steep. (6) Again, those whom an unfair lot has set on a knife edge will be safer by removing pride from circumstances themselves proud and lowering their fortune as much as they can to level ground. Many are obliged to stick to their summit, since they cannot come down from it except by a fall; but let them bear witness that this is their greatest burden, to be compelled to be burdensome to others, and that they are not exalted on high but impaled.

By justice, mildness, and humanity, let them prepare with a generous and kind hand many kinds of protection for the success that they expect with increased freedom from care. However, nothing will free us so well from these waves tossing the mind as always to set up some limit to growth, not leaving to fortune the decision to cease, but spontaneously stopping a long way short; just so some desires will sharpen the mind and, once limited, will not lead it into a vast or uncertain distance.

(11.1) This discourse of mine concerns men who are imperfect, in between, and lacking in health, not the wise man. He need not walk timidly or tentatively; such is his self-confidence that he doesn't hesitate to engage with fortune and will never yield his place to it. And he has no cause to fear here, because he counts not only slaves and property and rank but also his own body and eyes and hand and whatever makes life dearer to a man and even his own self as mere contingencies of chance, and lives as if he has it on loan and is ready to return it without sadness to those who claim it back. (2) But he is not therefore cheap in his own eyes because he knows he is not his own, but he will act as scrupulously and carefully in all things, as a devout and holy man is accustomed to protect what is entrusted to him. And whenever he is ordered to return it, he will not complain to fortune but will say: "Thank you for what I have possessed and owned. (3) I cherished your property at a great cost, but because you order me I give and yield it thankfully and gladly. If you want me to keep anything of yours even now, I will keep it. If you decide otherwise, I hereby return my silver, both in plate and minted coinage,[35] and my house and household." If nature has called for what it entrusted to us before,[36] we will say to it also: "Take back my mind, now improved from the state in which you gave it; I am not turning back or fleeing; you have here readily and willingly offered what you gave me unawares; take it back!" (4) What is bad about returning whence you came? Anyone who does not know how to die well will live badly. So we must first reduce our valuation of this matter, and count our breath cheap. As Cicero says,[37] "We loathe gladiators if they desire to obtain their life at all cost; we wish them well if they proudly show their contempt for it." You might guess that the same thing happens to us; for often cowardly dying is the cause of death. (5) Fortune, who plays her own games, says: "Why should I keep you safe, you wretched and trembling creature? You will be wounded and pierced even more deeply because you don't know how to offer your throat; but you will live longer and die more quickly for taking the steel, not by lowering your neck or fending it off with your hands, but with brave spirit." (6) The person who fears death will never do anything worthy of a living human being; but if he knows it was ordained when he was first conceived, he will live as prescribed and maintain his behavior with the same strength of mind, so that nothing which happens is sudden. By anticipating whatever is possible as about to happen, he will soften the onslaughts of all evils, since they bring nothing new to men prepared and awaiting them, whereas evils weigh down men free of care and expecting only happiness. (7) There is illness, captivity, collapse, and fire. None of these is sudden; I knew the troubled habitation in which nature had enclosed me. There has so often been the cry of death in my neighborhood; so often, torches and tapers have escorted premature funerals past my threshold; on my side there has often been the sound of a crash from the bricks of a collapsing building; a night has carried off comrades, many of those whom the forum and senate and conversation had bound to me, and torn apart the linked hands[38] of comrades <tied to Fortune>; should I wonder that dangers which always hovered around me have finally reached me? The majority of men do not think of storms when they are about to make a voyage.

(8) I shall never feel ashamed of quoting a bad source in a good cause. Publilius,[39] more passionate than tragic or comic talents whenever he abandoned the follies of the mime and words aimed at the gallery, among many other sayings more courageous than the tragic buskin let alone the mime curtain, also made this comment:

What can happen to one man can happen to any man.

If anyone lets this sink into his heart and gazes on all other men's misfortunes (and there is a vast supply of them every day) as if there was a free path to himself, he will arm himself long before he is assailed: it is too late for the mind to be trained in endurance of dangers after the dangers arise. (9) "I didn't think this would happen," and

"Did you ever believe this would come to pass?" Why not, then? What riches are there not followed at their back by need, hunger, and beggaring? What rank, whose magisterial toga and augural staff and patrician sandals,[40] are not accompanied by discredit and well-known reproach and a thousand black marks and extreme contempt? What kingdom is there for which ruin and trampling and a master and executioner are not ready and waiting? And those blows are not separated by great intervals, but there is a moment of an hour between the throne and another man's knees. **(10)** So know that every rank is reversible, and whatever befalls another man can befall you too. You are wealthy. Are you wealthier than Pompey? When Gaius, his old kinsman and new host, opened Caesar's house to him so as to close his own, there was no bread or water. Although he possessed so many rivers springing up and coming to an end in his own territory, he was a beggar for drops of water; he perished of hunger and thirst in his kinsman's palace while his heir commissioned a public funeral for his kin while he was starving.[41] **(11)** You have held the highest honors; were any as great or unhoped-for or universal as Sejanus held?[42] The day the senate escorted him to the forum, the people minced him up into shreds; the man on whom gods and men had bestowed whatever could be heaped up, had no remains for the executioner to drag along. **(12)** Imagine you are a king: I will not refer you to Croesus,[43] who saw his pyre both kindled and extinguished while still alive, and became a survivor not only of his kingdom but of his death; I won't refer you to Jugurtha, whom the Roman people saw on show within a year of dreading him.[44] We saw Ptolemy king of Africa and Mithridates of Armenia under guard appointed by Gaius;[45] one was sent into exile, the other kept wishing to be released on a better guarantee. In such turmoil of affairs turned topsy-turvy, if you do not treat whatever is possible as future, you are giving misfortune strength against you, strength that is crushed by anyone who foresees it.

(12.1) The next among our concerns is not to toil over superfluous things or from a superfluous motive, that is, not to desire things we cannot achieve, or to understand too late after much sweat the emptiness of these desires. I mean that our effort should not be futile and without result, or that the result be unworthy of our effort; for the consequence of these disappointments is sadness, whether the business does not succeed or its success brings shame.[46] **(2)** We should cut back on rushing about like most men, who go the rounds between houses and theaters and public places; they are submitting to other men's business, always acting as if they were making something happen. If you asked one of them leaving his house: "Where are you going? What are you planning?" he will answer you: "By Jove I don't know, but I am going to see some people and do some business." (3) They wander purposelessly, looking for business, but they do not what they intended but whatever they come upon. Their chase is ill considered and futile, like that of ants crawling over bushes, driven up to the tip and then down again empty. Most men lead a life like theirs, and one would quite fairly call their behavior restless idleness.

(4) You will feel pity for certain people rushing around as if they were called to a fire: so frantically do they push aside those in their path and knock down themselves and others, while running around to greet someone who will not greet them in return, or to follow the funeral procession of a stranger, or to attend the lawsuit of a frequent litigator or the wedding of a frequent bridegroom; and when escorting a litter, they have carried it in certain areas. After that they return home with superfluous exhaustion and swear they don't know why they went out or where they had been, although the next day they will wander along in the same tracks. (5) So let all your effort be directed to some purpose, and let it be focused somewhere. It is not industry that makes people restless, but false images of things are driving them to madness; for not even madmen act without some hope. The appearance of something eggs them on, and their deluded mind does not detect its emptiness. (6) Just like this, each of those who go out to swell the crowd is led all around the town by silly, trivial excuses. Even when a man has no cause for toil, the dawn drives him forth; and when he has been crushed in vain at many men's doorways and has thoroughly greeted their personal assistants, shut out by many, he finds it harder to meet himself[17] at home than anyone else. (7) This evil is the origin of that loathsome fault: eavesdropping, hunting out public and private matters, and knowing many affairs which are neither told nor overheard without risk.

(13.1) I think Democritus was following this principle when he began, "Whoever wants to live tranquilly should not do much business, public or private." Surely he was referring to superfluous affairs.

For if they are essential, then not just many but countless tasks have to be done both privately and publicly; but when no binding duty summons us, we should check our activities. **(2)** The man who has a lot of business often gives fortune power over himself. It is safest to test it seldom, and for the rest always to have it in mind and make himself no promises about it: "I shall make a voyage, unless something happens," "I shall be elected praetor, unless something prevents it," and "My business deal will work out well unless something forestalls it."⁴⁸ **(3)** This is why we say that nothing ever befalls the wise man against his expectations; we are exempting him not from the misfortunes of men but from their mistakes. For him, things turn out not as he wanted but as he anticipated; above all he anticipated that something could oppose his plans. Then too the pain of an abandoned desire necessarily falls more lightly on the mind when you have not promised yourself a good outcome.

(14.1) We ought to make ourselves flexible so as not to indulge too much in fixed plans, but to pass on to whatever chance has brought to us and not fear a change of either course or rank, provided that frivolity, a vice most hostile to calm, does not seize on us. For obstinacy, from which fortune often steals something, is necessarily anxious and wretched, and frivolity is much more troublesome since it never keeps itself under control. Both conditions are hostile to tranquility: not being able to change anything, and not being able to endure anything. **(2)** In any case the mind must be called back into itself from all externals. Let it have faith in itself, rejoice in itself, respect its own qualities, and as far as possible withdraw from what is alien to it and focus on itself, not feeling losses, interpreting kindly even adversities. **(3)** When Zeno⁴⁹ was informed of his shipwreck and heard that all his possession had sunk, he said: "Fortune is ordering me to practice philosophy less encumbered." A tyrant kept threatening Theodorus with death, and deprivation of burial. He said: "You have something to be satisfied with, a half pint of blood in your power. As far as burial is concerned: you are a big fool if you think it affects me whether I rot under the earth or upon it." **(4)** Iulius Canus, a very great man, who does not deserve any less admiration because he was born in our age, after a prolonged quarrel with Gaius, when that Phalaris said as he was leaving, "Don't deceive yourself with a foolish hope, I have ordered your execution," said: "Thank you, most excellent emperor!"

(5) I don't know what he thought, but many ideas come to me. He wanted to be insulting and show the cruelty of a world in which death was a kindness? Or was he reproaching Gaius for his daily madness? For men would thank him both when their children had been killed and when their property was taken away. Or did it mean that he gratefully accepted freedom? Either way he answered with great spirit. **(6)** Someone will say, "Gaius could have ordered him to live after this," but Canus was not afraid of that. Gaius's trustworthiness in that sort of command was notorious. Would you believe that Canus passed the ten days intervening before his execution without any anxiety? It is scarcely plausible what that man said and did and how he maintained tranquility. **(7)** He was playing "brigands" when the centurion leading a group of men to execution ordered him too to be called out. When he was called, he counted the pieces and said to his friend, "See that you don't tell a lie after my death, that you were victorious." Then he nodded to the centurion and said, "You will bear witness that I was one point ahead." Do you think Canus was playing with that board game? He was mocking. **(8)** His friends were sad to lose such a man, and he said, "Why are you mournful? You are trying to discover whether souls are immortal: I shall soon know." He never ceased from examining the truth and conducting an investigation into his own death, even at the end. **(9)** His private philosopher escorted him, and the tomb at which there was a daily sacrifice to Julius Caesar, our god, was not far; he said, "Canus, what are you thinking now? Or what is your state of mind?" Canus said, "I am determined to watch at that swiftest of moments whether the mind will feel its departure." And he promised that if he found anything out, he would go the round of his friends and show them what was the condition of souls. **(10)** See this tranquility in the midst of a storm, see a mind worthy of immortality, which calls up its destiny as evidence of the truth, and taking that final step questions his departing soul and does not just learn something until his death but even from it; no one continued philosophizing longer. We shall not leave this great man in haste, and he must be spoken of with devotion; we shall consign you[50] to lasting memory, most glorious hero, a great part of the disaster that was Gaius's reign.

(15.1) But it is useless to cast away the reasons for private sadness; for sometimes loathing for the human race takes possession of us.

When you think how rare honesty is and how unknown is innocence, and good faith is scarcely maintained at all unless it is in men's interest, and such a crowd of successful crimes confronts us, along with the profits and losses of lust, both equally hateful—not to mention ambition so unable to keep within its limits that its shamefulness is glaring—the mind is driven into night, and the darkness rises up as if the virtues had been overthrown, since one cannot hope for them and gains nothing from possessing them. (2) Therefore we must bend so as to make all the vices of the crowd seem not hateful but absurd, and imitate Democritus rather than Heraclitus. For whenever Heraclitus went into public places he wept, whereas Democritus laughed: to Heraclitus all our activities seemed wretched, to Democritus sheer folly.[51] So we must mitigate everything and bear it with an easy mind; it is more humane to make fun of life than to bewail it. (3) Add to this that the man who laughs at it rather than mourns does more service to the human race: the former has left it some hope of benefit; the other foolishly laments what he despairs of being able to be corrected. When you consider things at large, the man who does not control his laughter shows a greater mind than the one who cannot control his tears, since laughter stirs up the mildest emotion and thinks nothing great or serious or even unhappy from such a great to-do. (4) Let anyone set before his eyes the individual reasons for our gladness or sadness, and he will know that what Bion said was true: all the business of humans is very much like the beginning, and their life is no more holy or earnest than their conception; those born from nothing are reduced to nothing. (5) But it is better to accept common behavior and human vices calmly, dissolving into neither laughter nor tears; for it is everlasting wretchedness to be tormented by the misfortunes of others, and an inhuman pleasure to delight in them, just as it is a pointless act of humanity to weep if someone is burying his son and to feign an expression of grief. (6) In one's own misfortunes, a person should act so as to grant to grief only what nature demands,[52] not what is required by custom. Indeed, most men shed tears for show and have dry eyes whenever they have no onlooker, thinking it shameful not to weep when everyone is doing it. This evil of depending on other men's opinion has implanted itself so deeply that even the simplest matter, grief, has turned into pretense.

(16.1) The following considerations are customarily a just reason for making men sad and bringing on distress. When the deaths of good men are bad, when Socrates is compelled to die in prison and Rutilius to live in exile, and Pompey and Cicero to offer their throats to former dependents, while Cato, the living image of virtues, falls on his sword[53] and makes public the truth about himself and the republic, we must be tormented that fortune pays out such unjust recompense. What could each individual hope for when he saw the best persons suffering what is worst? **(2)** So what is the issue? Look at how each of them bears it, and if they were brave, feel their loss with the spirit of those persons. But if they died like women and cowards, nothing has been lost; either their virtue deserves your approval, or they do not deserve that you should regret their cowardice. Indeed, what is more shameful than for the greatest men to make others timid by their brave deaths? **(3)** Let us praise a man so often worthy of praise and say: "You are so much more fortunate as you are more brave! You have escaped all mischances, envy, sickness. You have left your imprisonment; you did not seem to the gods to deserve bad fortune: rather, you did not deserve that fortune should still wield any power over you." But if men recoil and look back toward life at the moment of death, we must seize them by force.[54] **(4)** I shall not weep for anyone happy, or weeping. The first has wiped away my tears himself; the other has shown by his tears that he is not worthy of any. Am I to weep for Hercules because he is burned alive, or Regulus[55] because he is pierced by so many nails, or Cato because he wounds his own wounds? All those figures discovered at the expense of a little time how to become everlasting, and reached immortality by their death.

(17.1) Another serious source of anxieties is if you present yourself anxiously and do not show your nature openly to others, as is the life of many, falsified and adjusted for display; for constant watching over ourselves torments us, fearing to be caught other than is usual. We are never free from care if we believe we are being evaluated as often as we are seen; for many things happen to bare men against their will, and even if such cautious concern over oneself succeeds, life is not pleasant or carefree for men living continually under a mask. **(2)** But what great pleasure is experienced by genuine and ungroomed honesty, thrusting no screen before its habits! Yet even this life suffers the risk of scorn, if everything is laid open to all, since there are those who disdain whatever they have come close to. But virtue runs no risk of being cheapened when it is set before the eyes, and it is better to be scorned for one's honesty than tormented by constant pretense. Only let us put a limit on it; it makes a great difference whether you live honestly or carelessly.

(3) One must also retreat into oneself frequently; for association with unlike companions disrupts a settled condition and stirs up emotions and inflames whatever is weak or neglected in the mind. Still, solitude and company must be blended and alternated. The first will bring on a longing for people, the second for ourselves, and each condition will be the cure for the other; solitude will heal loathing for the crowd and the crowd one's weariness of solitude.

(4) And we should not keep our mind always straining at the same level, but call it away to jesting: Socrates did not blush to play with young boys; Cato[56] eased his mind with wine when it was exhausted by public concerns; and Scipio bestirred that body of a triumphant general and soldier in the dance, not weakening it in soft motions as is the custom now for men mincing beyond womanly affectation even in their manner of walking, but as those men of old used to step out in manly fashion during play and public holidays, risking no loss, even if they were observed by their enemies. (5) We must give our minds relaxation: they will arise from rest better and more vigorous. Just as we should not impose commands on fertile lands—for uninterrupted fertility will quickly drain them—so constant toil will break down the impulses of our minds, which will recover strength after being released and relaxed for a short while: constant laboring leads to blunted and languid minds. (6) Our desire for this would not be so great if sport and play did not provide a natural pleasure; but frequent enjoyment of this often will take away all power and vitality from minds; for sleep is necessary for refreshment, but if you continued it night and day it will turn into death. It makes a great difference whether you relax something or slacken it. (7) The founders of our laws established feast days so that men should be assembled publicly for cheerful enjoyment, inserting it as a necessary moderation of labors. As I said, some great men gave themselves monthly holidays on fixed days; some again divided every

day between leisure and concerns. We remember the great orator Asinius Pollio, who let no business keep him after the tenth hour; he did not even read his correspondence after that hour, to make sure no new concerns arose from it, but put down the weariness of the whole day during those two hours.[57] There were some who interrupted work at midday and postponed some lighter business until afternoon. Our ancestors also forbade any new proposal to be brought before the senate after the tenth hour. The soldiery divides the watches, and the night is exempt from duty for those who had returned from a sortie by day. **(8)** We must indulge the mind and give it leisure in place of nourishment and energy. One must even wander on open strolls so that the mind may gain strength and raise itself with the open sky and abundant fresh air; sometimes riding on a journey and a change of place will give strength, as will company and more lavish drinking. Sometimes we should even come close to tipsiness, not so as to drown us, but to calm us down; for this washes away our cares and stirs the mind deeply and remedies sadness as it does some sicknesses. The inventor of wine was called Liber[58] not from the license of the tongue but because he frees the mind from enslavement to cares, supports it, and makes it lively and bolder for every enterprise. **(9)** But there is a healthy measure of wine as of liberty. People believe that Solon and Arcesilaus[59] indulged in wine, and Cato was reproached with drunkenness; whoever made this reproach will more easily make the charge honorable than Cato shameful. But we must not do this often, for fear our mind takes on a bad habit; but still at times it must be stretched in joyful liberty, and grim sobriety dispelled for a short time. **(10)** For whether we believe the Greek poet, "that is it sometimes pleasant to go crazy," or Plato, that "the man in control of himself knocked on the doors of poetry in vain," or Aristotle, that "no great intellect is without a mixture of craziness," a mind cannot utter anything great and above other men unless it is stirred up.[60] **(11)** When it despises common and routine things and rises more loftily with divine inspiration, then and only then does it intone something greater than mortal speech. Nothing sublime and set on high can come to it as long as it is at home with itself; it ought to desert its customary mode and be borne away and bite the bridle and carry off its rider and bear him where he feared to rise.

(12) Dear Serenus, you have heard what can preserve tranquility, what can restore it, and what offers opposition to creeping vices; but know this, that none of these devices is strong enough for those who maintain weakness, unless intense and constant care surrounds a failing mind.

Notes

Abbreviation

OLD   *Oxford Latin Dictionary*, ed. P. G. W. Glare, 2nd ed. (Oxford: Clarendon Press, 2012).

Introduction

1. See on this most recently "Seneca on Self Assertion," pp. 346–51 of Inwood 2005.

2. The parallel between physical and mental/moral sickness was a Hellenistic commonplace; cf. (after Seneca) Plutarch's essay "Whether the Sicknesses of the Mind or of the Body are Worse," *Moralia* 500b–502b; Loeb Classical Library vol. 6). Even the words *observatio sui* ("constant watching") in 17.1 evoke the medical practice of watching patients (*epitērēsis*) to observe the progress of their symptoms.

3. See Sorabji 1997 and Williams 1997.

4. See Griffin 1976, 447–48.

5. I refer here to the valuable exploration by Kaster 2005 in chap. 5, "The Dynamics of *Fastidium* and the ideology of disgust."

6. It is possible that Seneca knew Democritus only indirectly, but for a more positive assessment see chap. 2, "Epicurus and Democritean Ethics," in Warren 2002.

On Tranquility of Mind

7. The opening words put into Serenus's mouth announce the important topic of self-examination and the concern to heal the self; see further 2.7 and 2.9, with the corresponding stress on therapy in 14.2.

8. This is the first reference to Serenus's condition as a mental or moral disease.

9. Latin *animus* covers Greek *dianoia*, the moral and intellectual aspects of personality; usually it is best translated as "mind," but when it is associated with mood or morale I have translated it as "spirit," in the sense that we use *spirited*.

10. Like bulimics, Romans deliberately made themselves vomit to escape the consequences of overeating.

11. The forum was until the principate one public space, the Forum Romanum, to which Augustus added the Forum of Julius Caesar and Forum Augustum. Roman law courts both civil and criminal were held in the open forum, and men negotiated business with and for friends there. Service to friends, equal or dependent (clients), was a primary elite obligation, second only to serving the state itself.

12. Throughout the dialogue, incidental imagery of sea and storm recalls the original sense of *tranquility*—calm at sea.

13. On self-disgust (*fastidium sui*) and the different applications of *fastidium* in general, see chap. 5 of Kaster 2005.

14. This was well expressed by Horace *Epistles* 1.11.26 ("men who rush across the sea change their environment but not their state of mind") and by Lucretius before him. Seneca's short quotation from Lucretius 3.1068 is taken from an extended passage describing self-discontent and its effect on behavior.

15. Athenodorus of Tarsus was the young Augustus's instructor in philosophy and stayed on to advise the imperial family. We are not certain where the translated quotation and mere paraphrase of his teaching begins and ends. I have followed Reynolds' text (1977), which assigns to him all of 3.2–8.

16. Seneca is still thinking in terms of senatorial careers and magistracies. At Rome the praetor peregrinus supervised disputes between Romans and foreigners; the urban praetor presided over disputes between citizens.

17. Fortune is held responsible for all apparently undeserved misfortunes. Besides operating in political life, it takes on a more prominent role from chapter 8 onward.

18. A man condemned to exile or disgrace (*infamia*) would be barred from appearing in court or attending the popular assembly; nor could anyone appear on the speaker's platform unless invited by the presiding magistrate. Seneca points to the contrast by evoking the un-Roman offices of *prytanis*, *kerux*, and *Sufes*.

19. This recalls the legend of Aeschylus's brother, who lost both hands at Salamis but fought on; Seneca's nephew Lucan echoes this legend in his account of a fictitious hero in the sea battle at Massilia. In film comedy, Monty Python created the knight who fought on though deprived of all four limbs.

20. The thirty tyrants took over the government of Athens in 404 BCE at the behest of the victorious Spartans. Athens's democratic institutions included the Areopagus, an ancient religious court, the *boule*, or council of five hundred, and the *ecclesia*, the open assembly of citizens. The rhetorical plural, *Harmodii*, denotes imitators of Harmodius and Aristogeiton who assassinated the tyrant Hipparchus in 514 BCE. Socrates survived the tyranny but was condemned to death by representatives of the restored democracy in 399 BCE.

21. Curius was consul in 290 BCE and famous for his exemplary refusal of an enemy bribe and also his simple way of life (Valerius Maximus 4.3.5). I have not found the source for this saying.

22. This seems to be a list of Seneca's topics in sequence: first assessing one's own capacities, then the enterprise to be taken on, then the human associates or beneficiaries. But it is only a partial analysis of the forthcoming chapters 6–9.

23. This self-assessment recalls Serenus's initial self-scrutiny, and subsequent references to self criticism in 2.7 and 2.9, and 14.2 below.

24. This strange phrase condemns the giving of dinner invitations as fulfillment of obligation to clients and inferiors; it is as if the patron were using his dining hall as a cheap eating house, where humble people paid for what they ate.

25. Isocrates (436–338 BCE) instructed elite students in oratory, and it is said that he felt his pupil Ephorus needed the spur to rouse him; hence he was better suited to historical writing. His extensive historical work was famous but survives only in excerpts of later writers such as Diodorus.

26. Which Cato is this? The Censor, renowned for his virtue and vigor (b. ca. 235 BCE) or his descendant Cato "of Utica," famed for his Stoic integrity and living in the generation of the civil war. Most probably Seneca means the latter Cato.

27. Bion of Borysthenes was a Hellenistic Cynic street preacher associated with pithy sayings in the anecdotal tradition; see Diogenes Laertius 4.7.

28. In this discussion of external goods, fortune is shown as in control; compare 8.5 below, where worldly assets are called gifts of fortune (*fortuita*).

29. Diogenes of Sinope, the notorious fourth-century Cynic, celebrated in the anecdotal tradition (cf .Diogenes Laertius 6.20–83).

30. Romans regarded freedmen (that is, ex-slaves) as low class, but Greek freedmen such as Pompey's Demetrius were enormously wealthy and powerful. Plutarch's *Life of Cato Minor* 13 reports that a whole Asian city poured out to welcome and honor this Demetrius.

31. The Latin text of this phrase is damaged beyond restoration, but it contains a reference to shame.

32. This estimate of the holdings in the great library of Alexandria probably comes from the passage in Livy quoted in the same sentence. The library, assembled by Ptolemy Philadelphos in the early fourth century, was partly burned when Caesar was besieged on the island in 47 BCE, but different sources blame different attacks on Alexandria for the library's destruction.

33. Illuminated books were an Alexandrian invention; they came to Rome in the last century BCE, in time for Varro to compile an encyclopedia of great men, each illustrated with his portrait.

34. "On the left" presumably refers to the escort chained to his prisoner.

35. This is the typical language of wills and private agreements.

36. The gifts of nature are life itself and health; the rest are gifts of fortune.

37. This is a loose quotation of Cicero's defense speech "On Behalf of Milo" 92.

38. A possible interpretation of the Latin text here might take *copulatos* as an allusion to being bound to fortune, and treat it as subsequent to "the linked hands of comrades."

39. The mime writer Publilius Syrus was challenged by Julius Caesar to perform in his own mimes, a humiliating act for a gentleman. But he composed such powerful one-liners that a whole body of sayings developed and were taught in schools under his name. Cf. Seneca *Letters* 16.

40. These are the emblems of magistrates (*toga praetexta*), augurs (the *lituus*), and patricians: senators and patricians wore distinctive footwear, but this is the only example of *lora* = *shoestraps* cited by *OLD*.

41. This obscure story is not about the general Pompey and Julius Caesar, but about a later Pompeius whom Gaius Caesar (Caligula) imprisoned (as a guest!) and starved to death in his own palace. It is not attested elsewhere.

42. Aelius Seianus was Tiberius's prefect of the Praetorian guard. He ingratiated himself with the old emperor, slandering and destroying other members of the imperial family and isolating the emperor from affairs at Rome, until Tiberius was undeceived by a warning and sent a letter from Capri to Rome denouncing Seianus, who was executed overnight as a traitor. Tacitus' account of his fall in the *Annales* is lost, but there is a graphic description in Juvenal 10.66–77.

43. Croesus, the sixth-century king of Lydia famed for his wealth, is the center of Herodotus's moral tale in *Histories* 1.30–33, in which Solon warns him that no man can be called happy until he reaches death. Defeated by Cyrus, he was about to be burned on the pyre when he cried out that Solon had been right (Herodotus 1.86), and was spared. (Cf. Plutarch *Solon* 27.6–7 and 28.2.)

44. Jugurtha, the usurping king of Numidia, was betrayed and defeated, and brought to Rome to walk on display in Marius's triumph in 105 BCE.

45. These kings, successors of the ruling Ptolemies and the great Mithridates, were brought to Rome, tricked, and imprisoned by Gaius (Suetonius *Caligula* 26, 35; Dio 58.26.4, 59.25).

46. This section returns to the starting point of 6.1.

47. Given the opening of the dialogue in Serenus's self-discontent (cf. 1.4), this is the ultimate condemnation; such men have no time to know their inner selves.

48. This provisional anticipation resembles the Stoic practice of diluting the impact of misfortune by anticipating it (*praemeditatio malorum*); cf. Cicero *Tusculan Disputations* 3.29, 3.34.

49. As is his practice, Seneca follows two Greek anecdotes (about the Stoic Zeno and the Cyrenaic Theodorus, the latter threatened by Lysimachus with death) with a more detailed narrative of a Roman moral hero from the recent tyrannical reign of Caligula. The story is otherwise unknown. Within the story, Seneca equates Caligula with Phalaris, the notorious Sicilian tyrant who enclosed his victims in a bronze bull and roasted them to death.

50. Seneca apostrophizes Canus to mark his respect; this is the only apostrophe in this dialogue.

51. This contrast with the gloomy Heraclitus is the single most-quoted story about Democritus. Cf. Seneca *On Anger* 2.10.5.

52. Sorrow for the dead or grief at one's own bereavement is apparently accepted as natural; and nature here is contrasted with custom.

53. Opposed to Socrates' unjust death in prison are four Roman examples: the exile of the honest governor Rutilius in 91 BCE (much quoted by Cicero as a precedent for his own honor in exile); the murder of Pompey in 48 BCE by a Roman soldier acting on Egyptian order; the killing of Cicero by order of the triumvirate in 43; and Cato's suicide in 46, which was treated as a martyrdom and rehearsed in gory detail, because he reopened the wound he had himself inflicted (see below).

54. The normal context of the Latin idiom "lay hands on them" is the arresting of an offender to take him to court (see *OLD*, s.v. *inicere* 6b).

55. Hercules was believed to be mortal until, in agony from the poisoned shirt of Nessus, he burned himself to death on Mount Oeta. Atilius Regulus, Roman commander of an unsuccessful raid on Carthage in 257 BCE, was sent back to ask for ransom for the captive Romans. He persuaded the senate to refuse the ransom and went back to Carthage as he had promised, to be tortured to death. The story, told in detail by Cicero *On Duties* 3.99 and cited as an example of integrity in Horace *Odes* 3.5, was subsequently used by Seneca repeatedly in *On Providence* 3.3 and 3.9 (along with Rutilius, Cato, and Socrates).

56. The saintly Cato of Utica was known to spend the night drinking; men turned away so as not to see him staggering home. Playing with boys (not, perhaps, so innocent), drinking, and dancing are put on an equal footing with licensed relaxation.

57. Asinius Pollio (76 BCE–4 CE), a Late Republican orator, was made consul in 40 BCE, and won a triumph in Illyria. He then withdrew from partisan politics and established the first public library at Rome (before Augustus), winning respect as an advocate and promoter of culture.

58. The Italian fertility god Liber was equated with the Greek Dionysus, and his name was understood as "liberator," matching the Greek title *Lyaeos*.

59. The sources for this claim are unknown, but we see from, e.g., Horace *Epistles* 1.19.7 that it was customary to cite drinking as the inspiration of poets and other great men.

60. There are echoes here of Greek lyric, Plato's *Phaedrus* (as below), and Horatian lyric (*Odes* 2.7, 4.12.28). The passing echo of *Phaedrus* leads into the unmistakable analogy of the fiery horse in the chariot team of the soul (*Phaedrus* 246a–247c).

Editions and Translations

Costa, C. D. N., ed. 1974. *Seneca*. London: Routledge and Kegan Paul.

———. 1994. *Four dialogues of Seneca*. Translation and commentary. Warminster: Aris and Phillips.

———, ed. and trans. 1997. *Dialogues and Letters*. London: Penguin.

Reynolds, L. D., ed. 1977. *L. Annaei Senecae Dialogorum libri duodecim*. Oxford: Oxford University Press.

Bibliography

Griffin, M. T. 1974. "*Imago vitae suae*." In *Seneca*, ed. C. D. N. Costa, pp. 1–38. London: Routledge and Kegan Paul.

———. 1976. *Seneca: A Philosopher in Politics*. Oxford: Oxford University Press / Clarendon Press.

———. 1986. "Philosophy, Cato and Suicide." *Greece & Rome* 33:64–77, 192–202.

Inwood, Brad, ed. 2003. *Cambridge Companion to the Stoics*. Cambridge: Cambridge University Press.

———. 2005. *Reading Seneca: Stoic Philosophy at Rome*. Oxford: Oxford University Press / Clarendon Press.

Kaster, R. A. 2005. *Emotion, Restraint and Community in Ancient Rome*. Oxford: Oxford University Press.

Sorabji, Richard. 1997. "Is Stoic Philosophy Helpful as Psychotherapy?" In *Aristotle and After, Bulletin of the Institute of Classical Studies Supplement 68*, ed. R. Sorabji, pp. 197–209.

Warren, James. 2002. *Epicurus and Democritean Ethics: An Archaeology of Ataraxia*. Cambridge: Cambridge University Press. Williams, Bernard. 1997. "Stoic philosophy and the Emotions: Reply to Richard Sorabji." In *Aristotle and After, Bulletin of the Institute of Classical Studies Supplement 68*, ed. R. Sorabji, pp. 211–13.

Williams, G. D., ed. 2003. *Seneca: "De Otio," "De Brevitate Vitae."* Cambridge: Cambridge University Press.

On Leisure

Introduction

GARETH D. WILLIAMS

In our principal manuscript, the late eleventh-century Codex Ambrosianus, *On Leisure* is joined to *On the Happy Life* without a break. Marc Antoine de Muret, Montaigne"s tutor (1526–1585), first proposed that two separate works were conjoined at *On the Happy Life* 28; the two were separated in Justus Lipsius's edition of 1605. The title *De otio* is known from the table of contents of the Codex Ambrosianus, but the name of its addressee is effaced from the entry *Ad* [seven letters erased] *de otio*. Annaeus Serenus, prefect of the watch under Nero (d. 62/63 CE), is commonly accepted as Seneca's addressee, not least because his personality as drawn in *On Leisure* is in keeping with his characterization in *On the Constancy of the Wise Person* and *On Tranquility of Mind*, which are both addressed to him. If we accept Serenus as the addressee, *On Leisure* was composed no later than 63—a scenario that allows Seneca to have composed this justification of retirement from practical life in the period of his own *de facto* withdrawal from the Neronian court. As for the extent of the lacuna before the transmitted beginning of *On Leisure*, Seneca's formal division of his argument into two parts at 2.1–2 indicates that the surviving text begins soon after its opening.

An outraged interlocutory voice in 1.4 (whether attributed to Serenus or to an imaginary other) represents the orthodox Stoic view, allegedly contested by Seneca, that "we shall remain in active service right up to the very end of life." Seneca denies any breach of Stoic allegiance in proposing to argue (2.1–2) (i) that even from early age the Stoic may reject the practical life for that of contemplation, and (ii) that after a career in public service, the Stoic may retire to the contemplative life. The latter point in particular has been invoked to support the work's dating to the period of Seneca's withdrawal from court; but the treatise has a philosophical importance that far outstrips its possible biographical significance as a justification of his own retirement. Essential to Seneca's vindication of the contemplative life, whether "even from the earliest age" (2.1) or "when someone has already completed his official service and his life is far advanced"

(2.2), is that *even in contemplation* the Stoic is fully committed to active service of the sort pledged by the interlocutor in 1.4. Where they differ is in the interlocutor's failure, or refusal, to look beyond the confines of the localized *res publica* (4.1), and beyond a conventional view of service to the state, to the greater *res publica*—the cosmic megalopolis—that is envisaged in 4.2. The detached philosopher who resides intellectually in the latter is still committed to the goal of Stoic action, but he meets that goal not in the conventional sense understood by the interlocutor of 1.4. In terms of 2.1–2, the Stoic who retires to philosophy after a career in public service fulfills his duty "to remain in active service right up to the very end of life" through teaching (2.2) and by personal example (cf. 3.5: "Whoever serves himself well benefits others by the very fact that he provides what will be helpful to them"). As for the young philosopher who withdraws "even from the earliest age," he belongs in the category of Stoic who makes every effort to find a suitable state in which to serve (8.1–3); but from his detached viewpoint in the cosmic megalopolis, the pervasiveness of everyday corruption in the localized *res publica*—in *any* state, Athens, Carthage and (we might infer) even Rome—forces his withdrawal to the contemplative life (cf. 8.3: "But if no commonwealth is to be found of the sort that we visualize for ourselves, leisure turns out to be the inescapable option for all"). But even as he retires, he still engages in "active" contemplation that meets the Stoic mandate to public service, just as Zeno and Chrysippus, those Stoic preeminences, did in serving mankind by their philosophical influence and writings (6.4–5).

On this approach, a different but related controversy is open to resolution. Is *On Leisure* incomplete at its transmitted end as well as at its beginning? A main argument for its incompleteness at 8.4 (which, to some critics, is in any case a suspiciously weak and abrupt conclusion) lies precisely in the perceived need for Seneca to change direction in a lost portion of the work so as to accommodate the second proposition of 2.2; for if he maintains that all practical service in the localized *res publica* is ruled out because of the corrupt condition of any state (8.3), how can it be possible to embark in the first place on a public career from which eventual retirement is justified? How, that is, can Seneca's second proposition in 2.2 ever be a realistic option for the philosopher? If never, how can that second topic be anything other than redundant, at least in the treatise as we have it? Yet the counterargument for completeness again rests on the key point that the philosopher remains committed to action even in retreat. Both propositions in 2.1–2 are fully accounted for in the work as we have it, in that both fully observe the mandated Stoic commitment to action throughout life (cf. 1.4). If a suitable state can be found, the Stoic will serve publicly for as long as he practically can (hence the emphasis in 2.2 on retirement when "life is far advanced"); after retirement, he is no less committed to philosophical action to the very end; if no suitable state can be found despite his best efforts to serve in the localized *res publica*, he is fully entitled to withdraw to the contemplative life at *any* age; but action nevertheless remains the priority even in retirement.

Further Reading

Griffin, M. T. 1976. *Seneca: A Philosopher in Politics* (Oxford, Clarendon Press; repr. with postscript, 1992), esp. 315–21, 328–34.

Williams, G. D., ed. 2003. *Seneca: "De Otio," "De Brevitate Vitae"* (Cambridge: Cambridge University Press), esp. 10–18.

On Leisure

LUCIUS ANNAEUS SENECA

TRANSLATED BY GARETH D. WILLIAMS

(1.1) ... with great accord they make vices attractive to us. Even if we try out nothing else that may be curative, the very act of withdrawal from public life will itself be beneficial; we shall be better by ourselves. And further, we have the opportunity of withdrawing to the company of the best of men, and of selecting a given model by which to guide our lives. We can do this only in leisure: only then can we persist in our resolutions, when no one comes along to distort, with the help of the crowd, a judgment that is still vulnerable; only then can life, which we split apart by the most inconsistent aims, proceed on an even and uninterrupted course. (2) For the worst of our evils is that we keep changing our very vices, and so we can't even manage to stay consistent in a vice that we already know. One thing after another gives us pleasure, and what also causes us trouble is the fact that our judgments are not only perverse but fickle as well. We fluctuate, and we seize at one thing after another; what we've sought after we abandon, what we've abandoned we seek to recover, and we oscillate between our desire and regret. (3) For we are wholly dependent on the judgments of others, and we view as best what the many pursue and praise, and not what warrants praise and pursuit. Nor do we judge a path to be good or bad on its own merits, but by the mass of footprints on it—and none of them of people coming back![1]

(4) You'll say to me: "What are you saying, Seneca? Are you deserting your side? Surely your Stoics say: 'We shall remain in active service right up to the very end of life, without ceasing to apply ourselves to the common good, to help the individual, and to give assistance with an aged hand even to our enemies. We Stoics are the ones who grant no exemptions from service at any age, and as that most eloquent of poets puts it,

We clamp down the war-helmet on our gray hair.[2]

We are the ones who hold so strongly that there is no inactive moment before death that, if circumstance allows, death itself is not inactive.'[3] Why, in Zeno's very headquarters, are you talking to us of Epicurus's precepts? If you're weary of your side, why not desert it outright rather than betray it?" **(5)** For now, I'll say only this much in reply: "Surely you don't expect more of me than that I behave like my leaders? So what to do? I'll go not where they send me but where they lead me."[4]

(2.1) I shall now prove to you that I'm not abandoning Stoic precepts. For it's not the case that the Stoics themselves have abandoned them; and yet I'd have an excellent excuse, even if I did follow their personal examples and not their precepts. I shall separate what I have to say into two parts: first, that even from the earliest age someone can devote himself completely to the contemplation of truth, seeking a coherent intellectual basis for life and practicing it in private; **(2)** second, that when someone has already completed his official service and his life is far advanced, he can do this same thing with perfect right, and with the greatest insight communicate it to others, after the manner of the Vestal virgins who divide their years of service between different duties: they learn to perform the sacred rites, and when they have learned them, they begin to teach them.

(3.1) I shall show that this doctrine finds acceptance with the Stoics too. It's not that I've made it my rule to commit no offense against any saying of Zeno or Chrysippus, but rather that the simple fact of the matter allows me to support their opinion; if someone always supports the opinion of the same person, he belongs not in the senate but in a claque. If only everything were already understood, the truth obvious and generally accepted, and we never changed any of our convictions! As it is, we search for the truth along with the very people who teach it.

(2) The two schools, Epicurean and Stoic, very strenuously disagree on this question as on others, but in fact each directs us to leisure, but by different routes. Epicurus says: "The sage will not participate in public life unless in exceptional circumstances." Zeno says: "He will participate in public life unless something prevents him."[5] **(3)** The former aims for leisure on principle, the latter only on special grounds; but these grounds are wide ranging. If the state is too diseased to be helped, if it is seized by illness, the sage will not struggle unnecessarily and expend himself to no beneficial purpose.

If he has insufficient influence or power, if the state is not ready to accept him, or if ill health prevents him, he will not embark on a course that he knows is difficult to accomplish, just as he wouldn't launch a battered ship on the sea or enlist for military service if he were a cripple.[6] (4) Consequently, it's possible even for someone who has all options still open, before experiencing any of life's storms, to settle in a safe retreat and to devote himself from then on to liberal studies, and to spend his time in uninterrupted leisure, cultivating the virtues which even those furthest from public life can exercise. (5) To be sure, it is required of anyone to be of benefit to others—to many if possible, but if not, then to a few; if not to a few, then to those nearest to us; if not to those nearest, then to oneself. For when someone makes himself useful to others, he engages in public service. Just as a person who is responsible for his own moral deterioration harms not just himself but all those whom he could have benefited had he improved himself, so whoever serves himself well benefits others by the very fact that he provides what will be helpful to them.

(4.1) Let's embrace the idea that there are two commonwealths.[7] The one is vast and truly common to all, and includes the gods as well as mankind; within it, we look neither to this mere corner nor to that, but we measure the boundaries of our state by the sun's course. The other is the one in which we are enrolled by the circumstances of our birth—I mean Athens or Carthage or any other city that belongs not to the whole of mankind but to a particular population. Certain people give devoted service to both commonwealths, the greater and the lesser, at the same time; some serve only the lesser, some only the greater. (2) This greater commonwealth we can serve with devotion even in leisure; or rather, I'm inclined to think, even better in leisure, by inquiring what virtue is,[8] whether it is one or many, and whether a person is made good by nature or by training; whether this world body, which includes within it the seas and landmasses and the things connected to earth and water, exists alone, or whether god has scattered many such bodies; whether all the matter from which everything comes into being is continuous and with no intervals of space, or whether it is spread out and a void is intermixed with solid bodies; what kind of abode god inhabits; whether he looks on his handiwork in detachment or actively controls it, and whether he encompasses it from without or pervades its entirety; and whether the world is immortal or to be counted among things that are perishable and limited in life span. What service to god does the contemplator of such matters provide? That his great works are not without witness.

(5.1) We[9] commonly say that the greatest good is to live in accordance with nature. Nature has created us for both purposes—for contemplation and for action. Let me now prove the first statement. Yet why say more? Won't it be proved if each of us asks himself how much he craves knowledge of the unknown, and how excited he gets at every new report he hears? (2) Some sail the seas and endure the hardships of the furthest voyaging for the sole reward of discovering something hidden and distant. This is what causes people to crowd together for public spectacles, this is what makes them pry into things that are closed off, to inquire into the more abstruse, to uncover the past, and to hear about the ways of foreign nations. (3) Nature granted us an inquisitive disposition. Aware of its own skill and its beauty, it gave us life to be spectators of its great spectacle, since it would be sure to lose all pleasure in itself if it displayed its works, so vast, so distinct, so finely contrived, so bright and so beautiful in more ways than one, to an empty solitude. (4) For you to understand that it wanted not just to be seen but to be closely observed, consider the place to which it assigned us: it positioned us at the center of its creation, and gave us a commanding view of the universe. It not only caused man to stand erect. To equip him for contemplation, so that he could follow the stars as they glide from their rising toward their setting and could turn his gaze with the turning universe, it also set his head atop his body and placed it on a pliant neck. Moreover, by causing six constellations to rise by day and six by night, it revealed to view every single part of itself, so that through the wonders that it had presented to our gaze it aroused keen interest in the others as well. (5) For we cannot view all of them, or their real dimensions, but our vision opens a path of investigation for itself and lays a basis for the truth, allowing our research to progress from the obvious to the hidden and to discover things more ancient than the world itself: What was the origin of these constellations? What was the physical condition of the universe before the distinct elements began to separate to form its parts? What principle separated them out when they were plunged into darkness and confusion? Who assigned places to things? Was it by their own nature that heavy things sank downward and light ones flew up; or, quite apart from their thrust and weight, did some higher force lay down the law for individual bodies? Or is there truth to the argument that strives especially to prove that mankind is a part of the divine breath—that some portion, sparks, as it were, of the stars leaped down to the earth and clung to a place not their own?[10] (6) Our thought breaks through the ramparts of the sky, not content to know only that which appears to the eye. "I search," it says, "for what lies beyond the world. Is it an indefinite vastness, or is this space also enclosed by its own boundaries? What is the condition of things beyond those boundaries? Are they shapeless and mixed together, taking up the same space in all directions, or are they too divided up into some order? Are they physically attached to this world, or far removed from it, leaving it to revolve in a void? Is it out of atoms that everything that has or will come into being is constructed, or is the substance of things a continuum that is capable of transformation throughout? Are the elements hostile to each other, or, rather than battling among themselves, do they work harmoniously together in their different ways?" (7) Given that man was born to search into these matters, consider how little time has been granted to him, even if he claims every single moment of it for himself! Though he allows none of his time to be snatched away through his obliging nature and none to slip away through carelessness, though he guards his precious hours with the utmost miserliness and reaches right up to the furthest limit of the human life span, and though fortune upsets no part of what nature has ordained for him—nevertheless, man is too mortal to attain knowledge of things immortal. (8) So I live according to nature if I've devoted myself entirely to it, if I am its admirer and its worshipper. But nature wished me to do both—to be active and to be free for contemplation.[11] And I am doing both, since even contemplation entails action.

(6.1) "But it makes a difference," you say, "whether you turn to it only for pleasure, seeking nothing from it except unbroken contemplation with no practical outcome; for that existence is attractive in its special charms." To this my reply to you is that it matters equally in what frame of mind you go about your political life. Are you always preoccupied, taking no time for yourself in which to turn your gaze from human affairs to things divine? (2) To strive after wealth without any love of the virtues and without cultivating the intellect, and to be engrossed in bare work, are by no means commendable (these must be combined with each other and connected). Just so, virtue that is wasted on leisure without action, never presenting what it has learned for inspection, is an incomplete and idle good. (3) Who denies that virtue should test its progress by action, and not just consider what ought to be done but sometimes also act decisively and bring its ideas to the fullness of reality? But if there's no delay on the part of the sage himself, if what is lacking is not the doer but tasks to be done, surely you will then allow him to consort with himself?

(4) What are the sage's thoughts as he withdraws into leisure? He does so in the knowledge that then also he will be actively engaged in undertakings that will benefit posterity. Certainly we Stoics are ones to assert that both Zeno and Chrysippus accomplished greater things than if they had led armies, held high office, and brought in laws— and bring in laws they did, not for a single state but for the whole of the human race! So, then, why ever should leisure such as this not be right for the good man, if he uses it to give direction to later generations and to address not just a few but all peoples of all nations, both present and future? (5) In sum, I ask you whether Cleanthes, Chrysippus, and Zeno lived in accordance with their doctrines?[12] You'll doubtless reply that they lived just as they said life should be lived. Yet not one of them took part in civic life. "They had neither the fortune," you respond, "nor the civic status which normally allows people to participate in public administration."[13] Nevertheless, they didn't lead idle lives: they discovered how to make their particular kind of inactivity of greater benefit to mankind than the bustle and sweat of others. Therefore, though they played no public role, they were nonetheless deemed to have done a lot.

(7.1) Moreover, there are three modes of life,[14] and it is commonly asked which of them is best. One is devoted to pleasure, the second to contemplation, the third to action. If we first put aside our philosophical rivalry and the relentless hatred which we proclaim against those who follow paths different from our own, let us observe how all three come to the same thing under different labels. The person who commends pleasure is not devoid of contemplation; the person devoted to contemplation is not devoid of pleasure; the person whose existence is dedicated to action is not devoid of contemplation. **(2)** "But it makes a very great difference," you say, "whether something is a primary aim or an accessory to some other primary aim." There may certainly be a great difference; nonetheless, one doesn't exist without the other. The contemplator doesn't contemplate without action, the active man doesn't dispense with contemplation, and the third person—the one of whom we've agreed to have a low opinion[15]—doesn't sanction idle pleasure but pleasure that he makes stable for himself by his reason.[16] Accordingly, even this pleasure-loving school is itself committed to action. **(3)** How could it not be, since Epicurus himself says that at times, he'll withdraw from pleasure and even seek out pain, if regret looms over the pleasure, or if he'll take on a lesser pain in place of a greater one later?[17] **(4)** My point in saying this? To make it clear that all sides commend contemplation. For some it is the goal; for us Stoics, it is a place to ride at anchor, but not a harbor.[18]

(8.1) Consider also that you are allowed, in accordance with Chrysippus's prescription,[19] to live in leisure; I don't mean just tolerating leisure but actively choosing it. Our school refuses to accept that the sage will engage in public life in just any commonwealth. But what difference does it make how the sage arrives at leisure—whether because the right commonwealth isn't available to him, or because he's not available to the commonwealth—if no such commonwealth is going to exist for anyone? And in fact, no commonwealth will ever be available to those who search for it with a discriminating eye.[20] **(2)** I ask you, to what commonwealth is the sage going to attach himself? To that of the Athenians, where Socrates was condemned to death, and which Aristotle fled to avoid being condemned there?[21] Where the virtues are oppressed by envy? You can't tell me that the sage will attach himself to *this* commonwealth. To the Carthaginian one, then, where there is ceaseless political discord, and populist license threatens harm to all the best citizens; where there is the greatest contempt for fairness and right principle, and where inhuman cruelty toward enemies is even turned in enmity on their own citizens? This one too he'll run from. **(3)** If I wanted to make a complete survey of individual commonwealths, I wouldn't find a single one that could tolerate, or be tolerated by, the sage. But if no commonwealth is to be found of the sort that we visualize for ourselves, leisure turns out to be the inescapable option for all, because the one thing that might have been preferable to leisure exists nowhere. (4) If someone says that it's best to go by sea, and then forbids sailing in a sea where shipwrecks commonly occur and there are often sudden storms that sweep the helmsman in the wrong direction, he tells me, unless I'm mistaken, not to set sail, however much he praises sailing.[22]

1. Allusion to the Aesopic fable of the lion and the fox: the "sick" lion draws sympathetic visitors, but the wily fox notes the one-way direction of all the prints. So for Seneca, individuals are swept along toward ruination by the one way traffic of mass opinion.

2. Virgil *Aeneid* 9.612.

3. Presumably a reference to Stoic suicide.

4. Seneca exploits a notorious Stoic inconsistency (one that he will, in fact, deny later in *On Leisure*): Zeno of Citium (335–263 BCE) and Chrysippus of Soli (ca. 280–207 BCE), the first and third heads of the school, advocated public service but never actually performed it themselves, at least in the conventional sense (but cf. 6.4–5).

5. Not direct quotations, but a neat antithesis contrived by Seneca.

6. Given Seneca's own *de facto* retirement from the Neronian court after 62 CE, autobiographical overtones have been detected here. But the grounds for exemption from service in 3.3 are too well attested before Seneca, too conventional rather than personally revealing, to be interpreted as unambiguously autobiographical.

7. Zeno's dream in his *Republic* of a universal civic awareness (a notion influenced by earlier, especially Cynic, ideas) was adapted by Chrysippus to shape the "cosmic city" idea of later Stoics.

8. Of the three familiar parts of Hellenistic philosophy, logic, physics, and ethics, Seneca here begins with staple ethical questions before progressing to physics, first on the nature of the physical cosmos, then on its divine governance. Key differences between the Stoic and Epicurean worldviews in Seneca's survey of physical questions here—the Stoic material world continuum, god immanent throughout it, is contrasted with random atomic motion in the void, with no divine involvement in this or any other perishable world—revive the interschool rivalry featured in 1.4–5.

9. The Stoics.

10. In Stoic theory, the rational human soul is a portion of the universal fiery divine breath/*pneuma*. In 5.5–6, Epicurean and Stoic ideas are again in tension (cf. n. 8 above); but what transcends their rivalry here is the model of self- and world-questioning that Seneca presents as engaging any discerning mind at its peak performance.

11. A key Senecan emphasis also elsewhere (e.g., *On Tranquility of Mind* 4.8, *Letters* 3.6), with elaboration in 6.2–4 below.

12. Cf. 1.5 and n. 4.

13. Because they were not freeborn Athenians, Zeno, Cleanthes, and Chrysippus were ineligible for legal or political office there.

14. Formularized in Aristotle (*Nicomachean Ethics* 1095b 17–19), but the distinction extends back to Plato and his predecessors.

15. An Epicurean; Seneca possibly alludes to a point of discussion in the treatise's lost opening.

16. I.e., the Epicurean aims to achieve "katastematic" pleasure (e.g., not being hungry) as opposed to the "kinetic" sort (e.g., eating to relieve hunger).

17. Cf. Epicurus *Letter to Menoeceus* 129–30.

18. The distinction glances back to 2.1–2: in the case either of retirement to the contemplative life from early age (2.1) or withdrawal after a career in service (2.2), the Stoic is always committed to action; for even in retirement Stoic *contemplatio* (here in effect the anchoring place) is still directed to action for the common good.

19. Along the lines of Zeno's prescription in 3.2 above.

20. So *fastidiose*, which is rendered more pejoratively by other translators (to the effect of "fussy," "choosy"). Yet the sage delineated in chapters 4–6 is hardly disdainful of, or fussily selective about, public service *per se*. Active service within/to the community is his mandated goal, but on close inspection he is without a useful or relevant role to play within the (inevitably corrupt) states he surveys; hence retirement to philosophical action is the only realistic option (8.3).

21. After Alexander's death in 323 BCE, Aristotle, accused of impiety, left Athens, allegedly recalling the Socratic precedent (399 BCE) as he did so.

22. For resistance to claims that *On Leisure* is incomplete at its transmitted end, see my introduction to this essay.

On the Happy Life

Introduction

JAMES KER

Topic and Structure

Seneca's title *De vita beata* refers to the "happy life" or "happiness" (Greek *eu zên, eudaimonia*) that all the ancient philosophical schools agreed was the thing naturally desired by all human beings. Along with this general consensus, however, the schools expressed stark disagreement over what constitutes the highest good—the end, goal, or perfection of life, which each person needs in order to be happy: pleasure, freedom from pain and anxiety (Epicureans); virtue alone (Stoics); virtue accompanied by certain additional goods (Peripatetics). Our fullest surviving account of the debate is Cicero's dialogue *On the Ends of Good and Bad*, which examines the three answers in turn.

Seneca's work is a briefer and more selective sketch of the Stoic happy life constituted by virtue, but it still considers this life's relationship to pleasure and other circumstances. At the beginning of the work (1.1), Seneca announces to Gallio, his brother and the work's addressee, that he will address first "what it is we are seeking" and then "the way to get there most swiftly" (1.1). After an early focus on defining the happy life, however, the second topic, progress, will be intertwined with several additional debates.

In a preliminary discussion of the problem at hand (1.2–3.1), Seneca satirizes people's misdirection and emphasizes the need for an expert guide (1.2). This leads to his focus on defining the happy life (3.2–5.4), in which his professed independence from "any one Stoic authority" (3.2) is balanced by his adherence to the common Stoic principle of "agree[ing] with the nature of the world" (3.3)—the foundational principle of Stoicism, which becomes a leitmotif of the work as a whole (e.g., 8.1–2, 13.1, 20.5). He then proceeds to give not one but six definitions of the happy life, each of different length—he justifies his approach to definition by analogy with an army, which can be extended one minute and contracted the next, as strategy dictates (4.1).

A passing mention of pleasures cues the first major task of Seneca's dialogue: the refutation of pleasure as the highest good or as being combined with virtue as part of the highest good (6.1–15.4).[1] Each of the objections that follow (voiced by a third-person interlocutor, clearly not Gallio) corresponds to a specific component of the Epicurean doctrine on pleasure. In this exchange, Seneca shows himself to be familiar with Epicurus's writings and aware of, even sympathetic to, Epicurus's "sober and temperate" conception of pleasure (12.4). On the other hand, he asserts that the Epicurean school has given "a sponsor and a veil" (12.4) to reckless hedonists, and he holds the Epicureans responsible for these extremes. The topic of pleasure is then exorcised with a portrait of virtue's purity and freedom, and of virtue's status as the guarantor of "true happiness" (15.5–16.3).

Seneca's general sketch of the happy life provokes a new exchange with a more hostile interlocutor—or interlocutors (17–20). They ask: "Why, then, do you *speak* more bravely than you *live*?" (17.1). This ushers in an extensive catalogue of criticisms that prompt Seneca to explain that he is describing the wise person, not his all-too-imperfect self or the aspiring philosopher (20.3–5).

The objector's next line of questioning ushers in a debate focusing on the wise person's relationship to wealth (21–26.3).[2] Seneca's response is to sketch the Stoic theory of preferred indifferents (22.4) and to explain how the wise person gives gifts (*beneficia*; 20.4, 23.1–24.3), the topic dealt with at greater length in *On Benefits*. The debate is intensified by speeches from a wise person and then from Socrates, portrayed first in generic terms (24.4–25.8), then with greater biographic specificity (26.4–28.1). It is uncertain how much has been lost beyond the point where Socrates' acerbic attack on his opponents breaks off.

Seneca's Apology

Having chosen to focus on the "happy life," Seneca could easily have kept his focus on theoretical topics (6.1–15.4).[3] The shift in chapter 17, however, means that the work is now dedicated to defending a life spent progressing, however imperfectly, toward the Stoic happy life— an apologetic turn. But not just any Stoic happy life: this is a life lived expansively, managing preferred indifferents as part of the life of the body, the household, and the state.

Although the date of *On the Happy Life* is unknown, most scholars see the work as responding (sooner or later) to the informal attack made against Seneca in 58 BCE by the disgruntled professional prosecutor P. Suillius Rufus.⁴ Tacitus summarizes the kinds of charge leveled by Suillius against Seneca behind the scenes, praising Seneca's earlier banishment and highlighting contradictions between his philosophy and his wealth (*Annals* 13.42.2–43.1); Cassius Dio mentions these and other charges, including Seneca's supposed predilection for sex with "boys past their prime" (*Roman History* 61.10). Although, as Tacitus states, Suillius's charges were not uttered publicly, and were relayed to Seneca in exaggerated form (13.43.1), the accusations find a partial resonance, and a few seemingly more direct echoes, in the interlocutor's imagined accusations beginning in *On the Happy Life* 2.3, and later at 17.1–2, 21.1, and 27.5.

To address concerns about the philosopher's use of pleasure and wealth, Seneca did not have to use the rubric of the happy life. But doing so provided him with a ready-made structure in which to define his Stoic position through contrasting it dialectically with doctrines giving value to pleasure and externals, while articulating the qualified place of pleasure and externals *in* Stoic doctrine.

This material is given its own distinctive shape also by the rhetorical overlays employed by Seneca. By introducing Socrates, he infuses the work with the ambiance of Plato's *Apology of Socrates*, where the philosopher confronts his various accusers and uses this as an opportunity to scrutinize *their* views. And despite his claim to the contrary (17.3–4), Seneca seems happy to let his own voice blur into that of the wise person. The heavy use of Roman political terminology constitutes another rhetorical overlay, signaled early when Seneca employs the technical terms of political elections and senatorial deliberation to characterize the way in which he and his interlocutor decide how to vote or formulate their opinion (*sententia*) in relation to those of others (1.5–2.1, 3.2). At numerous later moments, Seneca builds on existing ideals of political behavior (e.g., 15.7, 20.5), even as he seeks to replace these political values with philosophical values.⁵

Seneca's apology, if we may call it that, remained influential in countering perceptions of Seneca's supposed hypocrisy. Diderot, for example, took *On the Happy Life* as a rhetorical blueprint for his *Essai sur la vie et les écrits de Sénèque* (1778), in which the *philosophe* defends both Seneca and himself against the modern-day Suilliuses of the "anti-Sénèque" camp.

Pleasure, Wealth, and the Craft of Living

Unlike Seneca's other shorter essays, *On the Happy Life* focuses on moral conduct in times of good fortune—as Seneca's wise person puts it, the "downhill" virtues (such as liberality, moderation, gentleness) rather than the "uphill" virtues (endurance, courage, persistence; 25.6–8). In this work, then, we have an opportunity to see how Seneca crafts this different material, and also to observe what his treatments of pleasure and of wealth have in common.

Seneca responds in somewhat opposite ways to the questions of pleasure and wealth.[6] His argument in chapters 6–15 combats those who would elevate pleasure and make virtue its instrument. In the case of wealth, conversely, Seneca's aim is to justify the wise person's preference for it, arguing against those who would see self-contradictions in a Stoic's possession of wealth.

But several concepts also help to unify the two sections. Both topics, for example, are articulated in terms that distinguish the wise person's unique and sublime form of joy (also tranquility) that is a defining thread of Seneca's portrait of how it feels to be happy.[7] Both topics are also articulated in terms of freedom, with virtue as freedom from pleasure (e.g., 3.4, 4.3)[8] and the wise person's generosity (*liberalitas*) originating in a "free mind" (*liber animus*; 24.3).

The philosopher's profile as an *artifex uitae suae*, "craftsman of his life" (8.3), is also applied equally to both pleasure and wealth. In the case of pleasure, being a craftsman involves the mind's taking its beginnings from the senses, but then, like god, asserting its power over them (8.3–4). In the case of wealth, the craftsman ideal is implicitly at work in Seneca's various mentions of wealth as giving the philosopher "greater material for unfurling his mind" (21.4, 22.1, 24.3).

The notion of life craftsman, and with it the nature of the lifestyle or life course conducted by the philosopher, is most fully encapsulated in chapter 25. In the wise person's formula ("Put me in fortune . . . put me in misfortune . . . I am ready for the misfortune . . . I prefer the fortune . . ."), Seneca adds as much gravity as he can to the exercise of downhill virtues by having a "Socrates" deliver this speech, since the overall trajectory of Socrates' life path, ending in prison and hemlock, helps to throw into relief the fleetingness of all those materials that allow an exercise of downhill virtues.

A characteristically Senecan focus on death, as a crucial component of the art of living and as the ultimate proof of freedom, is evident in the words of the aspiring student of philosophy (20.5) and in Seneca's description of the suicide of Diodorus, the Epicurean who "just a few days ago" cut his own throat, and whose last words make reference to his "good conscience" (19.1). Even if he does not himself praise Diodorus's Epicurean lifestyle, Seneca clearly saw in his death an opportunity to demonstrate the potential of a bravely chosen death to bear witness to an examined life. And an espousal of willingness to undertake death is *a fortiori* an espousal of detachment from pleasure, wealth, and all other indifferents, for death encapsulates freedom in its most fundamental sense as the freedom of soul from body.[9] To embrace death is also to remember how, within the temporal scheme of the happy *life*, it will always be the uphill virtues that are needed last. This is the theoretical, and biographic, framework within which Seneca situates his preference for external things.

Selected Reading

Asmis, Elizabeth. 1990. "Seneca on the Happy Life." In *The Poetics of Therapy*, ed. M. Nussbaum, *Apeiron* 23:219–55.

Griffin, Miriam T. 1992. "Seneca *Praedives*." In *Seneca: A Philosopher in Politics*, 2nd ed., 286–314. Oxford: Oxford University Press.

Ker, James. 2010. "Socrates Speaks in Seneca, *De Vita Beata* 24–28." In *Ancient Models of Mind: Studies in Human and Divine Rationality*, ed. A. Nightingale and D. Sedley, 180–95. Cambridge: Cambridge University Press.

On the Happy Life

LUCIUS ANNAEUS SENECA

TRANSLATED BY JAMES KER

(1.1) Everyone, brother Gallio, wants to live happily, but when it comes to discerning what it is that *makes* life happy, they are in the dark. And so difficult is it to attain a happy life that the faster a person rushes toward it, the further he departs from it, if he loses the path. When the path leads him in the opposite direction, his velocity results in a still greater separation.

So we must plan to address first what it is we are seeking. Then we must look around for the way to get there most swiftly so that we can learn on the way—so long as it is the *right* way—how much ground we have covered each day and how much nearer we are to that thing toward which a natural desire propels us. (2) Indeed, as long as we rove around this way and that, following not a leader but the discordant hue and cry of people calling us in different directions, our brief lives (brief, even if we work toward a good mind day and night) will be frittered away in mistaken wandering. Let us determine, then, both where we are headed and by what path, and let us have an expert who has already explored what we are advancing toward. For the terms here are not the same as with other travels: in them, we are prevented from erring by a recognized path and by locals who can answer our questions, whereas here the most worn and most crowded paths deceive us the most.

(3) There is nothing, then, that we need to ensure so much as that we not resemble cattle, following the herd of those that have gone before, proceeding not where we ought to go but where others are headed. Yet nothing gets us entangled in greater troubles than our conforming ourselves to rumor, when we judge as best those things that have met with great approval; or than our having many examples in place of what is good and living by imitation rather than reason. (4) That is where that great heap comes from, where one person falls over another. Just as happens in a crush of humanity, when the populace presses on itself, and no one falls without pulling another down onto him, and the first ones are the undoing of those that follow—this you can see happening in everyone's lives. No one's error

affects himself alone, but he is the cause and the author of another's erring. For it is harmful to be tangled up with those that have gone before, and as long as each individual prefers to take things on trust rather than to judge, there is never any judging about life, but always trusting; and we are spun around and thrown headlong by a hand-me-down error. We perish as a result of others' examples. We *will* be restored to health: only let us be segregated from the crowd. (5) But for the time being, the populace stands against reason, defending its own bad situation. So the same thing happens as in elections, where those who are amazed at the men elected praetors are the very ones who elected them, whenever capricious favor turns in the opposite direction. We approve of things, then find the same things reprehensible. This is the outcome of any judgment in which the majority is conceded to.

(2.1) When our topic is the happy life, there will be no benefit in your replying to me as follows, in the manner of divisions in the senate: "This side seems to be in the majority."[10] For in precisely that way is it more pernicious. Human affairs are not in such a good condition that the majority favors what is better: a crowd is proof of what is worst. (2) Therefore let us seek out what is best to do, not what is the most established practice, and what can place us in possession of eternal happiness, not what is approved of by the common crowd, the worst discerner of truth. By "common crowd" I refer as much to those who wear crowns as to those who wear cloaks, because I pay no heed to the color of the clothes by which our bodies are concealed. When it comes to human beings, I do not trust my eyes. I have a better and more reliable light by which I can distinguish true things from false: let the discoverer of the mind's good be the mind.

If this thing, the mind, is ever given time to take a breath and withdraw into itself, see how it will torture itself and confess to itself the truth, saying: (3) "Whatever I did up till now I would prefer to be undone. Whenever I reflect on what I said, I envy those that are mute. Whatever I wished for, I think of as the curses of my adversaries. Whatever I feared—good gods, how much lighter that was than what I desired! I conducted animosities against many, and then I returned from hate back to favor—if, that is, there is such a thing as favor among bad men. But I am not yet a friend to myself. I devoted all my energy to distinguishing myself from the many and to making myself famous by marrying into a dowry. What was I doing except putting myself directly in the path of missiles and showing envy where to bite me? **(4)** Do you see those men who praise eloquence, who pursue wealth, who fawn over favor, who exalt power? Everyone either is their enemy or, which amounts to the same thing, could be their enemy: as many as are in awe of them resent them. Why should I not rather seek out something that is good in practice—something I can feel, rather than display? Those things that are looked at, that make people stop and stare, that one person points out to another in astonishment, are shiny on the outside, but on the inside are pitiful."

(3.1) We should seek out something that is not good to look at, but robust and unvarying and more beautiful on its hidden side. We should recover this. It isn't placed far away. It *will* be discovered: you simply need to know where to extend your hand. For now, it is as if we are passing nearby things in the darkness, bumping up against exactly what we long for.

(2) But so I do not lead you around in circles, I will pass over the opinions of others, for enumerating them would be a long task, as would refuting them. So hear ours. But when I say "ours," I do not bind myself to any one Stoic authority: I too have the right to set forth my position. Thus I will follow one, will command another to divide his proposition, and even, perhaps, when summoned to speak after all the others, I will disapprove of nothing that the earlier ones decreed and yet will say: "I have this to add."[11] **(3)** In the meantime, I do something that is common to all Stoics: I agree with the nature of the world.[12] Not to deviate from nature, but to be formed according to its law and example—that is wisdom.

Happy, therefore, is the life in agreement with its own nature. And there is no other way for this to come about than if the intellect is, first, healthy and in unending possession of its own health; next, strong and energetic; then, enduring most nobly, fitted to the times, caring for its body, and for the things that pertain to the body, without anxiety; then, attentive to the other things that equip life, without admiring any of them, and ready to use the gifts of fortune and not be their slave. **(4)** You understand, even without my adding it, that once things that either provoke or terrify us have been expelled, there follow unending tranquility, freedom. For when pleasures and pains have been rejected,[13] a huge joy comes in to replace those things that are trivial and fragile and actually prompt self-disgust[14]—a joy unshaken and unvarying, followed by peace and harmony in the mind, and a greatness combined with gentleness, since ferocity always derives from weakness.

(4.1) Our good can also be defined in a different way—that is, the same proposition can be grasped with different words. Just as one and the same army is spread out more widely one moment and compacted more tightly the next, and it either arcs with the middle part curving out into wings or is arranged in a straight front, but no matter how it has been ordered it has the same strength and the same will to stand up for the same cause—so the definition of the highest good can sometimes be spread out and extended, and at other times be compressed and collected into itself. (2) It will be the same thing, then, if I say, "The highest good is the mind looking down on the things of fortune, joyous in virtue," or, "the mind's undefeated strength, well versed in the ways of the world, calm in action, with much humanity and concern for those with whom it has contact." One may also define it in such a way as to say that that human being is happy to whom nothing is good or bad except a good or bad mind; who is a cultivator of the morally good,[15] content with virtue; who is neither buoyed up nor broken by changes in fortune; who knows that there is no greater good than that which he can give to himself; to whom true pleasure will be scorning pleasures. (3) One may, if you wish to range further, translate it into one and another form, without endangering or damaging its power. After all, what prevents us from saying that the happy life is a free, upright, fearless, and stable mind, placed beyond fear and beyond desire, to whom the only good is what is morally good, the only bad thing, disgrace, and the rest are a worthless swarm of things that neither subtract anything from the happy life nor add anything to it, coming and going without any increase or diminution of the highest good?

(4) It is necessarily the case that when the mind has this kind of foundation, whether it wishes it or not, it will be accompanied by an unceasing cheerfulness and a joy that is deep and comes from deep within. For it rejoices in things that are its own and does not desire anything greater than what it has at home. Why should it not consider these things hefty compared with the tiny, trivial, and

impermanent movements of that meager thing, the body? The day on which someone succumbs to pleasure, he will also succumb to pain. But you see what a bad and harmful servitude someone will be

serving if he alternately falls into the possession of those unpredictable and unbridled masters: pleasures and pains. Therefore an exit must be made to freedom. (5) And freedom can be conferred by no other thing than a disregard of fortune. Then that priceless good will arise: the quiet of a mind residing in safety, and sublimity, and a magnificent and immovable joy ensuing upon the expulsion of error and knowledge of the truth, and friendliness and expansiveness of mind—things in which he will delight not as goods but as things arising from *his* good.

(5.1) Since I have begun to treat the topic lavishly: that person can be called happy who feels neither desire nor fear, owing to the gift of reason. For even rocks, and cattle too, lack fear and sadness, but no one would call them happy on that account, as they have no comprehension of happiness. (2) Put in the same category human beings whose dull nature and lack of self-knowledge have reduced them to the level of cattle and beasts. There is no difference between these men and animals, because the latter have no reason, whereas the former have a reason that is crooked and is perversely clever to their own detriment. The thing is, no one can be called happy if he has flung himself outside truth. (3) The happy life, therefore, is established in right and certain judgment, and unchangeable. The intellect is pure and is released from all bad things only once it has escaped not only injuries but even minor annoyances. It is prepared always to stand its ground and to defend its position, even when fortune is angry and hostile. (4) For as regards pleasure, even if it is infused from all sides and floods every pathway and soothes the mind with its characteristic blandishments and adds one thing after another to harass us in part and in whole, who among mortals that has any trace of humanity left in him would wish to be titillated day and night and to desert his mind and give in to the body?

(6.1) "But the mind also will have its pleasures," he says.[16] Let it have them, absolutely, and let it preside as arbiter of luxury and pleasures. Let it fill itself with all those things that customarily delight the senses. Then let it look back over things past, and, recalling its erstwhile pleasures, let it revel in what came before. And let it now look forward to those pleasures to come and arrange its hopes, and while the body wallows in its present feasting, let it send its thoughts ahead to the future. So much the more pitiful will it seem to me, since it is madness to count bad things as goods! No one is happy without health, nor is anyone healthy if he desires future things in place of what is best. (2) Happy therefore is the one right in his judgment. Happy is the one content with present circumstances no matter what they are, and a friend to his own affairs. Happy is the one whose disposition of his affairs is entirely as reason recommends.

(7.1) Even those who have said that the highest good is in the lower regions of the body can see in what a disgraceful place they have located it. That is why they deny that pleasure can be separated from virtue, and say that no one can live morally without living pleasurably, and no one can live pleasurably without living morally also.[17] I do not see how these things that are so divergent can be wedded. Why is it, I ask you people, that pleasure cannot be separated from virtue? I suppose, given that good things all take their beginning from virtue, from virtue's roots arise even those things that *you* love and seek after? But if these things were indistinguishable, we would not see certain things that are pleasurable but not morally good, and other things that are most definitely morally good, but arduous, attainable only through pain. (2) Now add the fact that pleasure comes even to the most disgraceful life, whereas virtue does not admit of living badly, and certain individuals are unhappy not without pleasure but indeed precisely on account of pleasure. This could not have come about if pleasure had blended itself with virtue. Virtue is often without pleasure, but it is never in need of it.

(3) Why do you combine things that are dissimilar and indeed divergent? Virtue is something sublime, elevated and regal, invincible, inexhaustible. Pleasure is lowly, servile, weak, transitory. It does duty in brothels and taverns; indeed, it dwells there. You will find virtue in a temple, in the forum, in the senate house, standing before the walls, covered in dust and browned by the sun, with callused hands. Pleasure you will most often find hiding, keeping to the shadows around the bathhouses and steam rooms and places that have reason to fear official inspectors,[18] soft and weak, dripping with wine and unguents, pallid or rouged, and embalmed with chemicals. (4) The highest good is immortal. It does not know how to depart, nor does it

feel glutted or regretful. You need to understand that a right intellect never falters, nor is it hateful to itself, nor does it change anything, being already the best.[19] But pleasure is extinguished precisely at the time when it delights. It does not have much space, and so it fills it quickly and it becomes tedious, fading after its first onset. And nothing is ever stable whose nature consists in motion. Thus there cannot even be any substance to a thing that comes in and passes through so speedily, and will perish precisely in its usage. You see, it hurtles toward its cessation, and even as it begins it looks to the end.

(8.1) What about the fact that there is as much pleasure in bad things as in good, and disgraceful men take as much delight in their dishonorable deeds as morally good men take in their outstanding ones? The reason why the ancients taught us to pursue the best life and not the most pleasurable was so that the will that is right and good might have pleasure as its companion, but not as its leader. For the leader we must use is nature: it is nature that reason looks to and consults. (2) To live happily, then, is the same thing as to live according to nature. As for what this is, I will explain. If, carefully and without fear, we preserve the benefits of the body and the equipment of nature, treating them as ephemeral and fleeting; if we do not enter into servitude to them, and things not our own do not take possession of us; if the things that please the body when it receives them have the same status for us as auxiliaries and light-armed soldiers have in an army camp, where they must serve rather than give orders—this, in the end, is how they can be useful to the mind.

(3) Let a person be uncorrupted by externals and unconquerable, and an admirer only of himself, "trusting in his mind and ready for either outcome,"[20] a craftsman of his life. Let his confidence be not without knowledge, his knowledge not without perseverance: let his decisions, once made, remain, and in his decrees let there be no erasures. It is understood, even without my adding it, that a man such as this will be composed and orderly, and in whatever he does he will be magnificent and at the same time friendly.

(4) Let reason, indeed,[21] be stimulated by the senses and take its beginnings from them. Certainly it has no other resource for its undertakings, or for its impulse toward the truth. But then let it return to itself. For even the all-encompassing world, god, the ruler of the universe, extends to external things, yet still he returns inward, into

himself. Let our intellect do the same thing. After it has followed its senses and through them has stretched out to externals, let it assert its power over the senses and itself. (5) This is the way in which a single force and power in harmony with itself will be produced, and that sure reason will come into existence which is not divided or hesitant in its beliefs and its apprehensions, or in its convictions. When this reason has arranged itself and has agreed with its parts and, as it were, sung in harmony with them, it has touched the highest good. (6) For there is nothing crooked or slippery left over, nothing causing it to totter or slide. It will do all things in accordance with its own command, and nothing will happen unexpectedly. Rather, whatever is done will result in good—easily, as planned, and without the doer's hanging back. For reluctance and hesitation are signs of conflict and inconsistency. And so you may with confidence conclude that the highest good is mental harmony. For the virtues will need to be in a place where there is agreement and unity: the vices are at variance.

(9.1) "But you also," he says, "do not cultivate virtue for any other reason than that you hope for some pleasure from it."[22] First, just because virtue is going to provide some pleasure does not mean that this is the reason why it is sought. It does not provide pleasure, you see, but provides it also. Nor does it toil for pleasure: rather, its toil will attain this as well, even though it is seeking something else. (2) Just as in a field that has been plowed for corn some flowers grow up in between, yet all that work was not undertaken for this little plant, however much it pleases the eyes (the sower had another outcome in mind, and this supervened)—so too, pleasure is not the reward or the motive of virtue but an accessory; and it is not approved of because it gives pleasure, but, if approved of, it gives pleasure also.

(3) The highest good is precisely in the judgment and disposition of the best mind. When such a mind has filled up what belongs to it and has enclosed itself within the ends of its own territory, the highest good is at its full height and does not long for anything more. For there is neither anything outside its totality, no more than there is anything beyond the end.[23] (4) You are off course, then, when you ask for what reason I seek virtue, for you are seeking something above the highest. Do you ask what I seek from virtue? Virtue. For it has nothing better: virtue is its own reward. Or perhaps this is not great enough? When I say to you, "The highest good is an unbreakable

rigor of the mind, and foresight and sublimity and health and freedom and harmony and splendor," even now do you demand something greater to which these things may be referred? Why do you speak to me of pleasure? I am searching for a human being's good, not the belly's. The belly is more capacious in cattle and beasts.

(10.1) "You are pretending not to see what I am saying," he says. "For I myself deny that anyone can live pleasurably unless at the same time he also lives morally—something that cannot be the case for mute animals or for those that measure their good in terms of food. What I am saying is that I clearly and publicly declare that this life that I call pleasurable does not come about without the addition of virtue." (2) But who does not know that the most foolish men are filled to the brim with your pleasures, and that their wickedness overflows with pleasurable things? And that their mind accumulates perverted forms of pleasure in great number: above all, arrogance and placing too great a value on oneself and an inflated ego that towers over others, and a passion for their own things that is blind and lacks foresight, and overexuberance for trivial and childish reasons; also, slanderousness and a self-importance that enjoys delivering insults; a sluggish mind that is lazy and dissolute, dripping with delights and falling asleep on itself. (3) Virtue shakes off all these things and pinches itself awake[24] and evaluates pleasures before it admits them. And it does not set much store by those it does approve of,[25] nor does it rejoice in using them but in tempering them. And temperance, in reducing pleasures, harms the "highest good." You embrace pleasure; I restrain it. You enjoy it; I use it. You think it the highest good; I do not even think it good. You do everything for the sake of pleasure; I do nothing for its sake.

(11.1) When I say that "I" do nothing for the sake of pleasure, I am talking about that wise person, the only one to whom you grant pleasure.[26] I do not, however, call a person wise who has anything above him, least of all pleasure. If pleasure is distracting him, how will he stand up to toil and danger, to poverty and the other menaces that vex human life in such great number? How will he bear the sight of death, how will he bear pains, how will he bear the shattering of the world and so many fierce enemies, when he has been vanquished by such a soft opponent? "He will do whatever pleasure has persuaded." Come on! Do you not see how many things it will try to persuade him into? **(2)** "It will not be capable of persuading him to do anything disgraceful," he says. "For it is conjoined to virtue." Once again, do you not see what kind of highest good it is that needs a guardian to make sure it is good? And how will virtue govern pleasure, if it follows it? For following is the act of one who obeys, ruling of one who commands. Are you putting the commander in the rear? What an excellent duty virtue serves for you, as the foretaster of your pleasures!

(3) But we shall see whether virtue still exists in your house,[27] where it has been treated so insultingly: "virtue" cannot keep its name if it has given ground. In the meantime, adhering to our topic, I will show that the pleasures have besieged many persons on whom fortune lavished all its gifts, and who you must admit are bad. **(4)** Look at Nomentanus and Apicius,[28] procuring the goods (as they call them) of land and sea, and surveying on their table the creatures of every nation. See these same men gazing down on their banquet from a heap of roses, titillating their ears with the sounds of voices, their eyes with spectacular sights, their tastebuds with flavors. Their bodies are stimulated all over with sweet and gentle applications, and to occupy their nostrils while this is happening, fragrances of different kinds are infused right into the room, where sacrifices are being given up to luxury. You will say that these men are immersed in pleasures. Yet it will not go well for them, for they are not rejoicing in good.

(12.1) "It will go badly for them," he says, "because many things will come along that disturb the mind, and their intellects will be disturbed by beliefs that contradict one another."[29] I concede that this is the case. But they themselves, while they are foolish and inconsistent and vulnerable to the pang of regret, will nonetheless experience great pleasures. So we must admit that on such occasions those men were as far removed from all pain as they were from a good mind, and as comes about for many, they were raving with a cheery insanity and were smiling in their madness. **(2)** By contrast, wise persons' pleasures are diluted and modest and practically powerless. They are contained and scarcely noticeable. For they come unasked for, and however much they arrive on their own initiative, they are not held in high regard or taken up with any joy by those who experience them. Indeed, wise persons blend the pleasures in, and place them in their life at intervals, much as serious business is relieved by a game or a joke.

(3) So let them stop joining things that do not go together, and stop tangling virtue up with pleasure—a vice that finds them encouraging the most wicked people. That dissolute hedonist, perpetually drunk and belching, because he knows that he is living with pleasure, upon hearing that pleasure is inseparable from virtue believes that he is living with virtue too. Next, he gives his own vices the title of wisdom and makes despicable pronouncements. (4) They do not, then, indulge in luxury at the urging of Epicurus, but rather, being devotees of the vices, they conceal their luxury in philosophy's lap and make a beeline for where they hear pleasure is praised. Nor do they appreciate how sober and temperate is that pleasure of Epicurus (this, by Hercules, is *my* opinion!), but they fling themselves toward his very name, seeking for their lusts a sponsor and a veil.[30] (5) And so they lose the one good thing they had in their bad actions: shame for their wrongdoing. Now, you see, they praise the things at which they used to blush, and they boast about their vice. Thus not even a resurgence of regret is allowed,[31] when a moral label is placed on disgraceful idleness. This is why your praise of virtue is dangerous: moral precepts are hidden within, while what is outwardly shown is that which corrupts.

(13.1) I am myself of the opinion—though my fellow Stoics would be unwilling to say what I say—that Epicurus's teachings are sacred and right and, if you approach more closely, sobering. The fact is that *his* pleasure is restrained to a small and meager amount, and he imposes the same law on pleasure as we do on virtue. He commands pleasure to obey nature. And what is sufficient for nature is insufficient for luxury. (2) What, then, is the problem? Whenever someone uses "happiness" (*felicitas*) to refer to inactive leisure and the alternations of gluttony and lust, he is searching for a good authority for a thing that is bad. And when he goes there, allured by the pleasing name, the pleasure he is following is not what he hears but what he has brought with him. And once he begins to think his own vices are similar to the teachings, he indulges in them without fear or secrecy, and from that point forward he even luxuriates in them with his head uncovered. I will not, then, say what most of my fellow Stoics say: that Epicurus's sect is a teacher of misdeeds. But I do say this: it is called names, and is infamous. "Yet it does not deserve it." (3) But how can anyone know this unless he has been admitted within? Its own exterior gives license for storytelling and incites wicked expectations. This is like a brave man dressed up in women's clothing: you are confident of your respectability, your masculinity is intact, and your body is not exposed to suffering anything disgraceful, yet you have a tambourine in your hand.[32] So select a label that is morally good, that inspires the mind simply by how it is inscribed. The existing label has been discovered by the vices.

(4) Whoever approaches virtue has given an indication of his noble nature. Whoever follows pleasure seems weak, broken, ignoble,[33] gravitating quickly toward disgrace unless someone shows him the distinctions between pleasures so that he knows which pleasures stand within the limits of natural longing[34] and which are carried headlong and have no limit, being the more unfulfillable the more they are filled. (5) Come on, then! Let virtue go in front, and every footstep will be safe. Further, pleasure is harmful when it exceeds, whereas in virtue there is no need to fear that there will be anything excessive, because there is a limit in virtue itself. A thing cannot be good if it labors under its own magnitude. Furthermore, for creatures who have been assigned a rational nature, what better aim is there than reason? Even if that pairing of yours pleases you—if this is the company with which you prefer to proceed toward the happy life— let virtue go in front, and let pleasure accompany, hovering around your body like a shadow. But to hand over virtue, a most sublime mistress, to serve pleasure as a handmaiden is the act of one who conceives nothing great in his mind.[35]

(14.1) Let virtue go first, and let these be the standards she bears. We will nonetheless have pleasure, but we will be its masters and its controllers. Pleasure will obtain something from us by asking for it: it will get nothing by coercion. By contrast, those who have yielded first position to pleasure are without both: they lose virtue, and what is more, they themselves do not have pleasure, but pleasure has them.[36] They are either tortured by a lack of pleasure or stifled by its abundance, being unhappy if they are deserted by it and still more unhappy if they are overrun—just as those caught in the Syrtian sea are left high and dry one moment, and flooded by torrential waves the next.[37] (2) And this comes about from excessive lack of self-control and a blind passion for a thing. For when someone seeks bad things instead of good, it is dangerous for him to attain them. Just as toil and danger attend our hunting of beasts, and even when we have captured them their possession gives us anxiety (since they often gore their masters), so it is with great pleasures: they do great harm when they get away from us, and when we capture them they capture us. The more numerous and the greater they are, the more diminished is that man whom the crowd calls happy, and the more things he is enslaved to. (3) I am inclined to persist in using the same image to describe this thing: consider how someone who hunts out the lairs of beasts, and who thinks it is a great thing "to catch the prey by snare" and "to circle round the wide woodlands with dogs"[38] so that he can close in on their tracks, abandons more important things and says no to many duties. In the same way, the pursuer of pleasure ranks all things behind it, and the first thing he neglects is his freedom. His spending is all on his belly, and he does not buy pleasures for himself but sells himself to pleasures.

(15.1) "But what prevents pleasure and virtue from merging into one thing," he says, "and what prevents the highest good from being fashioned in such a way that one and the same thing is both morally good and pleasurable?" Because there can be no part of the morally good that is not morally good, and the highest good will not have its own purity if it sees something in itself that is different from what is better. (2) Even the joy that derives from virtue, though it is a good, is still not part of the perfect good, no more than are joy and tranquility, even though they come into existence from the most excellent causes—for these are good, but they follow the highest good and do not complete it.[39] (3) If, however, someone makes an alliance between virtue and pleasure, and an unequal one at that, through the fragility of the one good he weakens whatever force is in the other, and he throws his freedom under the yoke, since it remains unbeaten only if it recognizes nothing else as more valuable than itself. For he begins to have need of fortune, which is the greatest servitude of all. The life that ensues is anxious, suspicious, fearful, afraid of events, hanging on the moments of passing time. (4) You are not giving virtue a foundation that is serious and stable, but rather you are ordering it to stand in an unstable spot. And what is so unstable as awaiting the things of fortune, or the changeability of the body and the things that affect the body? How can this person obey god, and accept whatever happens with a good mind, and not complain about fate but be a favorable interpreter of his own circumstances, if he is agitated by the slightest prickings of pleasure and pain? But he is not even a good guardian or avenger of his fatherland, nor is he a defender of his friends, if he veers toward the pleasures.

(5) The highest good must ascend, therefore, to a height from which it is not dislodged by any force, where neither grief nor hope nor fear have any access, nor any other thing that might diminish the highest good's authority. And an ascent so high can be made by virtue alone. That steep incline must be tamed by virtue's step. Virtue will stand bravely and will endure whatever happens, not only patiently but also willingly. It will always know that difficult times are a law of nature. And like a good soldier it will bear its wounds and count its scars, and as it dies, pierced with arrows, it will love the commander for whom it is falling. It will keep in mind that ancient teaching: Follow god. (6) On the other hand, whoever complains and laments and groans is compelled by force to follow orders, and though he is unwilling, he is nonetheless seized away to do what has been commanded. Yet what insanity it is to be dragged rather than to follow![40] What foolishness it is, by Hercules, and ignorance of one's own condition, to grieve because you lack something or because something rather harsh happens to you; and equally, to be surprised at, or to bear unworthily, those things that happen to good and bad people alike. I refer to sicknesses, funerals, the maiming of the body, and other things that suddenly smash into human life. (7) If, because of the way the universe is configured, there is something we must suffer, let us take it on with a great mind. This is the oath we took when we enlisted: to bear mortal things, and not to be disturbed by things that it is not in our power to avoid. We have been born under a king: freedom consists in obeying god.

(16.1) True happiness, then, is located in virtue. What will this virtue persuade you to do? To regard as neither good nor bad that which concerns neither virtue nor wickedness. Next, to be unmovable both against what is bad and in keeping with what is good so that you may, within the bounds of what is allowed, fashion an image of god. (2) What does virtue promise you for this expedition? Huge things, equal to what is divine: you will not be compelled to do anything, you will lack nothing, you will be free and safe from harm. You will never attempt anything in vain, you will never be prevented. Everything will go for you in accordance with your thinking, nothing will arise to stand in your way, nothing against your opinion or your will. (3) "What? Virtue is sufficient for living happily?" Why should it *not* be sufficient, and indeed overflowing, given that it is perfect and divine? For what can be lacking in something that is placed outside longing for anything? What outside needs are there for one who has collected all his own things into himself? But a person who strives toward virtue, even if he has advanced a long way, needs some leniency from fortune while he is still struggling amid human affairs— until he has undone that knot and every mortal bond. What, then, is the difference? It is that others are shackled, trussed up, or even tied on a rack, whereas he who has advanced to higher things and has raised himself aloft is tugging at a loosened chain, not yet free, but already as if free.

(17.1) So if any one of those who bark at philosophy says what they always say: "Why, then, do you speak more bravely than you live? How is it that you lower your voice for someone of higher rank and treat money as a necessary resource for you?[41] And that you allow yourself to be disturbed by a loss and shed tears when you hear that your wife or your friend has died? And that you look to your reputation and let yourself be touched by spiteful words? (2) How is it that your country estate is more cultivated than natural use requires? Why do you not dine in accordance with your own prescriptions? Why is your furniture so extravagant? Why is wine consumed at your house that is of an older vintage than you are? Why is there gold everywhere? Why have trees been planted to provide nothing more than shade? How is it that your wife wears in her ears assets equal to those of a wealthy household? How is it that your school of slave boys is decked out in expensive uniforms? How is it that in your house table service is a fine art, and the silverware is not laid out randomly and spontaneously but is expertly arranged, and there is a maestro appointed for the carving up of special dishes?"

Add, if you like: "Why do you have property overseas? Why do you have more than you are aware of? Why are you either so disgracefully negligent that you do not know even a few of your slaves, or so disgracefully luxurious that you have too many for your memory to retain knowledge of?"

(3) Later I will help your attacks and will throw more charges at myself than you can think of. For now, I will make this reply to you: I am not wise, and, just to nourish your ill will: I will not be wise. Demand from me, then, not that I am equal to the best but that I am better than the bad. It is enough for me to subtract something from my vices each day and to chastise my own mistakes. (4) I have not arrived at good health, nor will I indeed arrive. I am concocting balms rather than cures for my "gout," content if it visits me less often and less acutely. Yet compared with your feet, you weaklings, I am a runner. I am saying these things not on my behalf (for I myself am deeply mired in all manner of vices) but on behalf of one who has accomplished something.

(18.1) "You speak in one way and live in another," you say. This accusation, you spiteful creatures, bitter enemies of all the best, was made against Plato, against Epicurus, against Zeno.[42] All of them said not how they themselves were living but how they themselves ought to live too. I speak about virtue, not about myself; and when I attack the vices, I attack my own vices especially. I will live as I ought as soon as I can. (2) Nor will your spitefulness laced with all its poison deter me from the best things. Not even that venom with which you spatter others, with which you kill yourselves, will hinder me from continuing to praise the life *not* that I live but that I know *ought* to be lived, or from worshiping virtue and crawling after it from a huge distance behind. (3) Can I expect outright that resentment will leave all things unviolated, when it did not hold Rutilius sacred, or Cato?[43] Should someone be concerned if he seems too wealthy to people who regard Demetrius the Cynic as not poor enough?[44] A spirited man who combats all natural longings, made that much poorer than the other Cynics by the fact that, when they forbade themselves to have things,[45] he also forbade himself to want them—this man, they say, is not sufficiently poor! For you see, he professed knowledge not of virtue but of poverty.

(19.1) They say that Diodorus,[46] an Epicurean philosopher who just a few days ago put an end to his life with his own hand, did not act in accordance with the decree of Epicurus, because he cut his own throat. Some want this act of his to be called insanity, others rashness. Diodorus, meanwhile, happy and full of good conscience, gave testimony to himself as he departed from life and praised the restfulness of a life spent in port and at anchor. And he said what you people heard unwillingly, as if you too had to do it:

I have lived and I have run the course that fortune granted.[47]

(2) You people argue about one person's life and another's death, and in response to the reputation of those who are great on account of some outstanding glory, you bark like little dogs when they encounter unfamiliar people. For it suits you best that no one seems to be good, as if another's virtue is a rebuke to all your misdemeanors.[48] You jealously compare their splendors with your filth, and you do not understand how much you lose by your audacity. For if those who follow virtue are greedy, lustful, and ambitious, what are you, to whom the very name of virtue is hateful? (3) You deny that anyone delivers on what he says or lives up to the example of his own speech. Why is this surprising, when what they say is courageous, huge, venturing beyond all the tempests of human existence? Although they try to unfasten themselves from their crosses (while each one of you drives nails into his own cross), they are nonetheless brought up for punishment and are suspended on single posts. You whose punishment is self inflicted are stretched over as many crosses as you have desires. Yet you are slanderous and cleverly compose insults against others. I could have believed you had the time to do this, if some of you were not spitting down on spectators from a cross.[49]

(20.1) "Philosophers do not deliver on what they say." They do, however, deliver on much of what they say, of which they have a morally good conception. If only they *did* accomplish things equal to their words: what could be happier for them? In the meantime, there are no grounds for you to scorn their good words, or their hearts full of good thoughts. Their undertaking of wholesome studies deserves praise, even if they do not achieve their goal. (2) What is surprising if, having entered upon a steep path, they do not arrive at the top? But if you are a man, those who undertake great things, even if they fall, deserve your admiration. It is a noble thing to make an attempt on lofty things, looking not to one's own strength but to the strength of one's nature, and to conceive in one's intellect things greater than can be successfully achieved even by those endowed with enormous greatness of mind.

(3) He who proposes the following to himself: "I will see death with the same expression as when I hear about it. I will submit to my labors, however great they are, sustaining my body with my mind. I will scorn wealth equally whether it is present or absent, and I will be neither gloomier if it resides elsewhere nor more heartened if it glitters around me. I will pay no attention to fortune at either its coming or its going. I will look on all lands as my own, and my own lands as everyone's. I will live as if I know that I was born for others, and I will on this account give thanks to the nature of the world. For how else could it have served my interests better? It gave me, a single person, to all, and gave all to me. (4) Whatever I have, I will neither guard greedily nor recklessly scatter: I will believe that I possess nothing greater than what I have given well. I will calculate favors not according to their number or their weight, but only according to my evaluation of the recipient: that which someone deservingly receives, I will never consider costly. I will do nothing for the sake of people's opinions, but everything for the sake of my conscience. Whatever I do out of my conscience I will believe is being done with people looking on. (5) The limit to my eating and drinking will be to satisfy my natural longings, not to fill and then empty my belly. I will be pleasant to my friends, kind and yielding to my enemies. I will be won over before I am asked, and when morally good requests are made, I will come running. I will know that my homeland is the world and the gods who protect it, and that the gods stand above me and around me as censors of my actions and my words. And when either nature seeks my spirit back or reason gives it leave to go, I will exit testifying that I loved my good conscience and my good studies, and that no one's freedom, least of all my own, was ever diminished by my doing"—he who proposes to do these things, who wishes to do them and tries to do them, will be making a journey toward the gods. Indeed, that person, even if he does not reach them, "falls, but having dared great things."[50]

(6) You people, certainly, in hating virtue and its cultivator, are doing nothing new. For weak eyes fear the sun, and nocturnal animals

turn away from the bright daylight—they are stunned by its first rising, and they scatter in search of their lairs, or conceal themselves in some nook or cranny, afraid of the light. Keep moaning, and keep exercising your unhappy tongues with attacks on good people. Keep opening your mouths and biting down: you will break your teeth long before you leave any impression.

(21.1) "Why does this one study philosophy and live his life so wealthy? Why does he say that wealth is to be scorned, and yet have it? Why does he think that life is to be scorned, and yet live, and that health is to be scorned, and yet watch his health so carefully and prefer it to be at its best? And he thinks that exile is an empty word, and says, 'What harm is there in changing regions?' and yet, if he can, he spends his old age in his homeland? And he holds that there is no difference between a longer time and a shorter time, yet if nothing prevents it, he extends his life and he flourishes peacefully in extreme old age?"[51]

(2) He says that those things ought to be scorned, not so that he will not have them, but so that he will not have them anxiously. He does not reject them for himself, but when they depart he sees them on their way, free from anxiety. Where, indeed, can fortune make a safer deposit of wealth than in a place from which it can be received without any fuss from the one who hands it back? (3) Marcus Cato, when he praised Curius and Coruncanius and that age in which a few small coins of silver were a censorial offense, himself possessed four million sesterces—certainly fewer than Crassus, but more than Cato the Censor.[52] Should a comparison be made, it would be found that he had surpassed his ancestor by more than he was surpassed by Crassus. And if greater wealth had come his way, he would not have spurned it. (4) For the wise person does not think himself unworthy of any fortuitous gifts: he does not love wealth, but he does prefer it. He receives it not into his mind but into his house, and when he has it he does not reject it but holds on to it, and he wants his virtue to be supplied with greater material.

(22.1) But what doubt is there that here, in wealth, the wise man has greater material for unfurling his mind than he does in poverty? For in poverty the only kind of virtue is not being deterred or depressed, whereas in wealth there is a wide open field for temperance and liberality and diligence and management and magnificence.

(2) The wise person will not scorn himself, even if he is of the smallest stature; yet he will wish to be tall. And he will remain strong when emaciated in body or missing an eye, yet he will prefer to have a robust body—though he knows there is something else in him that is stronger. He will tolerate his health being poor, but he will wish it to be good. **(3)** You need to understand that there are certain things that, even if they are small within the larger scheme of things and can be taken away without ruining the principal good, nevertheless add something to the unending joy that comes into existence from virtue. Wealth affects him and exhilarates him, like a favorable wind that pushes a sailor along, or like a fine day and a sunny spot during the cold depths of winter. **(4)** Who, indeed, among wise persons—our wise persons, I mean, for whom virtue is the sole good—denies that even these things that we call indifferents have some value in them, and that some are preferable over others?[53] Some of these things are granted some honor, and others are granted much. And, to make sure you do not get it wrong: wealth is among the preferables.

(5) "Why, then, do you mock me," you say, "when wealth has the same place for you as it does for me?" Do you want to know how different a place they have? If wealth flows away from me, it will take nothing but itself. You will be stunned, and it will seem to you that you are devoid of yourself, if wealth departs from you. For me, wealth has a place; for you, the highest place. In sum, my wealth is mine, but you belong to yours.

(23.1) So stop forbidding philosophers to have money. No one has sentenced wisdom to poverty. The philosopher will have ample wealth, but not wrested from anyone or dripping with another's blood, and acquired without any harm to anyone or any filthy profiteering. Its exit will be as morally good as its entry, and no one except a stingy person would mourn for it. Pile it up as much as you wish: that wealth is morally good in which, even when there are many things that each person might wish to be called his, there is nothing that anyone can rightly call his. **(2)** In fact, the philosopher will not push fortune's generosity away from him, and he will neither boast nor blush over an estate that was gained by morally acceptable methods. He will actually have something of which he can boast, however, if he can open up his house and admit the citizenry among his possessions and say: "What each recognizes, let him take." What a great man he is, and wealthy in the best way, if he can say this and then retain exactly the same amount! What I mean is that if he can allow the people to scrutinize his things and not lose anything or feel anxious—if no one finds anything in his house to which he can lay claim—he will be wealthy boldly and publicly.

(3) The wise person will not allow a single denarius to make an entrance across his threshold if it is ill gotten. But the same person, faced with great wealth, a gift of fortune and the fruit of his virtue, will not reject it or refuse it access. For what reason is there for him to begrudge it a good place? Let it come and make itself at home. He will neither toss it around nor hide it away: the one is the act of a tasteless mind, the other of a mind timid and pathetic, as if it held a great good in its pocket. Nor, as I have said, will he cast it out of his house. (4) For what is he going to say: "You are useless," or "I do not know how to use wealth"? Just as he will be capable of completing a journey even on foot, but will prefer to climb aboard a carriage, so he will be capable of being poor, but will wish to be wealthy. So he will possess wealth, but treating it as light and likely to fly away: he will not allow it to weigh heavily on anyone else or on himself. (5) He will give—why did you prick up your ears, why are you preparing your pocket? He will give either to good men or to those whom he can make good. He will give, selecting with special care those who are most worthy, since he remembers that he must give an account of his expenses as much as of what he has received.[54] He will give for right and commendable reasons, because a bad gift is to be counted a shameful loss. His pocket will be open, but not riddled with holes: much will come from it, but nothing will fall from it.

(24.1) If someone thinks it is an easy thing to give, he is off course. This thing is exceedingly difficult, if one is to make informed donations rather than random and haphazard scatterings. To this person I do a favor, to that one I return one. This one I rescue, that one I take pity on. Another I provide for because he is worthy to be spared the distraction and the impediment of poverty. To certain people I will not give, no matter how much is lacking, because even if I give it will be lacking. To others I will offer, on others I will even tread! I cannot be negligent in this matter: I am never more carefully noting names than when I give.[55]

(2) "What?" you say. "You give with a view to receiving?" Actually, with a view to not wasting. Let a gift go somewhere from which it need not be sought back, but could be paid back. Let a favor be deposited like a treasure buried deep, which you would not dig up unless it were necessary. (3) Well? How great is the material for doing favors in a wealthy man's own household! For who requires that generosity be directed only toward those who wear the toga? Nature commands me to be helpful to human beings. What does it matter if these be slave or free, freeborn or freed, and possessing a legal freedom or a freedom conferred by one friend on another? Wherever a human being is, there is a place for a favor. Thus money can be distributed even inside one's own threshold, and can be an exercise in liberality, which is so called not because it is paid out to free individuals (*liberis*) but because it originates in a free (*libero*) mind. In the wise person's house, liberality is never thrust on the disgraceful or unworthy, nor is it ever so exhausted and off course that it cannot flow as if from a full reservoir whenever he finds someone worthy.

(4) There is no reason, then, why you should hear wrongly what is said morally, bravely, and spiritedly by those who are eager for wisdom. And pay attention to this first: there is a difference between one who is eager for wisdom and one who has attained wisdom. The former will tell you: "I say the best, but I am still tossed amid many bad things. It is not the case that you can hold me to my rule: I am making myself at this very moment, and shaping myself and raising myself up to the level of a huge example. If I advance as far as I have proposed, *then* demand that my actions correspond to my words." He, however, who has reached the highest point of human goodness will deal with you differently and will say: "First, you should not allow yourself to pass judgment on your betters. It has already turned out for me that I am displeasing to bad people—a sign that I am right. (5) But, to give you the account that I begrudge to no mortal person, hear what I promise and at how much I value each thing. I deny that wealth is a good. For if it were a good, it would make people good. As it is, since that which bad people are caught doing cannot be called good, I deny wealth this name. But I do admit that wealth is to be acquired and is useful and brings great advantages to life.

(25.1) "Hear, then, the reason why I do not count wealth as a good, and hear what I contribute in the case of wealth that is different from what you people do, seeing as we both agree that it is to be acquired.[56] Put me in the most lavish house, put me where gold and silver are in common use: I will not look up at myself because of things that, even if they are with me, are still outside me. Shift me to the Sublician bridge[57] and cast me among the needy: I will not on that account, however, look down on myself because I have joined the ranks of those who stretch out their hand for alms. For what difference does it make whether someone lacks a piece of bread, if he does not lack the capacity to die? Well? I prefer that splendid house to the bridge. (2) Put me among glittering contraptions and a luxurious retinue: I will not believe myself to be in any way happier because I have a soft garment, because purple is spread out under my guests. Change my bedding: I will not be unhappier if my tired neck rests in a handful of hay, if I lie over a patched circus cushion which leaks its stuffing. Well? I prefer to display my state of mind while wearing a noble's toga and cloak[58] rather than having my shoulder blades bare or half-covered.[59] (3) Let all my days proceed in accordance with my prayers, let one round of rejoicing follow on another: I will not be smug because of this. Change these favorable times to their opposite; let my mind be assaulted from all sides by loss, grief, and various attacks; let no hour be without lament: I will not for this reason say that I am miserable amid most miserable conditions. I will not for this reason curse a day, for I made provision that no day of mine would count as 'black.'[60] Well? I prefer to temper my joys than to combat griefs."

(4) The famous Socrates will say to you the following: "Make me conqueror of all the nations, have that luxurious chariot of Liber[61] carry me in triumph from the rising of the sun all the way to Thebes, let kings seek their laws from me:[62] I will be thinking of myself as human most of all when I am greeted by one and all as a god.[63] Then follow this lofty pedestal with a radical transformation. Let me be placed on someone else's float, to adorn the procession of a fierce and arrogant conqueror: I will not be any more humble when I am carried beneath another's chariot than I was when I stood in my own. Well? I nevertheless prefer to conquer than to be captured. (5) I will look down on the whole kingdom of fortune, but if I am granted an opportunity to make a selection, I will take what is better. Whatever

comes my way will be made good, but I prefer that easier and more pleasant things come, things less taxing to deal with.

"There is, indeed, no reason why you should think that any virtue is without effort. But some virtues are in need of goading, others of reining in. **(6)** Just as a body on an incline must be held back, but one facing a steep hill must be pushed, so some virtues are on an incline, others go up a slope. Or is there any doubt that there is a climb, an effort, a struggle, for endurance, courage, persistence, and whatever other virtues confront hard things and overcome fortune? **(7)** Well? Is it not equally obvious that there is a downhill ride for liberality, temperance, and gentleness? In the latter cases we restrain our mind from slipping forward; in the former we exhort it and spur it on most fiercely. So we will apply to poverty those braver virtues that know how to fight, and to wealth we will apply those more diligent ones that walk on tiptoe and hold back their heavy load. **(8)** Given this distinction, I prefer to use those virtues that must be exercised more calmly than those proved by blood and sweat. So I live no differently," says the wise person, "than I speak, but you people hear differently. Only the sound of my words reaches your ears: you do not investigate what it means."

(26.1) "What difference is there, then, between me, a fool, and you, a wise person, if we both wish to have wealth?" A vast difference. You see, in the case of the wise person, wealth is in servitude: in the case of the fool it is in command. The wise person gives no license to wealth: your wealth gives you all manner of license! You people get accustomed to wealth and cling to it, as if someone had promised you eternal possession of it: the wise man rehearses for poverty most of all when he stands amid wealth. **(2)** A general never trusts peace so much that he does not prepare himself for a war that, even if it is not being waged, has been declared. In your arrogance you have let yourselves be made senseless by a beautiful house, as if it could not burn or collapse, and by your wealth, as if it has transcended all danger, and as if it is too great for the strength of fortune to be able to exhaust it. **(3)** Ensconced in leisure, you play with your wealth and do not look ahead to its endangerment, just as foreign peoples who have been encircled but have no knowledge of battle engines often look on lazily at the efforts of their besiegers, and do not understand the purpose of those things that are being constructed in the distance. The same thing happens to you. You grow weak amid your possessions and do not consider how many incidents threaten from every direction, and even now you expect to carry off precious spoils. Whoever takes away a wise person's wealth leaves behind for him all that is his. For the wise person lives rejoicing in present circumstances, without a care for the future.

(4) "There is nothing," says Socrates, or some other with the same feelings and the same power regarding human affairs—"nothing of which I have persuaded myself more completely, than not to turn my life's conduct in the direction of your opinions. Bring together your usual words from every side: I will not think that you are attacking me but rather that you are wailing like the most pitiful babies." (5) This is what that one will say who has attained wisdom, whose mind, immune to vices, commands him to cry out at others, not out of hate but in order to offer a remedy. To this he will add the following: "Your assessment of me does not disturb me on my account but on yours, because to hate virtue and to challenge it with your outcries[64] is to forswear all hope of being good. You do not injure me. But then, neither do those who overturn altars injure the gods. Yet bad intentions and bad designs are manifest, even where no harm can be done. (6) I endure your hallucinations just as Jupiter the Greatest and Best endures the absurdities of the poets.[65] One of the poets put wings on Jupiter, another horns. Another made him an adulterer and a night reveler. Another made him cruel against the gods, another unjust to men, another even the rapist of freeborn people and of kin, another a parricide and a usurper of another's throne, including his father's. They accomplished nothing except that human beings, if they believed that the gods were like this, would lose their sense of shame toward wrongdoing.

(7) "But although your words do not hurt me, I still advise you for your own sake: Look up to virtue. Trust those who, having followed it for a long time, proclaim that they are following something great, that appears greater day by day. Worship virtue itself, in the same way as you would the gods; worship virtue's devotees as you would high priests. And whenever mention is made of sacred writings, show favor with your tongues (*fauete linguis*). This expression is not taken, as most believe, from showing favor (*fauore*),[66] but rather

it commands silence so that a ritual can be performed properly with no bad voice blurting out. It is even more necessary for this to be commanded of *you* so that whenever something is uttered from that oracle, you may concentrate and may hold your tongues while you listen. (8) But whenever someone shaking a rattle utters official lies;[67] whenever someone expert at lacerating his muscles bloodies his arms and shoulders with his lightly raised hand; whenever a woman crawling through the street on her knees lets out her wails, and an old man clothed in linen and wielding a laurel branch and a lantern in broad daylight cries out that one of the gods is angry—you rush in and listen, and you affirm that he is divine, feeding one another's amazement."

(27.1) Look, it is Socrates, who proclaims from that prison which he purified by entering, and rendered more moral than any senate house: "What madness is this, what nature hostile to gods and men, to defame the virtues and to violate sacred things with spiteful speech? Praise good men, if you can. If not, pass on by. But if you prefer to exercise your shameful freedom of speech, then make your attacks on one another. For when you direct your insanity at the heavens, I will not say you commit sacrilege, but you are wasting your time. (2) I have, on occasion, supplied Aristophanes with material for jokes,[68] and that entire cohort of comic poets has sprayed its poisoned witticisms on me. My virtue has been illuminated by the very things with which it was attacked. You see, it is beneficial for it to be drawn out and made trial of, and no one understands its magnitude better than those who have challenged it and felt its strength. No one knows the hardness of a rock better than those who have been dashed on it. (3) I offer myself like a lonely outcrop in a shallow sea, which the waves keep lashing, from whichever side they have been stirred up. Yet they do not for that reason either move it from its place or exhaust it with their endless onslaught through so many ages. Pounce, make your attack: I will defeat you by endurance. Something that crashes into things that are firm and cannot be overthrown exercises its strength to its own detriment. In future, search out some soft and penetrable material for sticking your weapons into. (4) "But do you really have the time to scrutinize the bad qualities of others and to pass judgments about anyone? 'Why does this philosopher live so lavishly? Why does this one dine so elegantly?' You inspect other people's pimples, when you are covered with so many sores? This is just as if someone were to deride the moles and warts on beautiful bodies, while he is being eaten away by horrible scabs. (5) Charge Plato with having sought money, Aristotle for having received it, Democritus for having neglected it, Epicurus for having consumed it.[69] Accuse me regarding Alcibiades and Phaedrus,[70] and I will call you most happy of all[71]—as soon as you are in a position to imitate even our vices! (6) But why do you not rather take a look at your own bad circumstances, which penetrate you on every side, some attacking you on the outside, others burning in your insides? Even if you are little aware of your own situation, human affairs have not reached the point where you have an abundance of leisure that leaves you free to exercise your tongue by reproaching better people.

(28.1) "You do not understand this, and you wear an expression inconsistent with your fortune, like very many who sit around at the circus or theater when meanwhile there has been a death in the family and they have not yet heard the bad news. I, however, am gazing forth from on high and can see what storms either threaten you and a little later will unleash their flood, or are already nearby and have come very close and will snatch away you and your things. What more? Surely even now, though you are too little aware of it, a whirlwind is spinning your minds, and is tangling you up, as you avoid the same old things and seek the same old things. Now your minds are lifted up on high, now dashed down to the depths . . ."[72]

Notes

Abbreviations

LS   Long, A. A., and D. N. Sedley, *The Hellenistic Philosophers*, 2 vols. Cambridge: Cambridge University Press, 1987.

OLD   *Oxford Latin Dictionary*, ed. P. G. W. Glare. Oxford: Clarendon Press, 1996.

Use.   Usener, Hermann. *Epicurea*. Leipzig, 1887.

Introduction

1. For analysis, including on the variations and subtleties in Stoic theories of pleasure, see Asmis 1990, 235–44. Background for the dispute can be found in Cicero *On the Ends of Good and Bad* 2.43–69; cf. Griffin 1992, 307.

2. Background for this emphasis, which probably derives from Panaetius, can be found, e.g., in Cicero *On Duties* 1.17; cf. Asmis 1990, 250; Griffin 1992, 179, 296–97, 307 n. 4.

3. For other discussions of the happy life with different emphases, see *Letters* 85 and 92.

4. On the work's chronology and approach, and the question of its relationship to Suillius's charges, see Griffin 1992, 19–20, 306–9, 396, 399; Asmis 1990, 246–47. For discussion of the charges and Seneca's relationship to money, see Levick 2003; for background on Suillius, Rutledge 2001, 111–13. The development of modern theories about the relationship of *On the Happy Life* to its historical context is helpfully traced by Chaumartin 1989, 1686–89.

5. As Schiesaro notes, Seneca even "offers an implicit model to the ruler" (1996, 26), especially in stressing the importance of respect for freedom.

6. On the heterogeneity of the debates, see Griffin 1992, 307.

7. On joy (*gaudium* = Gk. *chara*) and pleasure here, see Asmis 1990, 232–35, 244; joy and wealth, Griffin 1992, 179.

8. On Stoic values as freedom in this work, see Inwood 2005, 314.

9. As Hill 2004, 151–57 argues, suicide in Seneca serves as an exercise in "cognitive exemplarity."

On the Happy Life

10. These words were used by the president of the senate to declare the outcome of a vote after a *sententia* was put to the vote; see Talbert 1984, 282–83.

11. This phrase (*hoc amplius censeo*) has a technical application in senatorial procedure, where a senator can support a measure and yet amend it by addition; see Talbert 1984, 256.

12. The Stoics, beginning with Zeno, focused on living in agreement with nature. But this was adapted in various ways (see LS 63 ABC), especially concerning the exact reference of "nature." Seneca's phrasing a few lines below, "its own nature," recalls an addition by Chrysippus: the nature "of the human being" (cf. LS 63C2 and Chaumartin 1989, 1692), though Asmis 1990, 225–28 points out that Seneca, further, makes it specific to the nature of the individual person.

13. I fill the lacuna *uoluptatibus et *** pro illis* by following Reitzenstein, who inserts *doloribus spretis*.

14. I follow the conjecture of Gertz, *ipsa sui fastidio obnoxia* for the doubtful reading of the MSS †*ipsis flagitiis noxia*†.

15. "Morally good" is a translation of *honestum*, which I render throughout with either "morally good" or "moral" in keeping with the policy of the series.

16. An Epicurean interlocutor speaks up, unannounced. Here Seneca responds as if the objector were alluding to the Epicurean doctrine of recollection and anticipation of pleasures in the mind; see LS 21T, 22E1, F1, 24D.

17. For the doctrine (Epicurus frag. 506 Use.), compare Diogenes Laertius 10.138; Cicero *Tusculan Disputations* 3.20.49. See also LS 21B, P.

18. Literally, "aediles," the magistrates appointed to monitor standards in bathhouses and other public institutions.

19. The last two phrases are an approximate translation, since the text here is questionable (*nec quicquam* †*mutauit*† *optima*).

20. A quotation from Virgil *Aeneid* 2.61, where the phrase describes the Greek trickster Sinon, who knew that he might be put to death, but hoped to be well received by the Trojans, as in fact he was.

21. I follow the emendation of Russell, *[erat uera] Ratio uero*, against the MSS readings (†*erat uera. ratio uera*† and †*erat uera. ratio uero*†).

22. For this Epicurean criticism of the Stoics, see LS 21P; also, for the Epicurean theory, Epicurus frag. 504 Use.

23. Here "ends" and "end" translate forms of *finis*, which can refer to territorial boundary or any ending but also here alludes to *finis bonorum*, the regular Latin term for the *telos*, or highest good.

24. Literally "pulls its ear" (*aurem peruellit*).

25. I omit a poorly understood phrase in the text, †*utque enim*† *admittit*.

26. For clarifying discussion see Dyson 2010, defending the manuscript reading *concedis* ("you (*sg.*) grant") against the emendation of J. Müller followed by Reynolds, *concedimus* ("we grant").

27. The promise is kept at 14.1.

28. Cassius Nomentanus was a legendary glutton and spendthrift. M. Gavius Apicius, the gourmand (and recipe writer) from Minturnae, flourished during the age of Tiberius.

29. The objector apparently admits that Nomentanus and Apicius are wretched, but denies that they illustrate the Epicurean position. Seneca's refutation in the next lines, however, insists that they do in fact reach the Epicurean goal, or at least the hedonist's goal, and that they show this state to be compatible with, and vulnerable to, madness.

30. Usener 1887 excerpts this as frag. 460 in his survey of Epicurean theory on satisfying desires (frags. 454–84 Use.).

31. I read Reynolds's suggestion *paenitentiae* for †*adulescentiae*†.

32. An instrument of the Galli, the castrated priests of Magna Mater (Cybele).

33. I read Reynolds's suggestion *degener, cito* for †*degenerans uiro*†.

34. Usener excerpts this as frag. 455; see above on 12.4.

35. Epicurus frag. 514 Use. See also Cicero *On the Ends of Good and Bad* 2.69 = LS 210, on Cleanthes' word picture of the virtues as handmaidens to pleasure, a parody of Epicurean theory.

36. The latter two clauses directly contradict a famous utterance of the hedonistic philosopher Aristippus of Cyrene (Diogenes Laertius 2.75).

37. A reference to the notorious shallows off the coast of northern Africa.

38. Quotations from Virgil *Georgics* 1.139–40. The same verses are quoted for a different point at *Letters* 90.11.

39. For the distinction, see Cicero *De finibus* 3.55.

40. The language is close to Seneca's translation from Cleanthes' *Hymn to Zeus, ducunt uolentem fata nolentem trahunt* ("the fates lead the one who is willing; the one who is unwilling, they drag"), at *Letters* 107.10–11; the resonance is noted by Asmis 2009, 120.

41. On possible allusions here to the charges made against Seneca by P. Suillius Rufus in 58 CE, see my introduction to this essay.

42. For Plato as a target of criticism, see especially Athenaeus *Deipnosophistae* 11.504–9; for Epicurus, Diogenes Laertius 10.3–8; for Zeno of Citium (ca. 334–262 BCE), the first Stoic, Diogenes Laertius 7.33–34.

43. P. Rutilius Rufus (b. ca. 160 BCE) and Cato the Younger (95–46); see *On Providence* 2.9, 3.7, 3.14 with notes.

44. Seneca's contemporary and friend; see *On Providence* 3.3 with note.

45. For "they . . . themselves" rather than "he . . . himself," I am following Ruhkopf's emendation *interdixerint* (which makes the contrast with the other Cynics clearer).

46. Otherwise unknown.

47. Virgil *Aeneid* 4.653, words of Dido before her suicide. The line is a favorite of Seneca's, being quoted at *Letters* 12.9 and *On Benefits* 5.17.5.

48. I read *delictorum uestrum omnium sit* with Bourgery, for *delictorum †omnium† sit.*

49. This sentence has puzzled editors, and this translation is an approximation. In the final three sentences, I substitute "you" for Seneca's third-person plural "they," to clarify the reference to his opponents.

50. Ovid *Metamorphoses* 2.328, from the Phaethon episode, a comparison anticipated by the language at 20.2 above. Compare the similar but more extensive use of Phaethon in *On Providence* 5.10–11.

51. In the last two sentences we may see allusions to Seneca's own works *Consolation to Helvia* (concerning exile) and *On the Shortness of Life.*

52. "Marcus Cato" here is Cato the Younger, who evidently revered the frugality of the early third-century Romans M. Curius Dentatus and Tiberius Coruncanius, but possessed wealth of his own without blame. Cato's own wealth falls somewhere between that of the obscenely wealthy triumvir M. Licinius Crassus (d. 53 BCE) and his own moderately wealthy, but parsimonious, great-grandfather Cato the Censor (i.e., Cato the Elder, 234–149).

53. The theory of indifferents is discussed in detail at *Letters* 92.16–26; see also LS 58.

54. In contrast with the common tendency to give indiscriminately, criticized in *On Benefits* 1.1.2.

55. "I am … noting names" (*nomina facio*) is a technical term from accounting, referring to marking someone's status as a reliable or worthy debtor. Seneca applies this analogically to the recipients of his *gifts* (cf. *On Benefits* 1.1.2).

56. This speech has some similarities to a "premeditation of future bad events" (*praemeditatio futurorum malorum*); on *meditatio* in Seneca see Newman 1988, 1989; Bartsch 2006, 230–81.

57. Rome's oldest bridge and a location frequented by beggars.

58. Here no satisfactory solution has been offered for the corrupt text of *praetextatus et †causatus†*: "and cloak" is a guess.

59. I read with Lipsius *semitectis*, for *†sententiis†.*

60. "Black days," or *dies atri*, were the days after the Kalends, Nones, and Ides, considered unlucky.

61. Liber (identified with Dionysus, whose mother Semele was from Thebes) was the legendary inventor of the triumph procession; see Pliny *Natural History* 7.191.

62. I read with Madvig *a me petant* for *†penatium† petant.*

63. A theme of the Roman triumph, in which the triumphator was reminded by a slave: "Look behind you! Remember that you are human!"

64. An approximation, for *†clamitatis† odisse.*

65. There are similarities here to the fragments of Seneca's *On Superstition*, collected in Vottero 1998, 47–56.

66. Cf. *OLD* s.v. *faueo* 5. The Greek term *euphēmia* (lit. "good speaking") also often means "silence."

67. The details evoke various oriental religions, including worship of Isis (rattle) and Cybele (self-laceration).

68. I.e., in Aristophanes' *Clouds*.

69. For Democritus's abandonment of wealth, see *On Providence* 6.2; for corresponding anecdotes on the others, see Diogenes Laertius 3.3 (Plato), 5.4 (Aristotle), 10.7 (Epicurus).

70. Two of Socrates' younger interlocutors, accusations of pederasty were part of the anti-Socratic tradition (e.g., Lucian *Symposium* 39). On the similar accusations against Seneca, see my introduction to this essay.

71. I have adopted the general sense of Grimal's suggestion, *uos quos <tunc> maxime felices <dicam>*, for the corrupt text †*o uos usu†maxime felices*.

72. The transmitted text breaks off here, followed by what survives of the next work in the *Essays*, namely, *On Leisure*. Evidently, in an earlier manuscript from which the surviving manuscripts derive, the pages containing the end of the present work and the beginning of the next were lost.

Editions and Translations

Basore, John, trans. 1932. *Seneca, Moral Essays*, vol. 2. Loeb Classical Library. Cambridge, MA: Harvard University Press.

Davie, John, trans. 2007. *Seneca, Dialogues and Essays*. Oxford: Oxford University Press.

References

Agonigi, Donatella, trans. 1996. Seneca, *Sulla felicità*. Milan: Rizzoli.

Asmis, Elizabeth. 1990. "Seneca on the Happy Life." In *The Poetics of Therapy*, ed. M. Nussbaum, *Apeiron* 23:219–55.

———. 2009. "Seneca on Fortune and the Kingdom of God." In *Seneca and the Self*, ed. Shadi Bartsch and David Wray, 115–38. Cambridge: Cambridge University Press.

Bartsch, Shadi. 2006. *The Mirror of the Self: Sexuality, Self-Knowledge, and the Gaze in the Early Roman Empire*. Chicago: University of Chicago Press.

Chaumartin, François-Régis. 1989. "Les désillusions de Sénèque devant l'évolution de la politique néronienne et l'aspiration à la retraite: Le 'De vita beata' et le 'De beneficiis.'" *Aufstieg und Niedergang der römischen Welt* 2.36.3:1686–1723.

Dyson, Henry. 2010. "Pleasure and the Sapiens." *Classical Philology* 105:313–18.

Griffin, Miriam T. 1992. *Seneca, A Philosopher in Politics*. 2nd ed. Oxford: Oxford University Press.

Hill, Timothy. 2004. *Ambitiosa Mors: Suicide and Self in Roman Thought and Literature*. New York: Routledge.

Inwood, Brad. 2005. *Reading Seneca: Stoic Philosophy at Rome*. Oxford: Clarendon Press.

Ker, James. 2010. "Socrates Speaks in Seneca, *De Vita Beata* 24–28." In *Ancient Models of Mind: Studies in Human and Divine Rationality*, ed. A. Nightingale and D. Sedley, 180–95. Cambridge: Cambridge University Press.

Levick, Barbara. 2003. "Seneca and Money." In *Seneca uomo politico e l'età di Claudio e di Nerone*, ed. A. De Vivo and E. Lo Cascio, 211–28. Bari: Edipuglia.

Newman, R. J. 1988. "Rediscovering the *De Remediis Fortuitorum*." *American Journal of Philology* 109:92–107.

———. 1989. "*Cotidie Meditari*: Theory and Practice of the *Meditatio* in Imperial Stoicism." *Aufstieg und Niedergang der römischen Welt* 2.36.3:1473–1517.

Rutledge, Steven. 2001. *Imperial Inquisitions: Prosecutors and Informants from Tiberius to Domitian*. London: Routledge.

Schiesaro, Alessandro. 1996. "Felicità, libertà e potere nel *De vita beata*." Introduction to Seneca, *Sulla felicità*, trans. D. Agonigi, 5–26. Milan: Rizzoli.

Talbert, Richard J. A. 1984. *The Senate of Imperial Rome*. Princeton, NJ: Princeton University Press.

Vottero, Dionigi. 1998. *Lucio Anneo Seneca: I frammenti*. Bologna: Pàtron.

On Providence

Introduction

JAMES KER

Title and Topic

The work known as *To Lucilius on Providence* is referred to in the earliest surviving manuscript with the longer title *Why Some Misfortunos
Happen to Good Men, though Providence Exists.* This title derives from
a question which, we are told in the work's opening lines, Lucilius has
recently asked Seneca.[1] As Seneca goes on to explain (1.1), his friend's
question would most properly have been answered in a larger work
on providence—something he is not writing here, and evidently never
wrote. Had he done so, Seneca would no doubt have given his own cast
to the doctrines we read about in Cicero's *On the Nature of the Gods*,
our fullest surviving source for Stoic theology and providentialism—
and for the contrasting Epicurean view that the world is the product
of chance and that the gods have no interest in human affairs.[2]

Seneca effectively announces that the work he *is* writing—which
is, in fact, the shortest of the *Essays* that survive complete[3]—belongs
within the more circumscribed area that has become known, since
Leibniz, as the "theodicy" question: how the existence of bad things
(or, in post-Christian terms, "evil") in the world can be reconciled
with the world's having been designed by a divinity. Its focus on
theology and theodicy helps to explain why *On Providence* is among
the most frequently quoted Senecan texts in early Christian literature, even if Christian notions of original sin, eternal life, and divine
judgment transfigured the debate.[4]

But there is little trace here of the kinds of explanation that we
know Chrysippus and other Stoics offered for the existence of bad
things, for example as necessary opposites of goods or minor byprod-
ucts of a major good.[5] Seneca alludes to such topics elsewhere in his
writings, pointing out in one discussion of the gods, for example, that
they are "sometimes neglectful of individuals" (*Letters* 95.50). In the
present work, Seneca does not entertain Lucilius's complaint at all regarding bad things happening to good men, but argues, paradoxically,
that the "bad things" not only are not bad but actually are among

providence's most beautiful provisions. The problem, like so many other problems addressed by the Stoics, is reduced to a matter of correctly recognizing which things are valuable and which are not.

The work's focus is narrowed further by another term of Lucilius's question: the focus on "good men" (*boni uiri*). The focus on *good* men is motivated, from Lucilius's point of view, by the fact that they are the ones to whom bad things ought least to happen, so that the question seemingly exposes one of providentialism's most flagrant self-contradictions. But for Seneca the question becomes an opportunity to explain how the matching of good men with bad fortune is something of ethical and epistemological benefit, both for those who endure it and for those who look on.

Seneca, Lucilius, Audience

On Providence is the first item in Seneca's collection of *Essays* (*Dialogi*). But the *Essays* are not arranged chronologically (e.g., the early work *Consolation to Helvia* is positioned last), and when we turn to the question of where *On Providence* fits in Seneca's life, it is no easier to date it precisely than it is to date most of Seneca's tragedies.[6] A number of circumstantial factors make it less likely that it belongs to Seneca's exile years (as a few scholars have believed) or to his time in Nero's court than to the last years of his life, following his retirement in 62 BCE.

The clearest indication of a later date for the work is its dedication to Lucilius, the friend to whom Seneca also addresses the two major works of his last years, *Natural Questions* and *Letters to Lucilius*.[7] *On Providence* casts Lucilius in the role of an ingrate who complains about the world, when in fact the problem lies in his own mistaken values. This gives Seneca a chance to promise his friend: "I will reconcile you with the gods" (1.5; cf. *Letters* 74.10–11). Being portrayed in this way, Lucilius stands in for any reader who fails to appreciate the beneficial potential of misfortune. Indeed, Seneca's main interlocutor becomes more anonymous as the work proceeds, and occasionally a plural "you" is addressed (e.g., 4.6).

The work has an obvious relevance to Seneca and his aristocratic contemporaries in light of their vulnerability to sudden changes of fortune in Julio-Claudian Rome, and especially given how easy it was to view the Roman Empire as coextensive with the world and the emperor as god. The work's message: endure calamity, and do so in an aggressively dismissive way, not only by refusing to value calamity as bad but by turning it to good or even seeking it out. Yet apart from two quotations from his contemporary Demetrius the Cynic (3.3, 5.5), Seneca discusses misfortune almost exclusively via Cato and other republican heroes, together with Socrates. This wide-ranging inventory of the different forms that calamity can take makes the work a generalized and versatile form of preemptive consolation.

The Structure of the Discussion

On Providence has been described as less like a line and more like a spiral.[8] The work implicitly makes good on its promise to be a kind of defense speech, comprising what scholars have identified as an exordium (1), narration (2), division of topics (3.1), argument (3.2–6.2), and peroration (6.3–9). But Seneca frequently surprises the reader with unexpected turns. For example, after announcing in the opening lines that he will not be writing a work on providence (1.1), he immediately embarks on a sublime and vivid description of law-like movements in nature (1.2–4) to appeal to the reader's sense of wonder and to set the scene for an earthly spectacle.

Seneca characteristically refrains from outlining his argument until he has introduced some general ideas that are basic to the work (1.5–2.12), above all the gods' use of tough love, and their "impulse to watch great men wrestling with some calamity" (2.7). His main example, Cato's suicide at Utica in 46 BCE, belongs in the long tradition of evaluating the merits and significance of Cato's suicide. Here he emphasizes Cato's acquisition of "freedom" (*libertas*) and the gods' role as spectators (2.10). In the latter, Seneca would seem to be exploiting the strongly visual aspect of Latin *prouidentia* (lit., "foresight, looking forth") that is absent in Greek *pronoia* ("forethought").

Seneca's formal outline (3.1) serves as a clear guide, at least initially. He says he will be seeking to show "how things that seem bad are not," and sure enough, Lucilius's question and Seneca's response are repeated throughout the work in ever-changing language. The outline also breaks the topic up into separate points, which do indeed define the work's main structure (approximately 3.2–4.16, 5.1–2, 5.3–6, 5.7–11, 6.1–2), though the transitions become less perceptible as the work unfolds.

Other rhythms and units add a sense of continuity. The analogies from parenting, from athletics, from military discipline, and from spectacle, all introduced in the preliminary discussion in chapters 1 and 2, recur and are viewed from different angles. The typology of misfortunes is embodied in the recurring catalogue of moral exemplars, especially in the crescendo of repeated rhetorical questions (3.5–14) in which each individual is juxtaposed to an example of despicable behavior in the same general sphere of activity or using the same body part.

Seneca also introduces different speakers to the text in a series of evenly spaced monologues. In addition to Cato, Demetrius, and the interlocutor, we hear from fortune and nature (3.3, 3.14); and in the work's final chapters, the fading formal outline is succeeded by two more extensive speeches: one from the Phaethon episode in Ovid's *Metamorphoses* (5.10–11), the other in the voice of "god" himself (6.3–9). This final speech constitutes the work's fullest presentation of the divine, which Seneca has stealthily allowed the reader to glimpse in multiple guises throughout, as nature, fortune, providence, fate, and god (cf. *Natural Questions* 2.45.2–3). And in the work's final lines, god catalogues different forms of suffocation corresponding to the four elements of nature (water, air, earth, fire; 6.9), thus returning to the theme of suicide while also recalling the sketch of nature's orderliness in chapter 1.

Misfortune and Self-Knowledge

At the work's exact middle point, Seneca represents nature explaining why she made Cato's life so full of "grievous" things (3.14). Nature's statement lays bare the most basic lesson of the work: things considered bad, even if they are grievous, are not in fact bad, *and* nature wants "all" to "know" it. At some moments Seneca seems to allow that misfortunes are genuinely regrettable (5.9, 6.6). Yet good men's misfortunes *are* deliberate, sent with a teaching purpose, and the main instructor is god: with the assistance of fortune, god trains good men "to be as good and outstanding as they can be" (2.7) and to become as like to god as is permitted.

Seneca's notion of "a spectacle worthy to be looked on by god as he inspects his own creation" was to become a central motif in the discourse of Christian martyrology, and it is probably Seneca's most tangible influence on the Christian tradition (2.9 with note). Seneca's god, however, is in one sense inferior to humans: as god himself explains in the work's final chapter, god "is *beyond* suffering bad things, you are *above* suffering them" (6.6; emphases added). So when god devises misfortunes to test humans (4.8), he has something new to learn from how they rise above their suffering.

Seneca places equal emphasis on the potential for human beings themselves to learn through misfortune (4.3). The attempt at self-knowledge (*notitia sui*, 4.3), even if we go down in flames like Phaethon (5.11), demonstrates a man's willingness to obey god and to "offer himself up to fate" (5.8). This, ultimately, is the sense in which calamity is "in the interest of the very men to whom" it happens (*pro ipsis*, 3.2): it is an opportunity to act, and especially to *think*, in a way that agrees with the nature of the world. But in explaining the sense in which calamity is "in the interest of everyone" (*pro uniuersis*), Seneca only alludes briefly to the idea that good men or women in Roman public life can benefit others through their toil (5.3–4): his emphasis is on how good men give a lesson (*documentum*, 3.9, 4.12), being "born to serve as an example" (*nati . . . in exemplar*, 6.3).

Seneca presents this heuristic potential of misfortune as part of the teleology of nature. When he compares the courageous man to the sea which colors all the water that enters it (2.1), the simile is more than a simile: it locates human rationality and virtue within a broader spectacle of nature where, as demonstrated in *Natural Questions*, many lessons of moral import can be learned—as in the Roman amphitheater or in animal sacrifice (1.8, 6.8). Seneca makes his words complicit in this natural teleology, demonstrating how grievous events can be converted into, or revealed as, an opportunity for the highest form of self-knowledge—the knowledge gained by Cato and Phaethon alike.

Selected Reading

Dragona-Monachou, Myrto. 1994. "Divine Providence in the Philosophy of the Empire." *Aufstieg und Niedergang der römischen Welt* 2.36.7:4417–90.

Setaioli, Aldo. 2007. "Seneca and the Divine: Stoic Tradition and Personal Developments." *International Journal of the Classical Tradition* 13:333–68.

On Providence

LUCIUS ANNAEUS SENECA

TRANSLATED BY JAMES KER

(**1.1**) You have asked me, Lucilius, why it is the case that, if the universe is governed by providence, many bad things happen to good men. It would have been more fitting to answer this in the context of a work in which we were proving that providence is in charge of absolutely everything and that god is in our midst. But since you want to extract a small part from the whole and to resolve one dispute while leaving the larger controversy untouched, I will do a thing that is not difficult: I will plead the case of the gods.

(**2**) It is redundant in the present circumstances to show that a work of such grandeur does not exist without some kind of protector, and that the heavenly bodies do not gather together and move about in this way by a chance impulse—that things propelled by chance frequently fall into disorder and soon bump into one another, whereas this rapid motion continues without collision, obeying an eternal law and carrying along with it such a quantity of things on land and sea, so many lights shining and reflecting in ordered arrangement.[9] It is redundant to show that this order is not the product of matter moving randomly, and that things that came together haphazardly could not be suspended so artfully that, as a result, the tremendous weight of the earth could sit without moving and watch the flight of the heavens zooming around it; that the seas could pour into valleys and soften the earth and not be caused to overflow by rivers; that huge things could be born from seeds so small. (**3**) Not even those things that seem disordered and unpredictable—I mean rain, clouds, lightning bolts shooting down, and fires erupting from the sundered peaks of mountains, and the ground subsiding and quaking, and other things that the restless parts of the universe set in motion around the earth—not even these, however sudden they are, happen without reason. They too have their own causes, no less than things in strange places that are wondrous to look on, such as hot waters amid the tides and new archipelagos breaching in the wide open sea. **(4)** And again, if someone observes the shores being laid bare by the ebbing sea and in a brief time covered over, he will believe that the waves are first being drawn together and inward by some unseen turbulence, and then are breaking forth and rallying to recapture their position. In fact, however, the waves proportionately grow and decline with the hours and days, now greater now smaller, corresponding to how they have been drawn out by the lunar star, at whose command the ocean swells. These things can be saved for their own occasion, especially as you are not expressing doubts about providence, but leveling a complaint.

(5) I will reconcile you with the gods: they are the best to the best people. You need to know that the nature of the world does not allow that good things should ever be harmful to the good. There is a friendship between good men and the gods sealed by virtue. Did I say friendship? Actually there is a kinship and resemblance, because the only difference between a good man and god is time. He is god's pupil, his imitator,[10] and his true offspring, and that noble parent makes rigorous demands on his virtues and raises him strictly. That is what stern fathers do. **(6)** So when you see that good men who are favorites of the gods toil, sweat, and climb a steep road to the top, whereas bad men laze about immersed in pleasures, you should think about this: in our sons we are delighted by moderation, but in home-born slaves by license; and the former are restrained by a more severe discipline, whereas impudence is fostered in the latter.[11] The same thing should be obvious to you in the case of god. He does not treat the good man as his darling. He tests him, hardens him, readies him for himself.

(2.1) "Why do so many adversities arise for good men?" Nothing bad can happen to a good man. Opposites do not mix. Just as the flavor of the sea remains unchanged and is not even diluted, despite so many rivers, despite such an abundance of rains pouring down from above, despite such strongly tainted springs, so too the mind of a courageous man, faced with an onslaught of adversities, does not falter. It stays where it stands and it converts any happening to match its own color, being, as you know, more powerful than all external things. **(2)** I do not mean he does not feel them, but he defeats them; and although at other times he is resting and calm, when an attack comes he rises to meet it. He thinks of adversities as training exercises. And what man, so long as he *is* a man and is poised for morally good things, is not hungry for honest work and ready to undertake duties at great risk? What conscientious man does not find relaxation a punishment? **(3)** We see that athletes who care about their strength engage in bouts with the toughest men they can find, and demand that these men, who are helping them to prepare for a contest, use every ounce of their strength against them. They let themselves be battered and thrown around, and if they cannot find a single opponent who is their equal, they pit themselves against several at once. **(4)** Without an adversary, their manliness (*uirtus*) wastes away: its size and its power can be seen only when it shows what it can stand up to. Clearly good men must do the same. They must not flinch at hardships and difficulties, and must not level complaints against fate; but whatever happens, they must find the good in it—should turn it to good. It is not what you face that counts, but how you face it.

(5) Do you not see how fathers care for their children in one way, mothers in another? Fathers order their children to get up early to attend to their learning, and do not allow them to relax even on holidays, exacting sweat from them and sometimes tears; whereas mothers coddle them and wish to keep them sheltered, never encountering hardship, never weeping, never toiling. **(6)** God has a father's attitude toward good men. He gives them tough love, saying, "Let them be stirred up by labors, pains, and losses so they can become truly robust." Fattened animals are lazy and inactive, and their strength fails them not only when they are put to work but simply when they move the burden of their own weight. Good fortune that has known no wound cannot endure a single cut. But if someone has had to do constant battle with his misfortunes, his injuries give him a thick skin, and he yields to no bad thing. Rather, if he falls, he still fights—from his knees.

(7) Are you surprised if that god who loves good men so much and wants them to be as good and outstanding as they can be allots them a fortune to exercise against? I, for one, am not surprised if sometimes the gods have an impulse to watch great men wrestling with some calamity. **(8)** Sometimes we feel pleasure if a young man with a steadfast mind has intercepted an oncoming beast with his hunting spear or has endured a lion's attack without showing any fear. This spectacle pleases us all the more in proportion to how nobly he accomplished it. [Yet] such childish and frivolous entertainments for human beings are not sufficient to attract the gods' attention. (9) Here is a spectacle worthy to be looked on by god[12] as he inspects his own creation; here is a god-worthy duel: a brave man matched against misfortune, especially if the man has issued the challenge himself.

What I am saying is that I do not see what on earth Jupiter could have that is more beautiful, if he wishes to turn his attention to it, than the sight of Cato,[13] his party already devastated more than once, nevertheless standing upright amid public ruin. (10) "The whole world may have yielded to a single man's authority," says Cato, "and the lands may be guarded by legions and the seas by fleets, and Caesar's soldiers may be at the gates. Yet Cato has a way out: with one hand he will make a broad path to freedom. This sword, which remained unstained and blameless even in civil war, will now at last accomplish good and noble deeds: it will give to Cato the freedom it was not able to give to his fatherland. Mind of mine, set about the task you have long rehearsed. Tear yourself out of human affairs. Petreius and Juba have already fought each other and lie slain by each other's hand, in a brave and splendid death pact.[14] But this does not befit our greatness. It is as disgraceful for Cato to seek his death from another as it is for him to seek his life."

(11) It is clear to me that the gods watched with great joy as that man, that fierce self-liberator, gave thought to others' safety and eased the escape of those who were departing, as he took up his studies even on that final night,[15] as he thrust his sword into his sacred breast, as he splayed his guts and used his hand to extract that soul of his, which was too pure to be sullied by a blade. (12) I can believe that this is why his wound was not sufficiently decisive and fatal.[16] For the gods, who do not die, it was not enough to watch Cato once: his virtue was brought back and recalled, to show itself in a more challenging role. After all, entering into death does not take as great a mind as seeking it over again. Why would they not have watched willingly as their progeny escaped in such a conspicuous and memorable exit? Death surely sanctifies those men whose exit earns praise even from those who fear it.

(3.1) But in the course of my discussion, I will show how things that seem bad are not. Now I say this: first, that those things that you call harsh, that you call adverse and detestable, are in the interest of the very men to whom they occur; next, that they occur in the interest of everyone, for whom the gods have greater concern than for individuals; and after this, that the men to whom they occur are willing, and that if they are not willing, they are deserving of bad. To these points I will add that these things come to pass like this due to fate, and they come about for good men by the same law by which the men are good. Then I will persuade you never to feel pity for a good man. Yes, he can be called pitiable, but he cannot be so.[17]

(2) Of all the things I have proposed, that which I said first seems the most difficult: that those things we shudder and tremble at are in the interest of the very men to whom they happen. "Is it in these men's own interest," you ask, "to be cast into exile, to be dragged down into poverty, to carry out their children or their wife for burial, to be broken by dishonor, to be maimed?" If you are surprised that these things are in someone's interest, you will be surprised that some people are healed by fire and blade, and equally by hunger and thirst. But if you consider for yourself how some people for therapeutic reasons have their bones shaved and picked out and their veins extracted and certain limbs amputated that were not able to remain attached without their killing the whole body, you will also allow this to be proved to you: that certain difficulties are in the interest of those to whom they occur—just as, by Hercules, certain things that are praised and sought after are *against* the interests of those whom they delight, like feasts, drunkenness, and other things that kill through pleasure.

(3) Among the many magnificent sayings of our Demetrius[18] is this—I heard it recently and it still rings and echoes in my ears: "Nothing seems to me more unhappy," he said, "than someone to whom nothing adverse has ever happened." For such a man has never been allowed to test himself. Though everything has flowed for him in accordance with his wish, or even before he wished it, still the gods have made a scathing judgment of him. He has seemed unworthy of ever defeating fortune, which retreats from any really cowardly man, as if to say: "What? Am I to take *that* man as my adversary? He will immediately put down his weapons. Against him I do not need all my power. He will take flight at the slightest threatening sign: he cannot even look at me. Let us scout around for someone else with

whom I can enter into combat. I am ashamed to fight with a human being who is ready to be defeated!" (4) The gladiator thinks it a dishonor to be matched with an inferior opponent, and knows that there is no glory in defeating one who can be defeated without danger. Fortune does the same. It seeks the bravest men as matches for it and passes over others in disgust. It approaches the most scornful and upright men to direct its force against. It tests fire on Mucius, poverty on Fabricius, exile on Rutilius, torture on Regulus, poison on Socrates, death on Cato.[19] A great example cannot be found except in bad fortune.

(5) Is Mucius[20] unhappy because he clutches the enemy's fires with his right hand and exacts his own punishment for his error, because by scorching his hand he puts to flight the king whom he was not able to put to flight when the same hand was armed? Well? Would he have been happier if he had warmed his hand in a lady friend's lap?

(6) Is Fabricius[21] unhappy because, in the time he has left over from the republic, he tills his fields? Because he wages war as much on wealth as he did on Pyrrhus? Because at his hearth he dines on those very roots and grasses he picked as he cleared his land, an old man who once celebrated a triumph? Well? Would he have been happier if he had crammed into his belly fish from distant shores, and exotic birds? If he had roused his slow and sickened stomach with shellfish from the upper and lower seas?[22] If he had arrayed a huge pile of fruits around highly sought-after beasts caught at great loss of hunters' lives?

(7) Is Rutilius[23] unhappy because those who condemned him will need to plead their case for all the ages? Because he greeted his removal from his fatherland with a calmer mind than he did the removal of his exile from him? Because he alone refused the dictator Sulla and, when he was recalled, nearly went backward and fled further away? "*They* will see," he said, "—those whom Your Happiness[24] caught at Rome. Let them see the abundant blood in the forum, and senators' heads above the Servilian lake (for that was the storage depot for the spoils of Sulla's proscription),[25] and bands of cutthroats roving this way and that throughout the city, and many thousands of Roman citizens butchered in one place even after assurance had been given—indeed, while assurance was being given. Let these things

be seen by those men who are not able to go into exile."²⁶ **(8)** Well? Is Lucius Sulla lucky because when he goes down to the forum a path is cleared for him with the sword, because he allows the heads of former consuls to be shown to him, and he has the profit of the massacre counted out by the quaestor and in public records? And all this was done by the very one who passed the Cornelian law!²⁷

(9) This brings us to Regulus.²⁸ What harm did fortune do to him when it made him a lesson in trustworthiness, a lesson in endurance? His skin is pierced by nails, and in whichever direction his exhausted body leans, it rests on a wound. His eyes have been held open in unending wakefulness. The greater his torture, the greater his glory will be. Do you wish to know how little he regrets having valued his virtue at this price? Unfasten him and send him to the senate, and he will express the same opinion. **(10)** Do you therefore think Maecenas happier?²⁹ He, anxious about his love affairs and lamenting over daily rejection by his moody wife, tries to send himself to sleep using musicians playing in harmony, echoing gently from afar. Though he may tranquillize himself with undiluted wine and may use the splashing of waters to distract his anxious thoughts and deceive them with a thousand pleasures, on his feather bed he will lie as wide awake as Regulus on the cross. But Regulus has comfort in tolerating hardships for the sake of what is morally good, and he looks away from his suffering toward its cause; whereas Maecenas, weak from pleasures and toiling with excessive happiness, is vexed less by the things he suffers than by the cause of his suffering. **(11)** The vices have not taken possession of the human race to such an extent that there is doubt regarding whether, given a choice of fate, more would wish to be born Reguluses than Maecenases. Or, if there is anyone who would dare to say he would have preferred to be born a Maecenas than a Regulus, that same person, even if he does not say so, would have preferred himself to be born a Terentia.³⁰

(12) In your judgment, was Socrates³¹ badly treated because he swallowed that publicly mixed potion no differently than a tonic of immortality and discussed death right up to death? Was he badly done by because his blood congealed, and the coldness creeping in little by little brought the vigor of his veins to a standstill? **(13)** How much more ought we to envy him than those to whom wine is served in a jeweled cup, or for whom a male sex slave, who has been taught

to endure all things and whose manhood has been cut off or is ambiguous, melts snow floating in a cup of gold. They will measure back
out in vomiting whatever they drank, reluctantly re-tasting their own
bile. But Socrates will gulp down poison joyfully and willingly.

(14) As for Cato, enough has been said, and all human beings will
agree in acknowledging that the greatest happiness fell to him, whom
the nature of the world selected to collide with things that are objects
of fear: "Enmities with the powerful are grievous: let him be set in
simultaneous opposition to Pompey, Caesar, Crassus.[32] It is grievous
to be surpassed in political office by the worst sort of men: let him
be placed below Vatinius.[33] It is grievous to be involved in civil wars:
let him soldier around the whole world for a good cause with equal
determination and lack of good luck. It is grievous to lay one's hands
on oneself: let him do this. What will I accomplish through these
things? That all may know that these things are not bad. After all, I
deemed Cato worthy of them."

(4.1) Prosperity comes even to the common people and to worthless minds. But subjugating the misfortunes and terrors of mortals
is unique to a great man. The fact is that always being happy and
passing through life without one's mind being challenged is not to
know the other part of the nature of the world. (2) You are a great
man. But how do I know, if fortune does not give you an opportunity
to show virtue? You have gone to the Olympic Games, but no one
except for you has gone. You have a crown; victory you do not have.
I do not congratulate you as though you were a brave man, but as
though you had attained the consulship or praetorship: your increase
is from a conferred honor. (3) I can say the same thing even to a
good man, if no difficult event has given him occasion to show the
force of his mind: "I judge you pitiable because you have never *been*
pitiable. You have passed through life without an adversary. No one
will know what you were capable of—not even you yourself." The
thing is, self-knowledge requires a test: no one ever discovered what
he was capable of except by trying. That is why there are men who,
when bad things were slow to come, spontaneously put themselves
in their path and, when their virtue looked like it would pass into
obscurity, sought out an occasion for it to shine forth. (4) What I am
saying is that great men sometimes rejoice in adversities, just as brave
soldiers rejoice in war. I myself once heard the gladiator Triumphus

lamenting the rarity of spectacles under Tiberius Caesar: "What a fine era has passed away!" he said.[34]

Virtue is greedy for danger and does not think about what it is going to suffer but what it is striving toward, because even what it is going to suffer is part of its glory. Men in the army glory in their wounds. They joyfully display blood flowing, as a stroke of good fortune. Even if those who come back from the battle line unwounded have accomplished the same, he who returns wounded is looked on more. (5) What I am saying is that whenever god provides people with the material for doing something spiritedly and courageously, he is showing concern for them, whom he desires to be as morally good as possible. This is something that requires events of a certain difficulty. It is in a storm that one may recognize a captain, in a battle line a soldier. How can I know how much spirit you have against poverty, if you are immersed in wealth? How can I know how much resilience you have against dishonor and infamy and being hated by the people, if you are living your old age amid applause, if you are followed by a popularity that cannot be assailed and somehow turns minds favorably toward you? How do I know how calm your mind will be when you confront deprivation, if the children you have raised are there before your eyes? I have heard you when you were consoling others. I would have taken notice only if you had consoled yourself, if you had forbidden yourself to grieve.

(6) My plea to you[35] is that you not allow yourselves to fear those things that the immortal gods apply to our minds like spurs. Calamity is an opportunity for virtue. The ones that can deservingly be called pitiable are those who grow numb from excessive good fortune, who are held in a lazy tranquility as if on a motionless sea. If anything happens to them, it will come as a novelty. (7) Harsh things come as a greater shock to those who lack experience. The yoke feels heavy to a neck that is tender. The new recruit blanches at the sight of a wound. The veteran soldier looks on his own bleeding boldly, knowing that he has often been victorious after blood. That is why god hardens, examines, and exercises those whom he approves of, those whom he loves, whereas those whom he seems to be indulging, whom he seems to be sparing, he is keeping soft for bad things to come. You are wrong if you judge that an exception has been made for someone: though he has been fortunate for a long time, his share

will come to him too. Whoever seems to have been dismissed has been postponed.

(8) Why does god assail all the best men with bad health or grief or other misfortunes? Because also in an army camp, the most dangerous missions are given to the bravest. A leader sends his most select troops to attack the enemy in a night raid or to scout out a path or to dislodge a garrison from its post. None of them says as he departs, "The general has done badly by me," but rather, "He judged well." Let the same thing be said by any who are ordered to suffer things that fearful and cowardly men would weep over: "We seemed to god to be worthy of a test of how much human nature could endure."

(9) Flee from delights, flee from good fortune that drains your strength. In good fortune your minds are dissolved, and unless something intervenes to remind you of your lot as human beings, your minds fade as if put to sleep in an unending drunkenness. If someone has always been protected from gusts by windows, if his feet are warm from a succession of heated applications, if his dining rooms have been tempered by heat coming from under the floor and piped through the walls, the touch of a light breeze will be dangerous. (10) Because all things are harmful that have exceeded due measure, an excess of good fortune is exceedingly dangerous. It disturbs the brain. It lures our thoughts into baseless fantasies. It infuses a great deal of fogginess between fiction and truth. Why would it not be more preferable to endure unending misfortune by summoning virtue than to be broken asunder by "good" things lacking limit or measure? Death by starvation is gentler: from feasting men explode.

(11) With good men, then, the gods follow the same reasoning that instructors follow with their pupils: they demand more work from those who give them greater reason to hope. You cannot think that the Lacedaemonians hate their children just because they test their abilities with public floggings?[36] Their own fathers urge them to endure the lashes of the whip courageously, and though they are lacerated and half-unconscious they beg them to keep offering up their wounds for further wounding. (12) Why is it strange if god puts noble spirits through hard tests? A lesson in virtue is never soft. Fortune flogs us and lacerates us: let us suffer. It is not cruelty but a trial, and the more often we come to it the more courageous we will

be. The most robust part of the body is that which constant use has put into action. We ought to offer ourselves up to fortune so that *by* it we can be hardened *against* it. It will gradually make us equal to it: the frequency of our endangerment will give us scorn for dangers. **(13)** The reason why sailors have bodies hard enough to endure the sea, why farmers have callused hands, why soldiers' arms are strong enough to wield weapons, and why runners have agile limbs is this: what is most robust in each is what he has exercised. The mind comes to scorn suffering *by* suffering.

You will realize what suffering can produce in us if you observe what a contribution hard work makes to nations who are naked and become more courageous by what they lack. **(14)** Consider all the races in which the *pax Romana* reaches its limit—I mean the Germans and whatever nomadic races are encountered around the lower Danube.[37] They are oppressed by unending winter and gloomy skies. The barren soil sustains them grudgingly. They keep the rain out with straw and leaves. They range over lakes hardened into ice. For nourishment they catch beasts. **(15)** Do they seem pitiable to you? Nothing is pitiable if habit has carried it to the point where it is natural: things that began by necessity have little by little become a pleasure. Those races have no dwellings and no settlements except what is determined by their fatigue at the end of each day. Their nourishment is base and must be sought out by hand, the sky is hostile and terrifying, their bodies are uncovered. What seems calamitous to you is the life of so many races.

(16) Why are you surprised if good men are buffeted so that they can be made stronger? A tree is not robust or strong unless a continuous wind has been blasting it, for the harassment makes it solid and its roots become more securely fixed. Trees that have grown up in a sunny valley are susceptible to breaking. In order to be able to be fearless, then, it is in good men's own interest that they be much thrown around amid terrifying things, and that they endure things with a calm mind—things that are not bad except for someone who bears them badly.

(5.1) Now add the fact that it is in *everyone's* interest for the best men to be "soldiers," as it were, and to perform labors. This is god's plan and the wise man's alike: to show that the things that the crowd desires and fears are neither good nor bad.[38] But it will be clear that things he has allotted to no one but the good man are good, and that things he has imposed only on bad men are bad. (2) Blindness will be hateful if no one has lost their eyes except those who deserved to have them gouged out: therefore let Appius and Metellus lack sight.[39] Wealth is not a good: therefore let even Elius[40] the pimp have it so that although people have consecrated their wealth in temples, they can see it also in a brothel. God has no better way of removing people's desire for things than by conferring them on the most disgraceful men and taking them away from the best men.

(3) "But it is unfair for a good man to be maimed or crucified or bound in chains, while bad men walk around free and indulgent, their bodies unharmed." And? Is it not "unfair" for brave men to take up arms and spend the night encamped and stand before the rampart with wounds bandaged up, and meanwhile for the castrated and the devotees of shamelessness to live in the city without a care? And? Is it not "unfair" for the noblest virgins to be awakened in the night to perform sacred rituals, while the corrupted ones enjoy the deepest of sleeps? (4) Toil requires the very best. The senate often deliberates the whole day long while at the same time the most despicable individuals either pass their leisure on the Campus (Martius) or lurk in taverns or waste their time standing around talking. The same thing happens in this republic of the world: good men toil, they expend and are expended—and this willingly. They are not dragged away by fortune: they follow it and match its pace. If they had known, they would have anticipated it.

(5) I remember hearing this other saying of Demetrius, that bravest of men:[41] "I can," he said, "make only this one complaint to you, immortal gods: that you did not make your will known to me beforehand. For I would have come earlier to these things at which I am now present, in response to your summons. Do you want to take my children? I raised them for you. Do you want a part of my body? Take it: it is not a great thing for me to promise, as I will soon leave the whole of it. Do you want my breath? Why would I cause any delay for your receiving back what you gave? Whatever you seek you will take from one who is willing. Well? I would have preferred to offer it than to be asked to give it. Why was there a need to take it? You could have received it. Still, even now you will not be taking it, because nothing is seized except from someone who is holding on."

(6) I am coerced into nothing. I suffer nothing unwillingly. I do not serve god, but rather I agree with him—all the more so because I know that all things come to pass by a law that is fixed and is decreed for eternity. **(7)** The fates lead us, and the amount of time that remains for each person was stipulated at our first hour when we were born.[42] Cause hangs on cause. Things both private and public are drawn along in a long order of events. Each thing must be suffered bravely because all things do not simply occur, as we think, but rather they arrive. It was decided long ago what you would have that you could rejoice about, what you would have that you could cry about. And however much the lives of individuals seem to be distinguished by great variety, the total comes to one thing: the things we receive will perish, as will we. **(8)** Why, then, do we get angry? Why do we complain? We were made ready for this. Let nature use its bodies as it wants. We should be joyful and courageous toward all things, and we should consider how nothing perishes that is ours. What belongs to a good man? To offer himself up to fate. It is a magnificent consolation to be carried away with the universe. Whatever it is that has commanded us to live in this way, to die in this way, binds the gods too with the same necessity. Human and divine are carried along equally on a course that cannot be revoked. Yes, the founder and ruler of everything inscribed the fates himself, but he also follows them: having commanded them once, he obeys them always.

(9) "But why was god so unfair when distributing fate that he matched good men with poverty and wounds and untimely deaths?" An artisan cannot change his material: nature has not allowed this.[43] Certain things cannot be separated from certain other things: they hold together, they are indivisible.[44] Minds that are sluggish and liable to fall asleep or to be awake in a way that is no different from sleep are woven from inactive elements. To fashion a man who can genuinely be called a man, a stronger fate is needed. For him, the way will not be flat: he must go up and down, he must be tossed by waves, and must guide his vessel on a stormy sea. He must hold his course against fortune. Many things will happen that are hard and rough—but things he can soften and smooth out himself. Fire proves gold; misery, brave men.

(10) See how high virtue ought to ascend. You will realize that the way he needs to go is not free of cares:

The first part of the road is steep, and even fresh in the morning
the horses can scarcely struggle up it. The highest part is in the
    middle of the sky,
and to look on the sea and the lands from there is something I
    myself
am often afraid to do, and my heart trembles in quivering terror.
The road's furthest part is steep and calls for firm control:
even then, Tethys looks up from below, fearing that, before she
    receives me
in the waves that lie beneath, I may be thrown headlong.[45]

(11) When that noble-born young man (Phaethon) had heard this,
he said: "This road appeals to me: I will ascend. So valuable is it to
go through those things, even if I will fall." *He* (the Sun) persists in
trying to scare his eager mind with causes for fear:

And even if you hold to the road and are not drawn to err
    from it,
still you will go amid the horns of the Bull who stands opposite,
and the Haemonian Bow, and the face of the fierce Lion.

After this *he* says: "Give me the chariot and harness it. These things
you think deter me goad me on. I wish to stand in the place where
the Sun himself trembles." It is lowly and lazy to follow the safe path:
virtue takes the high road.

(6.1) "But why does god allow anything bad to happen to good
men?" Actually he does not allow this. He has taken all bad things
away from them—crimes and misdeeds and wicked thoughts and
greedy designs and blind lust and avarice that hovers over what belongs to another. The men themselves he watches over and protects.
Surely no one can demand from god that he take care of good men's
baggage too? They themselves discharge god of this responsibility:
they scorn external things. (2) Democritus cast away his wealth, reck-
oning it to be burdensome to a good intellect.[46] Why, then, are you
surprised if god allows to happen to a good man what a good man
himself sometimes wants to happen to him? Good men lose their
sons: why not, when sometimes they actually kill them? They are
sent into exile: why not, when sometimes they leave their fatherland themselves, with no intention of seeking it again? They are

killed: why not, when sometimes they lay their hands on themselves? (3) Why do they suffer certain hardships? So they can teach others to suffer them: they are born to serve as an example.

Imagine, therefore, god saying: "What do you[47] have that you can complain to me about, you who have approved of what is right? I have surrounded others with false goods, and I have deluded their empty minds as if with a long and deceptive dream. I have adorned them with gold and silver and ivory. There is nothing good within. (4) Those whom you gaze on as if they are happy, if you look not at their exposed part but at their hidden part, are pitiable. They are filthy and disgraceful, decorated on the exterior just like their walls: that happiness is not robust and pure; it is a shell, and a thin one at that. That is why, so long as they are permitted to stand and show themselves just as they choose, they shine and deceive. When something happens that unsettles them and uncovers them, then it is plain to see what profound and genuine squalor that incongruous splendor was concealing. (5) To you I gave goods that are certain and will endure, things that are better and greater the more someone turns them and inspects them from different angles. I have permitted you to scorn things that would be fearful, to treat desires with disgust. You do not dazzle on the outside: your goods are turned inward. In just this way has the world scorned external things, finding joy in the spectacle of itself. I have placed every good on the inside. *Your* good fortune is not to need good fortune.

(6) "'But many things happen that are sobering, terrifying, and hard to bear.' Because I was not able to save you from these, I have armed your minds against all things. Bear them bravely! This is the way in which you surpass god: he is beyond suffering bad things, you are above suffering them. Scorn poverty: no one lives in as much poverty as he was born in. Scorn pain: it will either be dissolved or will dissolve you. Scorn death: it either finishes you or takes you somewhere else.[48] Scorn fortune: I did not give it any weapon by which it could strike your mind. (7) Before all else I took measures that no one could hold you against your will. An exit is there: if you do not wish to fight, you are permitted to flee. That is why, of all the things that I wanted to be necessary for you, I made none easier than dying. I placed your life on a downward slope. If it is drawn out,[49] just look and you will see what a brief and direct road leads to freedom. I

did not place as long a delay for you in exiting as I did for when you entered. Otherwise, if a human being were to die as slowly as he is born, fortune would have held a great sovereignty over you. **(8)** Let every moment, every place, teach you how easy it is to give notice to nature and to press its gift back onto it.

"Even at the altars and solemn rites of sacrificers, while life is being prayed for, learn death. The fattened bodies of bulls collapse from a tiny wound, and animals of great strength are laid low by a blow from a human hand. The connection of the neck is sundered by a thin blade, and when that joint connecting the head and neck has been cut through, the whole great mass crashes down. **(9)** Your breath does not lie hidden, and does not need to be dug out with a blade. There is no need to grope around in your breast through a wound pressed deep inside.[50] Death could not be closer at hand. I did not stipulate a fixed spot for these blows: wherever you wish, a road can be made. The thing itself that is called death, by which the soul departs from the body, is too brief for such speed to be felt. Whether a noose strangles your throat, whether water cuts off your breathing, whether you fall on your head and are shattered by the hard surface of the underlying ground, whether a gulp of fire interrupts the passage of your returning breath—whatever it is, it comes fast. Are you embarrassed? You spend a long time fearing what happens so quickly!"

Abbreviations

LS   Long, A. A., and D. N. Sedley, *The Hellenistic Philosophers*, 2 vols. Cambridge: Cambridge University Press.

SVF   *Stoicorum Veterum Fragmenta*, ed. Hans F. A. von Arnim. Leipzig, 1903–24.

Introduction

1. Compare the title used by Lactantius: *Why Many Bad Things Happen to Good Men, though There Is Providence* (*Divine Institutes* 5.22.11).

2. On providence in the ancient philosophical tradition and in Seneca, see Dragona-Monachou 1994 (with discussion of the present work, 4440–42); also Traina 1997, 7–20; Dionigi 1997, 54–70. For Stoic texts, see *SVF* II, 1106–86.

3. The implausible theory that the work is in fact incomplete is discussed and dismissed by Traina 1997, 22.

4. On providence (and Seneca's work) in the Christian tradition, see Traina 1997, 13–20; on Augustine in particular, Dionigi 1997, 51–54, 62–70.

5. For these two arguments, see Aulus Gellius *Attic Nights* 7.1.1–13 (= *SVF* II, 1170 = LS 54Q); Plutarch *On Stoic Contradictions* 1050e (= *SVF* II, 1176).

6. For discussion of the work's date, see Griffin 1992, 396, 400.

7. The confrontation of Lucilius at 1.1 seems plucked from the epistolary to and fro, especially in *Letters* 96.1.

8. The spiral metaphor is credited to Grimal by Traina 1997, 22. On the work's structure, see Wright 1974, 48–54; Abel 1967, 97–123.

On Providence

9. Seneca's sketch of what he supposedly is not going to mention (*praeteritio*) touches on the material of *Natural Questions* (e.g., 1.pref.15).

10. Perhaps even "rival": as Traina 1997, 86 notes, the term used here, *aemulator*, suggests something more than the standard resemblance (*similitudo/homoiôsis*) to god.

11. Home-born slaves (*uernae*) were typically treated better than other slaves, and also less strictly than freeborn children, sometimes with a view to their providing cheeky entertainment.

12. For Christian echoes, see, e.g., Minucius Felix *Octavius* 37.1: "What a beautiful spectacle for god, when a Christian comes into combat with pain"; also Lactantius *On the Deaths of the Persecutors* 16.6–7.

13. Cato the Younger (95–46 BCE), who committed suicide at Utica (hence his conventional title Cato Uticensis) after the defeat of Pompey and the advance of Julius Caesar's forces. On Seneca's use of Cato here and elsewhere, see Isnardi Parenti 2000; Hutchinson 1993, 273–79; Griffin 1992, esp. 190–94; Abel 1967, 111–13; and in the tradition more generally, Goar 1987.

14. M. Petreius was a commander of Pompeian forces, Juba a Numidian king who fought with the Pompeians. When their cause became hopeless after the battle of Thapsus in 46, they agreed to kill each other.

15. Cato supposedly read "Plato's dialogue on the soul," i.e., *Phaedo* (Plutarch *Cato the Younger* 68.2); Seneca elsewhere refers to him reading a "book of Plato's" at *Letters* 24.6.

16. Cato's initial wound, made earlier the same night with a sword or dagger, had been sewn up; he subsequently tore it open with his bare hands.

17. These topics correspond more or less to 3.2–4.16 (in the men's interest); 5.1–5.2 (in everyone's interest); 5.3–6 (the men are willing); 5.7–11 (these things are fated); and 6.1–2 (they are not in fact unhappy).

18. Demetrius the Cynic, a philosopher exiled by Nero and again by Vespasian, is mentioned frequently in Seneca's later works (e.g., *On Benefits* 7.1.3–2.1), though he is also mentioned often by historians and other philosophical writers such as Epictetus and Lucian.

19. The list recurs at *Letters* 98.12–13 and elsewhere, with minor changes. On its functions and variations, see Mayer 2008, 304–6.

20. Q. Mucius Scaevola (= "Left-handed"), early Roman hero, was captured after attempting to kill Lars Porsena, the king of Clusium, who was besieging Rome. Mucius thrust his hand into a fire to show his indifference to being condemned to death, and was set free by the king.

21. C. Fabricius Luscinus (early 3rd c. BCE) resisted the attempts of king Pyrrhus to bribe him during war, and was famous for living in poverty on his farm.

22. A reference to the Adriatic and Tyrrhenian Seas, to the east and west of Italy.

23. P. Rutilius Rufus (b. ca. 160 BCE), a Roman statesman who was also a Stoic (being a student of Panaetius), was exiled in 92 on charges of corruption; his defense speech was modeled on the *Apology of Socrates*. He refused Sulla's invitation to return to Rome.

24. A mocking allusion to Sulla's epithet, *felix*, "lucky, fortunate."

25. After becoming dictator in 82/81, L. Cornelius Sulla (138–78 BCE) proscribed and executed thousands of Romans (cf. Plutarch *Sulla* 31). Severed heads were displayed at the *lacus Seruilius,* located next to the Roman Forum, to the west of the Basilica Iulia.

26. I.e., because they are dead.

27. The *lex Cornelia de sicariis et ueneficiis*, a law on homicide and poisoning, introduced by (Cornelius) Sulla in 81 BCE.

28. M. Atilius Regulus was a commander in the First Punic War; in 250, as a captive of the Carthaginians, he was sent to Rome to negotiate terms of peace, but told the Romans to continue the war, insisted on returning to Carthage, and was tortured, with his eyelids sewn open, and put to death.

29. C Maecenas (d. 8 BCE) was the major patron of the arts in the age of Augustus; Seneca chiefly refers to his own florid writing and luxurious lifestyle, as well as to his ostentatious erotic life with his wife Terentia.

30. I.e., Maecenas's wife.

31. Around sixteen of the twenty-six mentions of Socrates in Seneca focus on his death. On Socrates in Seneca, see Isnardi Parenti 2000.

32. I.e., the first triumvirate of the 50s BCE.

33. P. Vatinius, though the butt of jokes for his physical deformities and the target of invective from Cicero, held a series of high political offices during the first triumvirate, and beat Cato in the election for praetor in 55.

34. Tiberius put on relatively few shows compared with Augustus (cf. Suetonius *Tiberius* 47).

35. Seneca shifts from "you" singular to "you" plural.

36. I.e., the Spartans, whose legendary austere regimen for raising their children (the *agôgê*) is a staple example in moral philosophy.

37. Nations celebrated for their tough character, supposedly due to the harsh elements.

38. I.e., they are indifferents. For explanation of the theory, see LS 58.

39. Appius Claudius Caecus and L. Caecilius Metellus, statesmen of the Middle Republic; Metellus lost his sight when rescuing statues of the gods from fire in the temple of Vesta.

40. Otherwise unknown.

41. Mentioned already at 3.3 above.

42. This passage partly echoes the verses of Cleanthes reproduced at *Letters* 113.26. For the broader Stoic background on fate and free will, see LS 55.

43. The text is corrupt: †*hoc passa est*†. I have followed Reynolds's suggested *hoc <natura non> passa est.*

44. For Chrysippus's notion of events whose fates "hold together" (*cohaerentia*), see Aulus Gellius *Attic Nights* 7.1.9 = LS 54 Q (2).

45. Ovid *Metamorphoses* 2.63–69, then 79–81; Seneca supplements the verse quotations with prose paraphrase. The speaker is the Sun, who fails to deter his son Phaethon from driving his chariot across the sky and causing a conflagration. Compare the use of Phaethon in *On the Happy Life* 20.5.

46. The philosopher Democritus of Abdera, roughly contemporary with Socrates. For the story, see Diogenes Laertius 9.35, 39.

47. Plural.

48. The options, that death is either an end or a transition, are the same as those given by Socrates in the last pages of Plato's *Apology of Socrates;* compare *Letters* 65.24.

49. Reading Reynolds's suggested <*si*> *trahitur,* though it remains awkward.

50. I.e., as Cato did (cf. 2.12 above).

Editions and Translations

Basore, John, trans. 1928. *Seneca, Moral Essays*, vol. 1. Loeb Classical Library. Cambridge, MA: Harvard University Press.

Davie, John, trans. 2007. *Seneca, Dialogues and Essays*. Oxford: Oxford University Press.

References

Abel, Karlhans. 1967. *Bauformen in Senecas Dialogen*. Heidelberg: C. Winter.

Dionigi, Ivano. 1997. "Problematica e fortuna del *De Providentia*." In Seneca, *"La provvidenza,"* trans. A. Traina, 41–74. Milan: Rizzoli.

Goar, Robert J. 1987. *The Legend of Cato Uticensis from the First Century B.C. to the Fifth Century A.D. with an Appendix on Dante and Cato*. Brussels: Latomus.

Griffin, Miriam T. 1992. *Seneca: A Philosopher in Politics*. 2nd ed. Oxford: Oxford University Press.

Hutchinson, G. O. 1993. *Latin Literature from Seneca to Juvenal: A Critical Study*. Oxford: Clarendon Press.

Isnardi Parenti, Margherita. 2000. "Socrate e Catone in Seneca: Il filosofo e il politico." In *Seneca e il suo tempo*, ed. P. Parroni, 215–25. Rome: Salerno.

Mayer, Roland. 2008. "Roman Historical Exempla in Seneca." In *Seneca*, ed. J. Fitch, 299–315. Oxford: Oxford University Press.

Traina, Alfonso, trans. 1997. Seneca, *La provvidenza*. Milan: Rizzoli.

———, ed. 1999. *L'avvocato di dio: Colloquio sul "De providentia" di Seneca*. Bologna: Pàtron.

Wright, J. R. G. 1974. "Form and Content in the *Moral Essays*." In *Seneca*, ed. C. D. N. Costa, 9–69. London: Routledge and Kegan Paul.